PLANETARY

Warren Ellis & John Cassaday
Writer/Co-Creators/Artist

Laura Martin
Colorist

Bill O'Neil issues 13-15
Richard Starkings issues 16-18
Letterers

PLANETARY: LEAVING THE 20th CENTURY, Published by DC Comics, 1700 Broadway, New York, NY 10019. Cover and compilation Copyright © 2004 DC Comics. All Rights Reserved. **Originally published by WildStorm** in single magazine format as PLANETARY #13-18, © 2001, 2003, 2004.

DC Comics, a Warner Bros. Entertainment Company.

ISBN: 978-1-4012-0294-1

SUSTAINABLE FORESTRY INITIATIVE
Certified Chain of Custody
Promoting Sustainable Forest Management
www.sfiprogram.org
Fiber used in this product line meets the sourcing requirements of the SFI program.
www.sfiprogram.org SGS-SFI/COC-US10/81072

LEAVING THE 20TH CENTURY

John Layman & Scott Dunbier
Original Series Editors

John Cassaday
Cover Art

John Layman, Editor **Bob Harras,** Group Editor-Collected Editions
Robbin Brosterman, Design Director-Books **Larry Berry,** Art Director

Diane Nelson, President
Dan DiDio and Jim Lee, Co-Publishers **Geoff Johns,** Chief Creative Officer
John Rood, Executive Vice President-Sales, Marketing and Business Development
Patrick Caldon, Executive Vice President-Finance and Administration
Amy Genkins, Senior VP-Business and Legal Affairs **Steve Rotterdam,** Senior VP-Sales and Marketing
John Cunningham, VP-Marketing **Terri Cunningham,** VP-Managing Editor
Alison Gill, VP-Manufacturing **David Hyde,** VP-Publicity
Sue Pohja, VP-Book Trade Sales **Alysse Soll,** VP-Advertising and Custom Publishing
Bob Wayne, VP-Sales **Mark Chiarello,** Art Director

A COMPLETE NEW **ELIJAH SNOW** ASTONISHING ADVENTURE

CHAPTER THIRTEEN

WILDSTORM

THE PLANETARY MAGAZINE

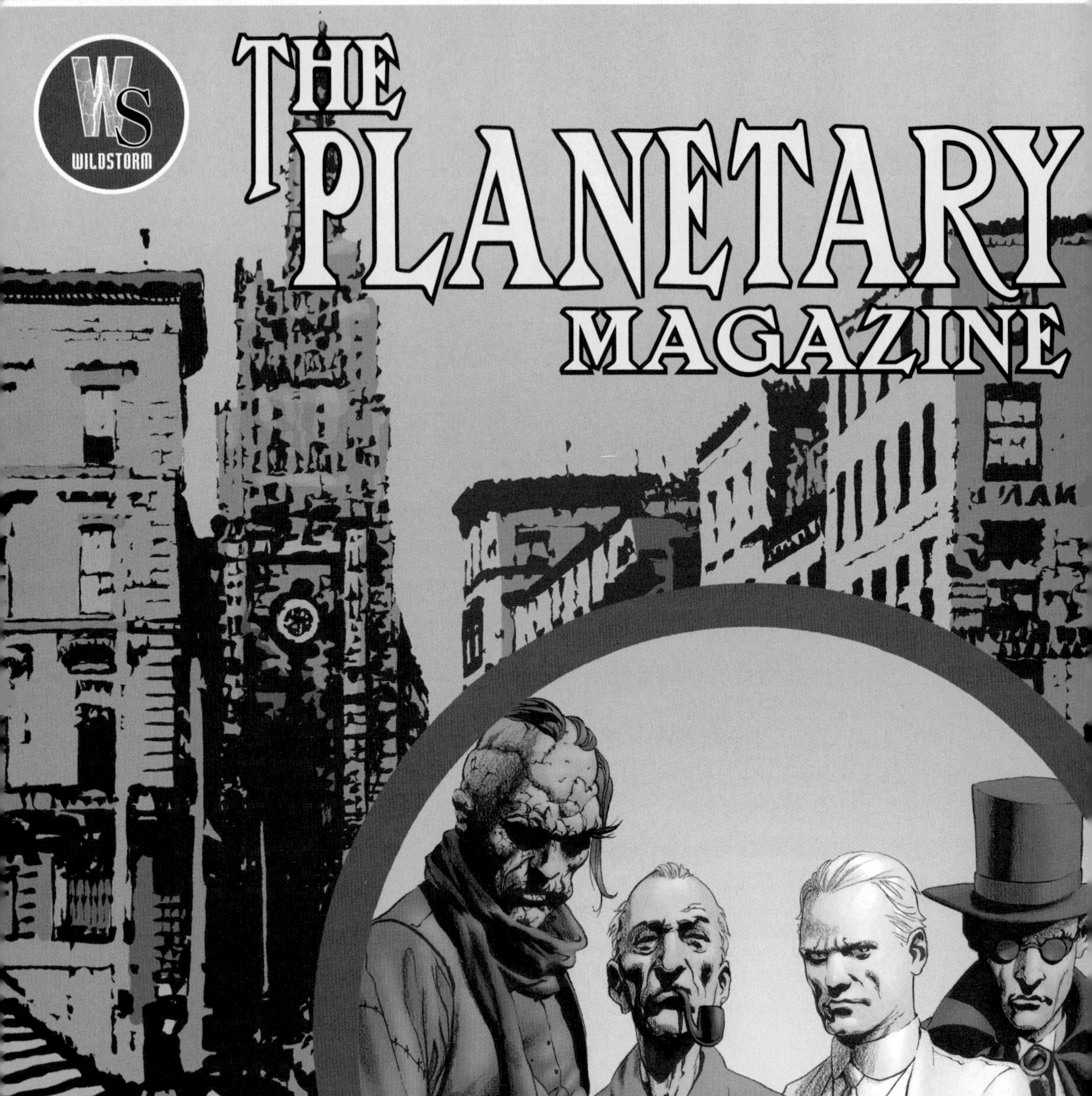

FEATURING THE TALENTS OF

WARREN G. ELLIS ESQ.
&
MR. JOHN M. CASSADAY
FROM THE COLONIES

WITH MISS LAURA J. DePU

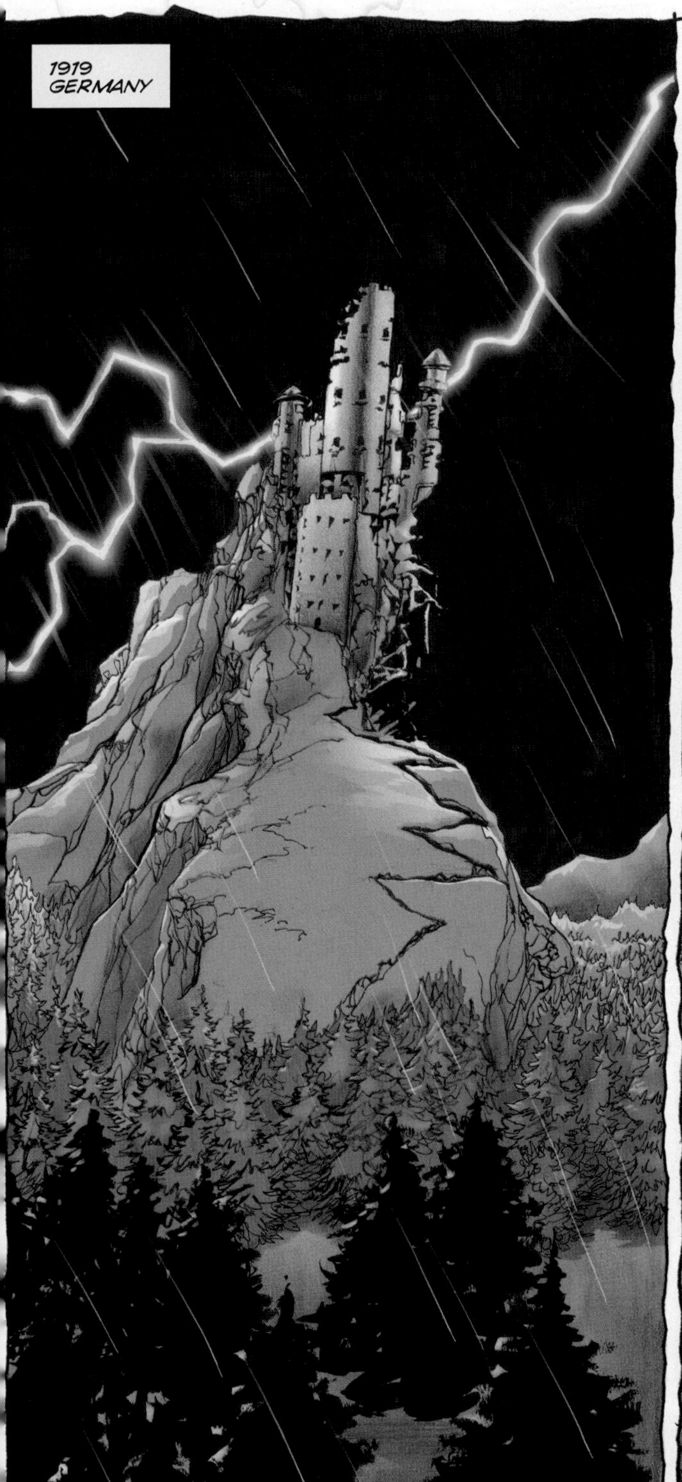
1919
GERMANY

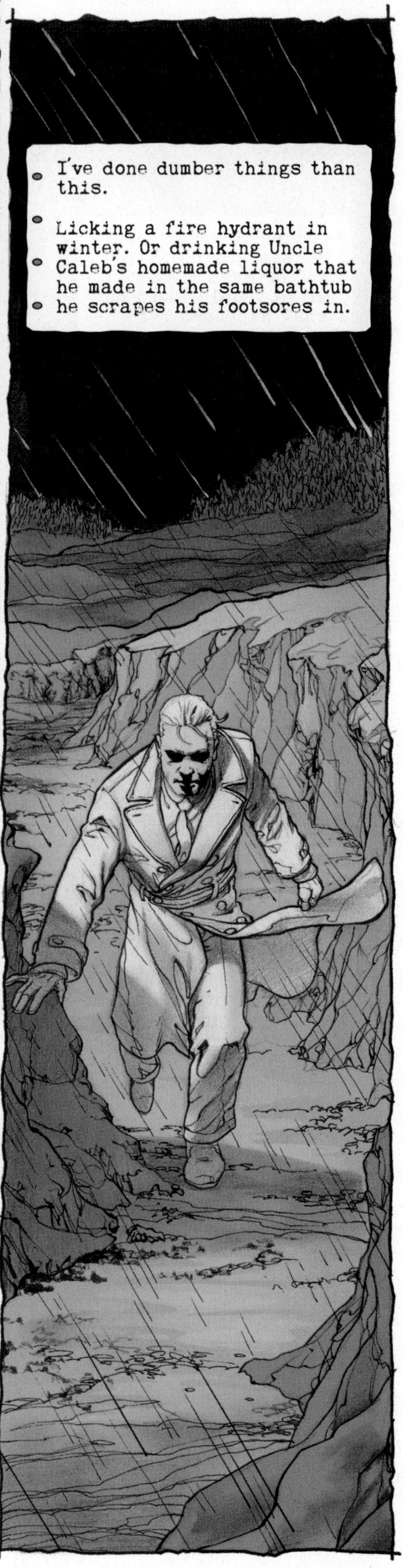
I've done dumber things than this.
Licking a fire hydrant in winter. Or drinking Uncle Caleb's homemade liquor that he made in the same bathtub he scrapes his footsores in.

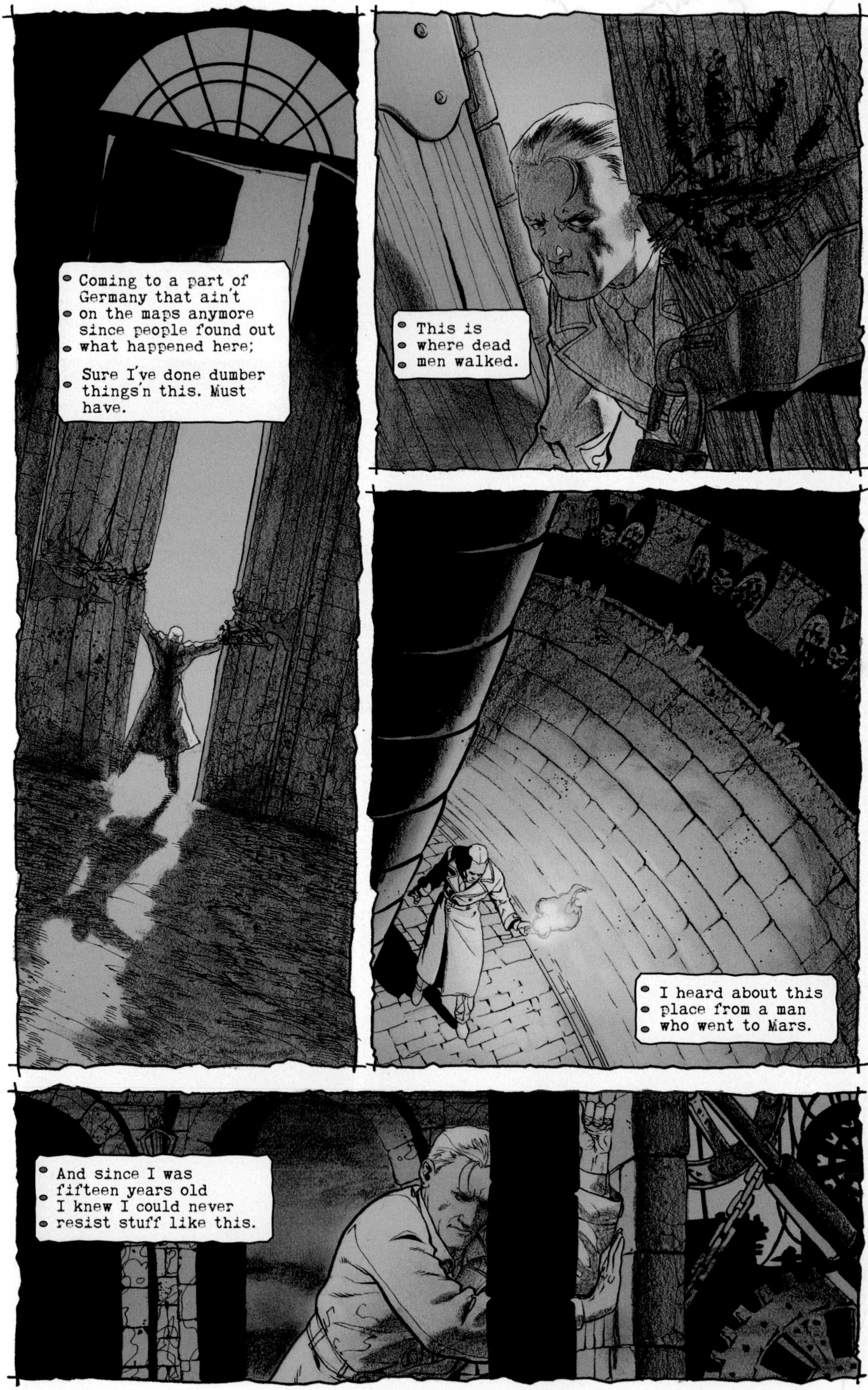
Coming to a part of Germany that ain't on the maps anymore since people found out what happened here;
Sure I've done dumber things'n this. Must have.
This is where dead men walked.
I heard about this place from a man who went to Mars.
And since I was fifteen years old I knew I could never resist stuff like this.

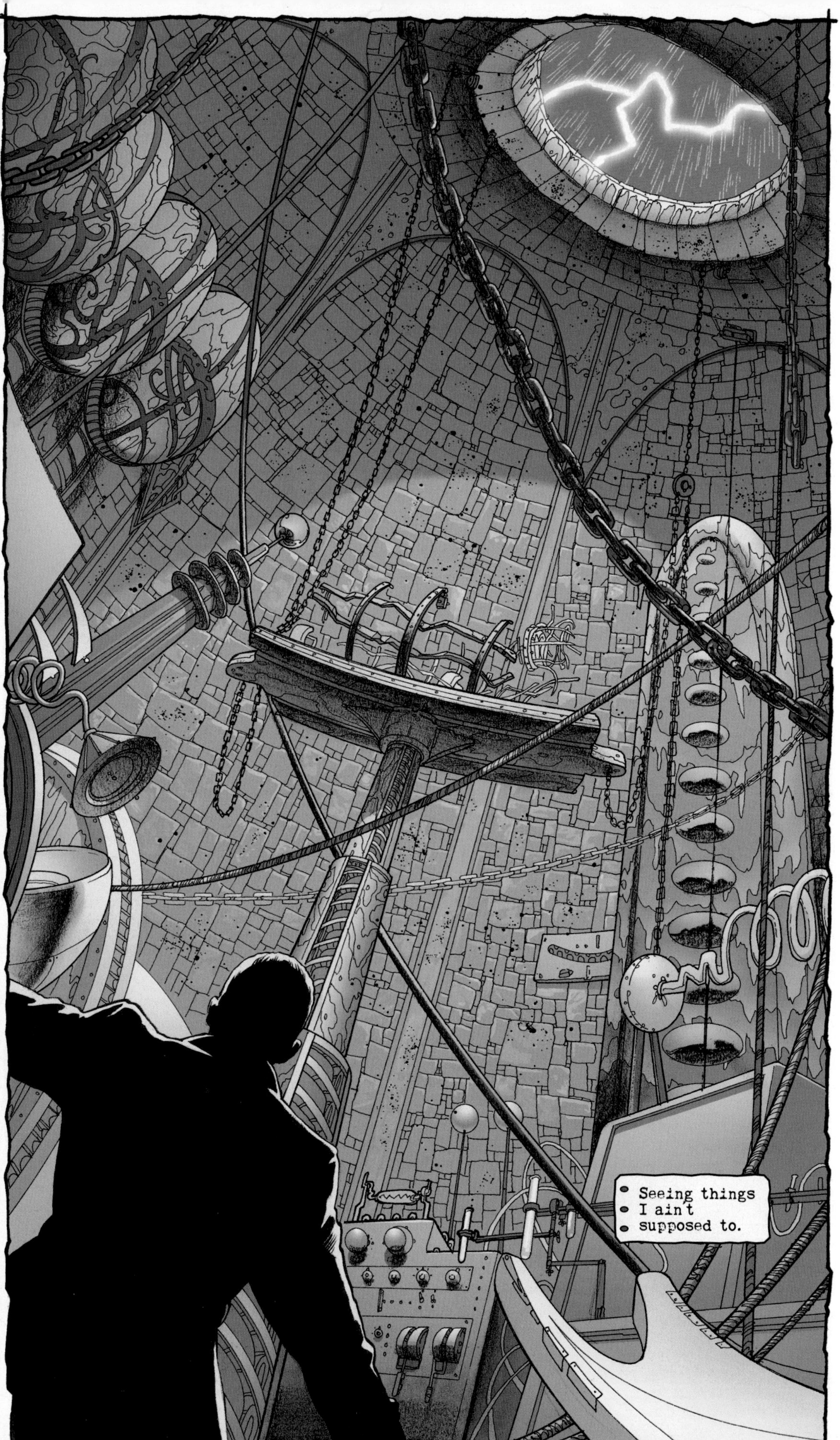
Seeing things
I ain't
supposed to.

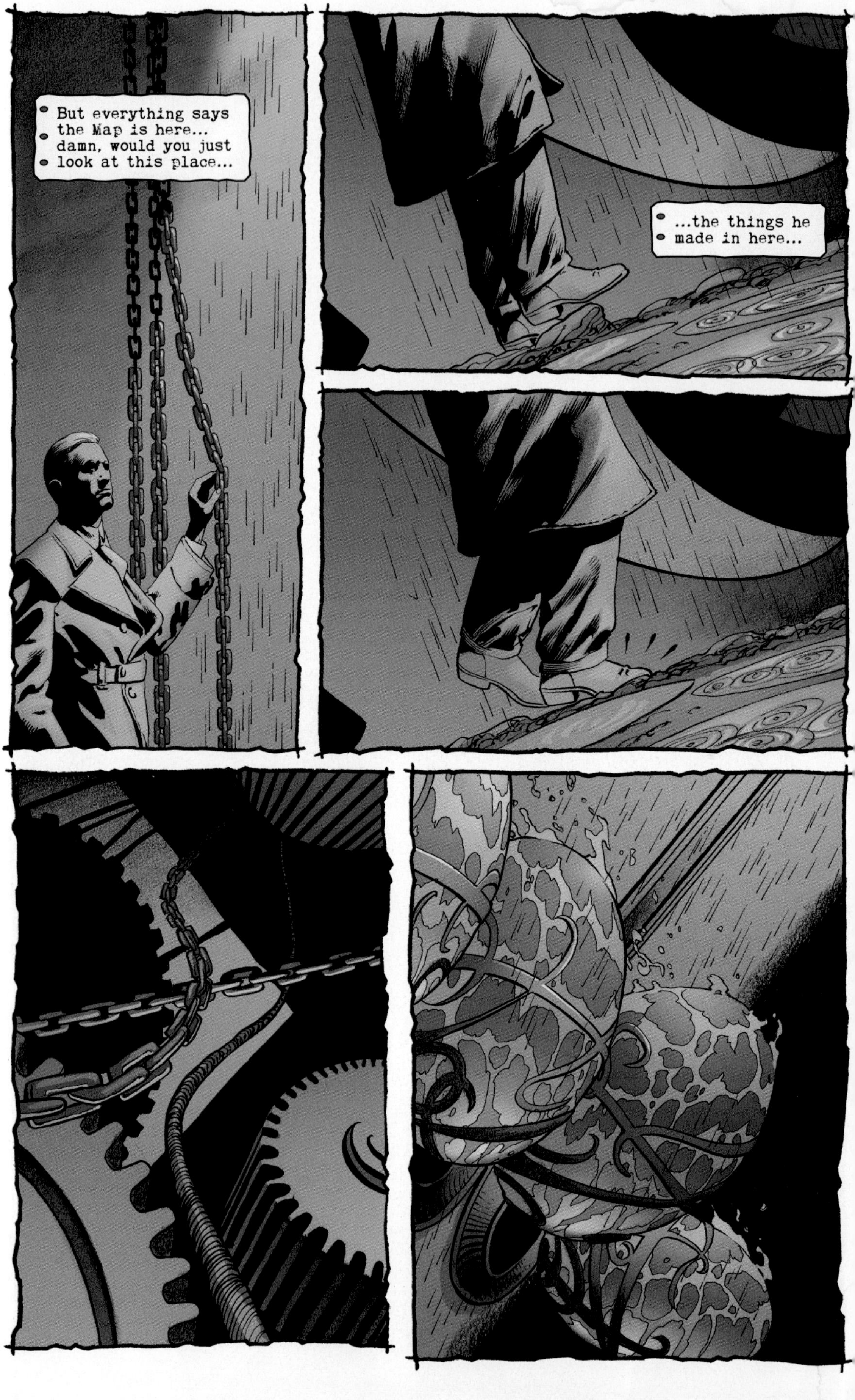
But everything says the Map is here... damn, would you just look at this place...
...the things he made in here...

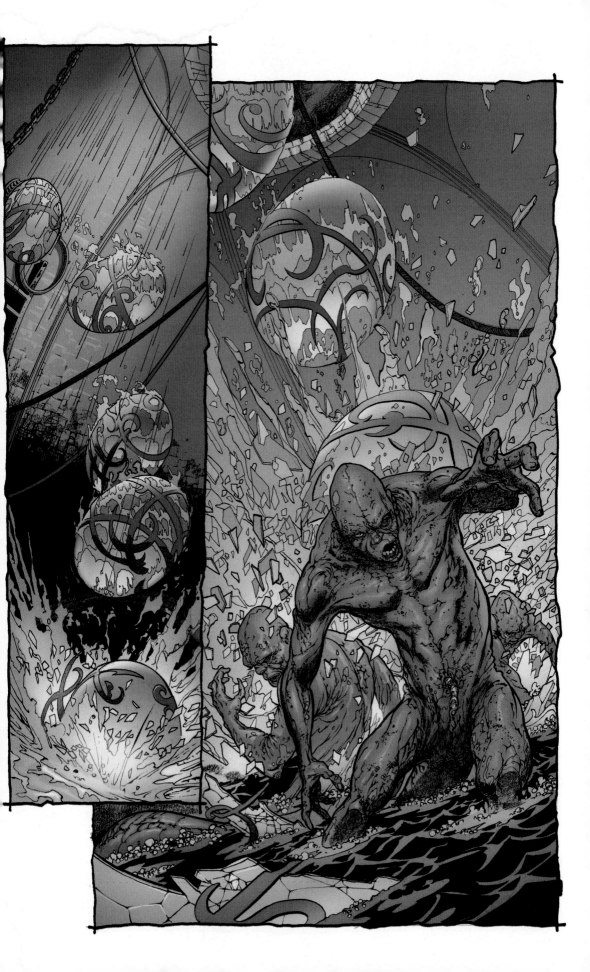

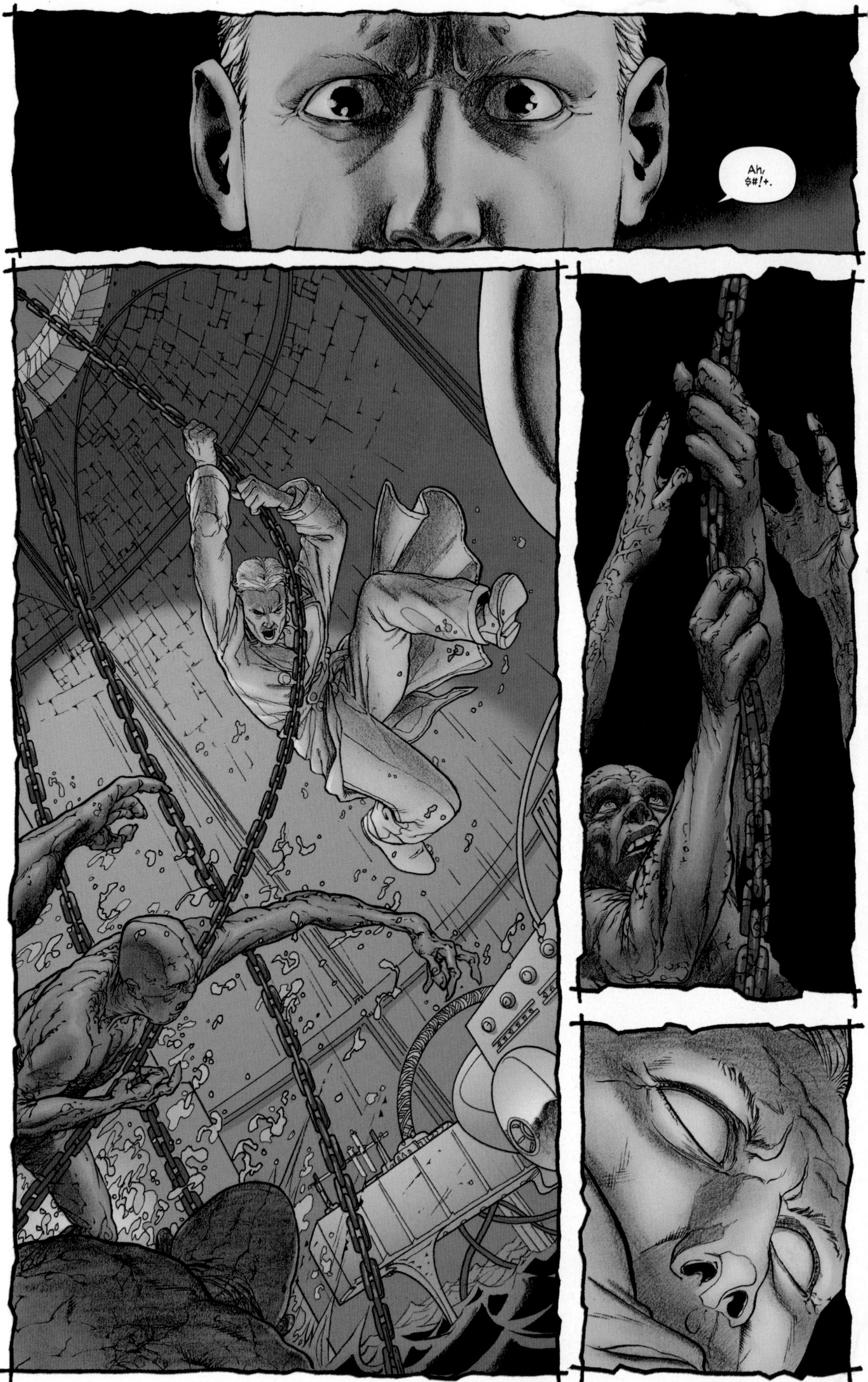
Ah, $#!+.

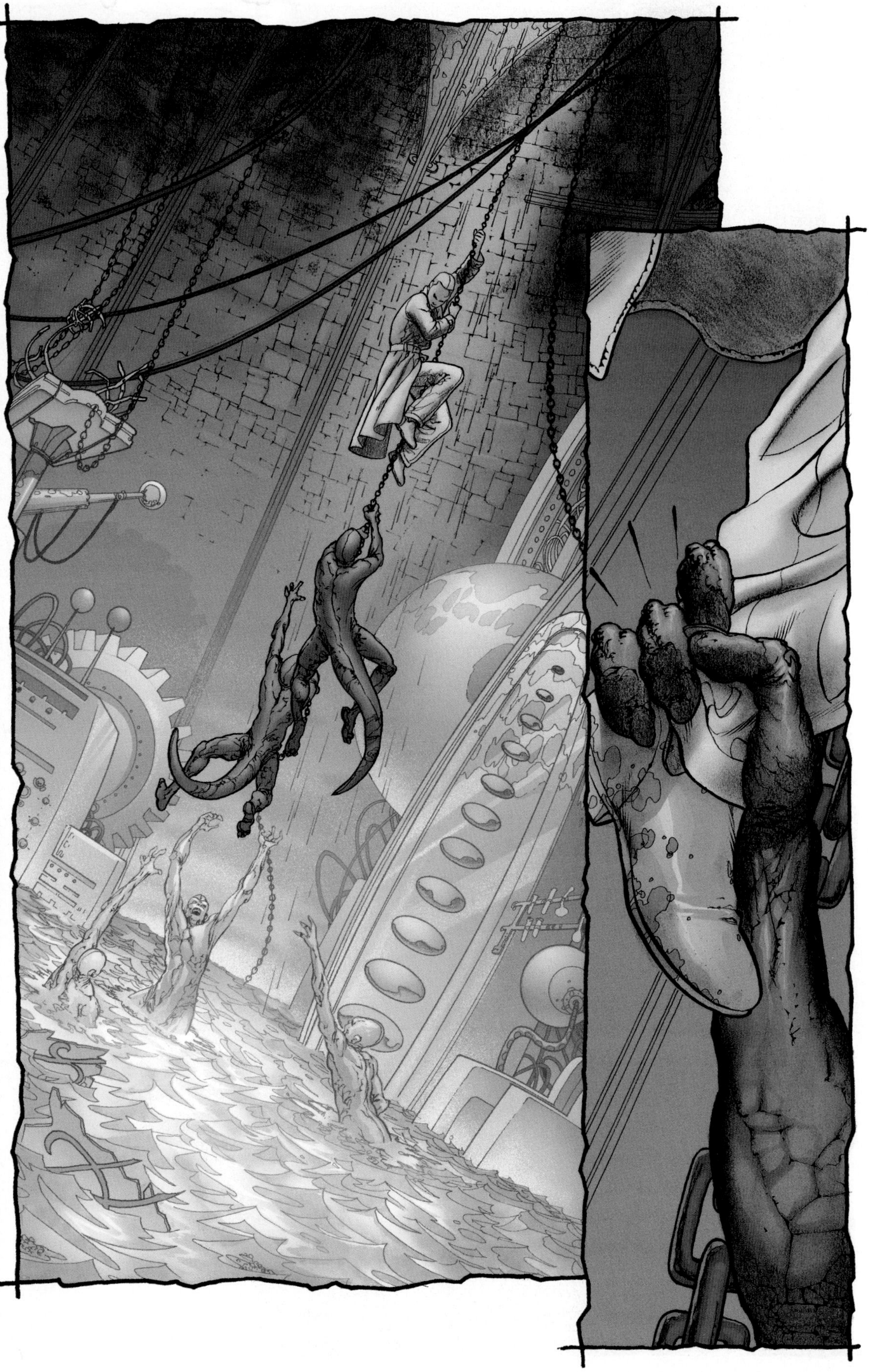

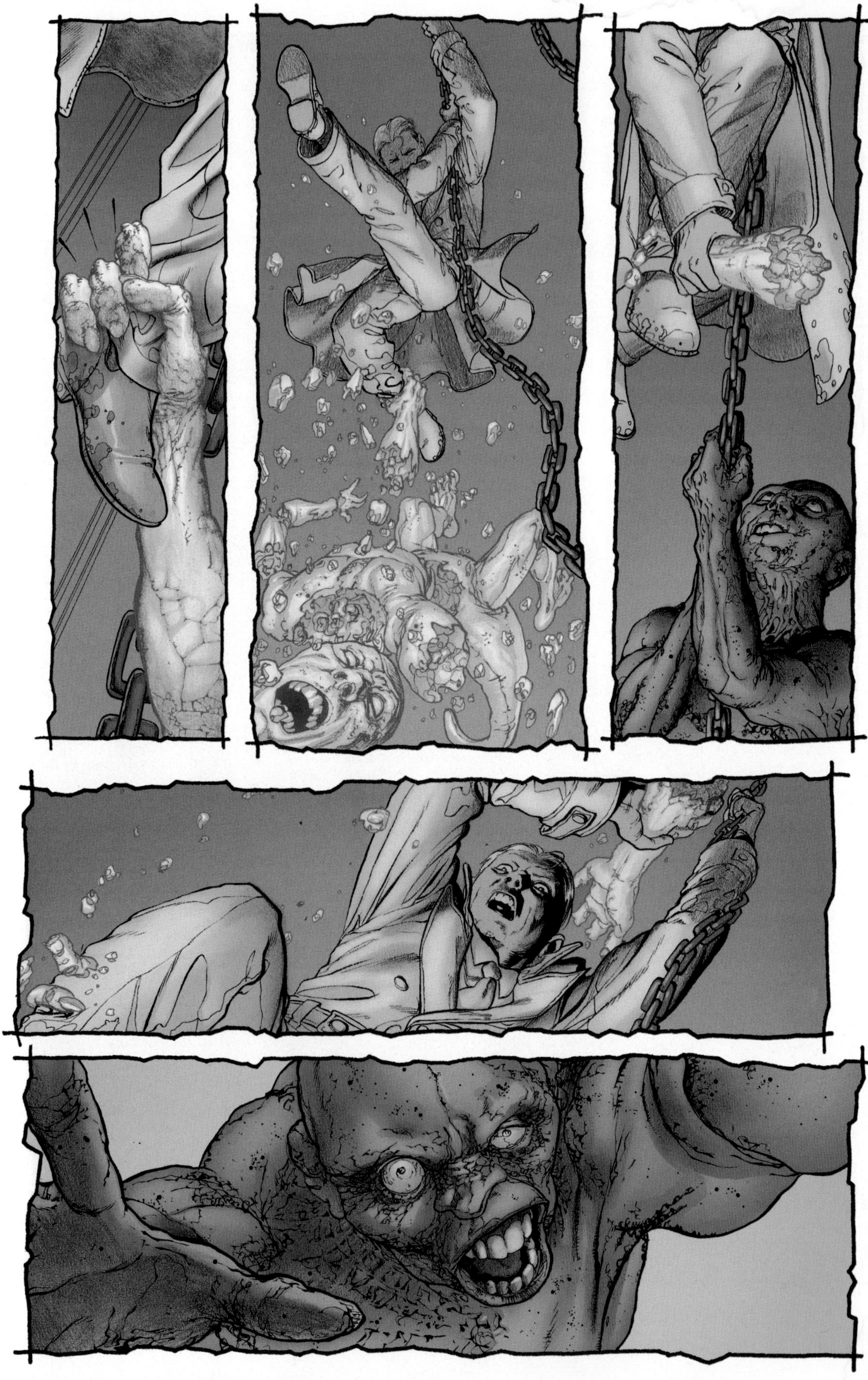

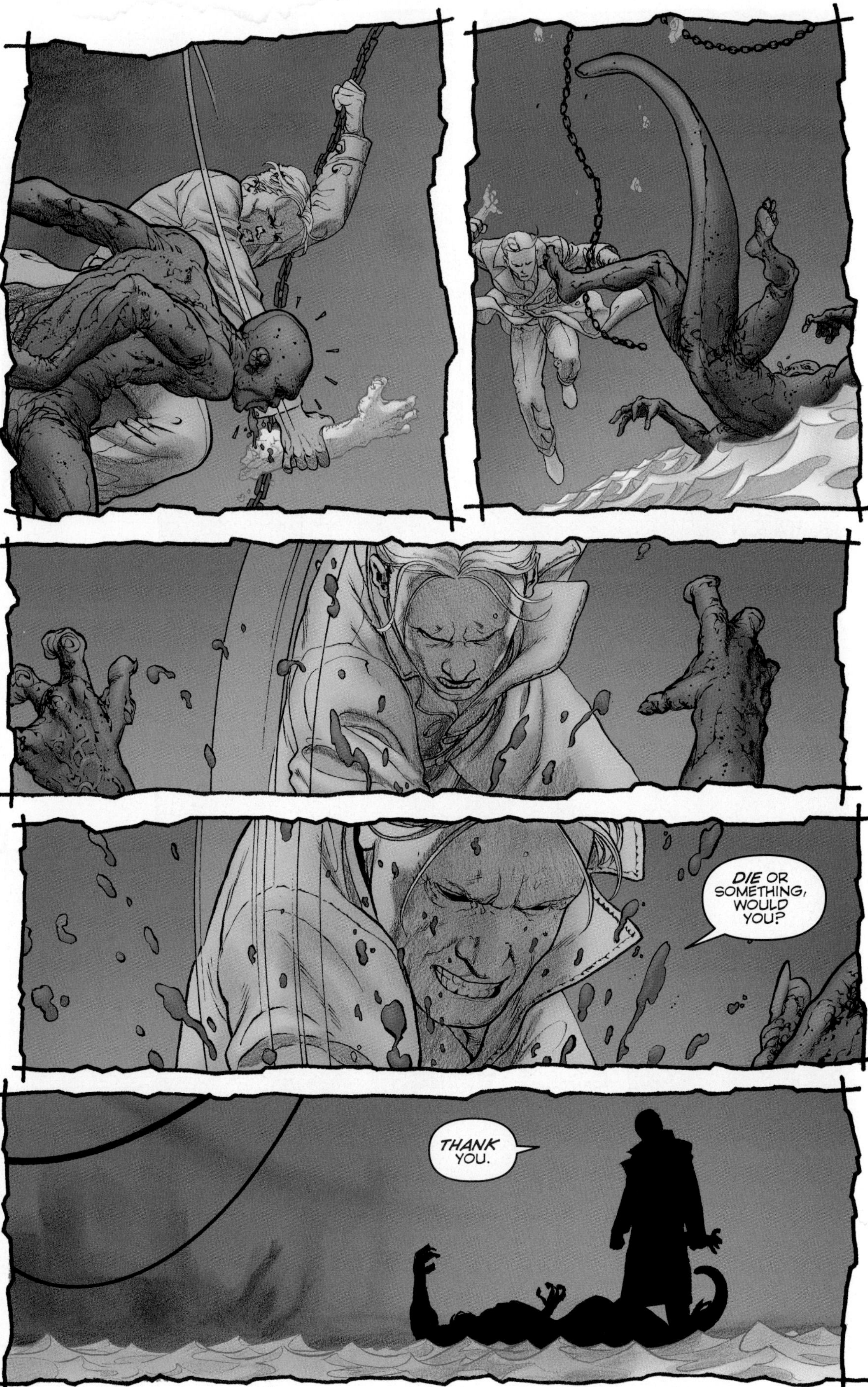
DIE OR SOMETHING, WOULD YOU?
THANK YOU.

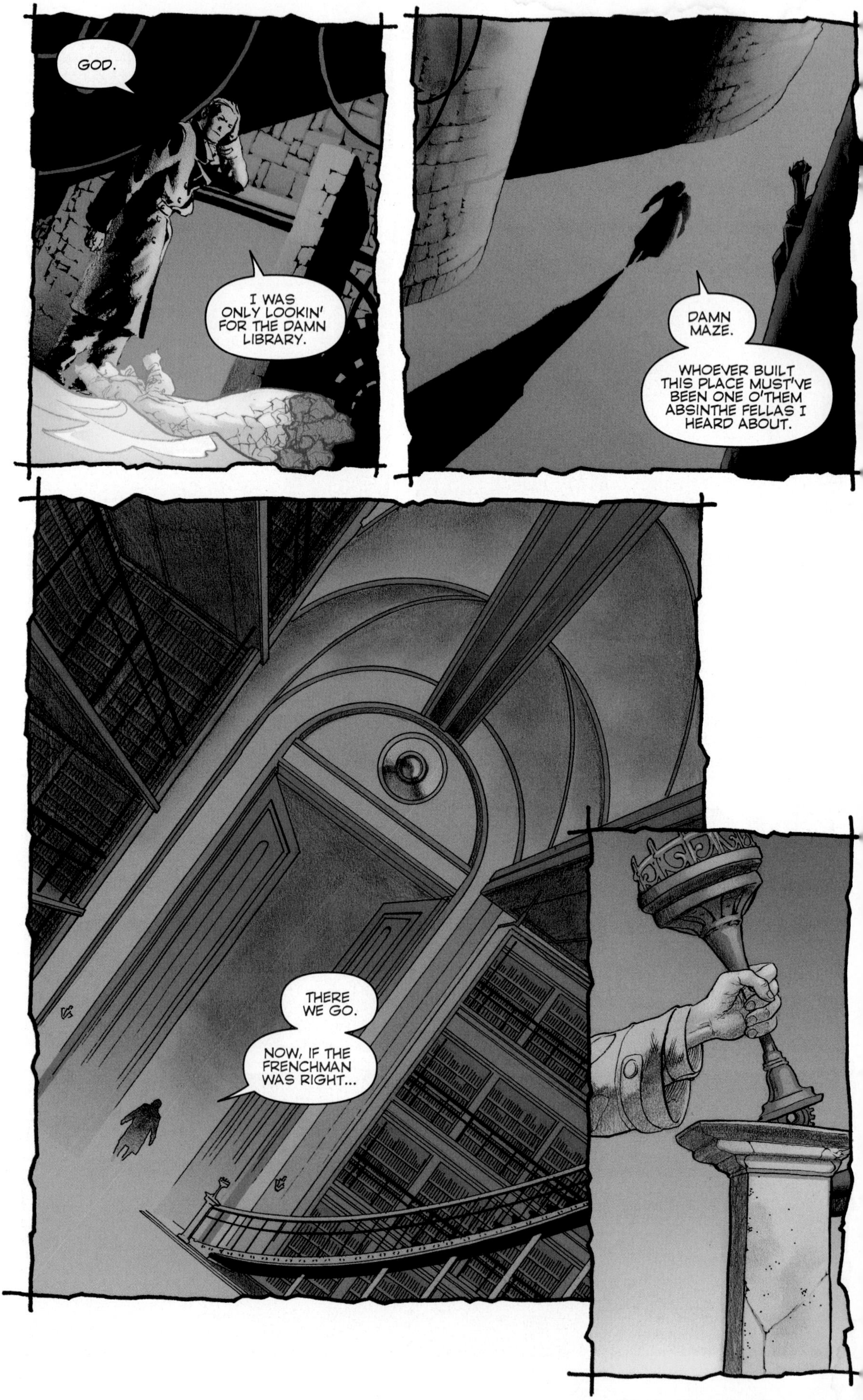
GOD.
I WAS ONLY LOOKIN' FOR THE DAMN LIBRARY.
DAMN MAZE.
WHOEVER BUILT THIS PLACE MUST'VE BEEN ONE O'THEM ABSINTHE FELLAS I HEARD ABOUT.
THERE WE GO.
NOW, IF THE FRENCHMAN WAS RIGHT...

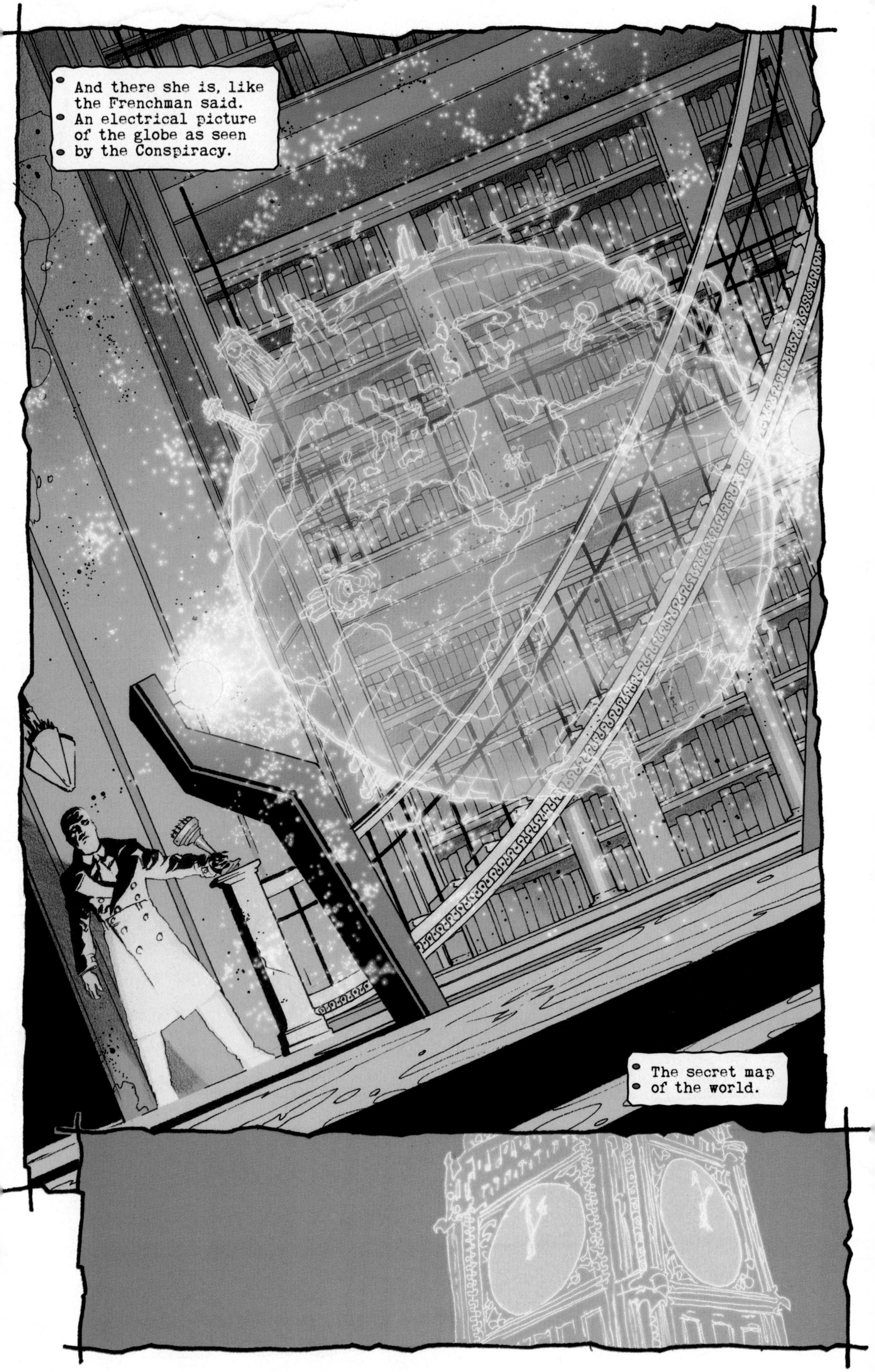
And there she is, like the Frenchman said.
An electrical picture of the globe as seen by the Conspiracy.
The secret map of the world.

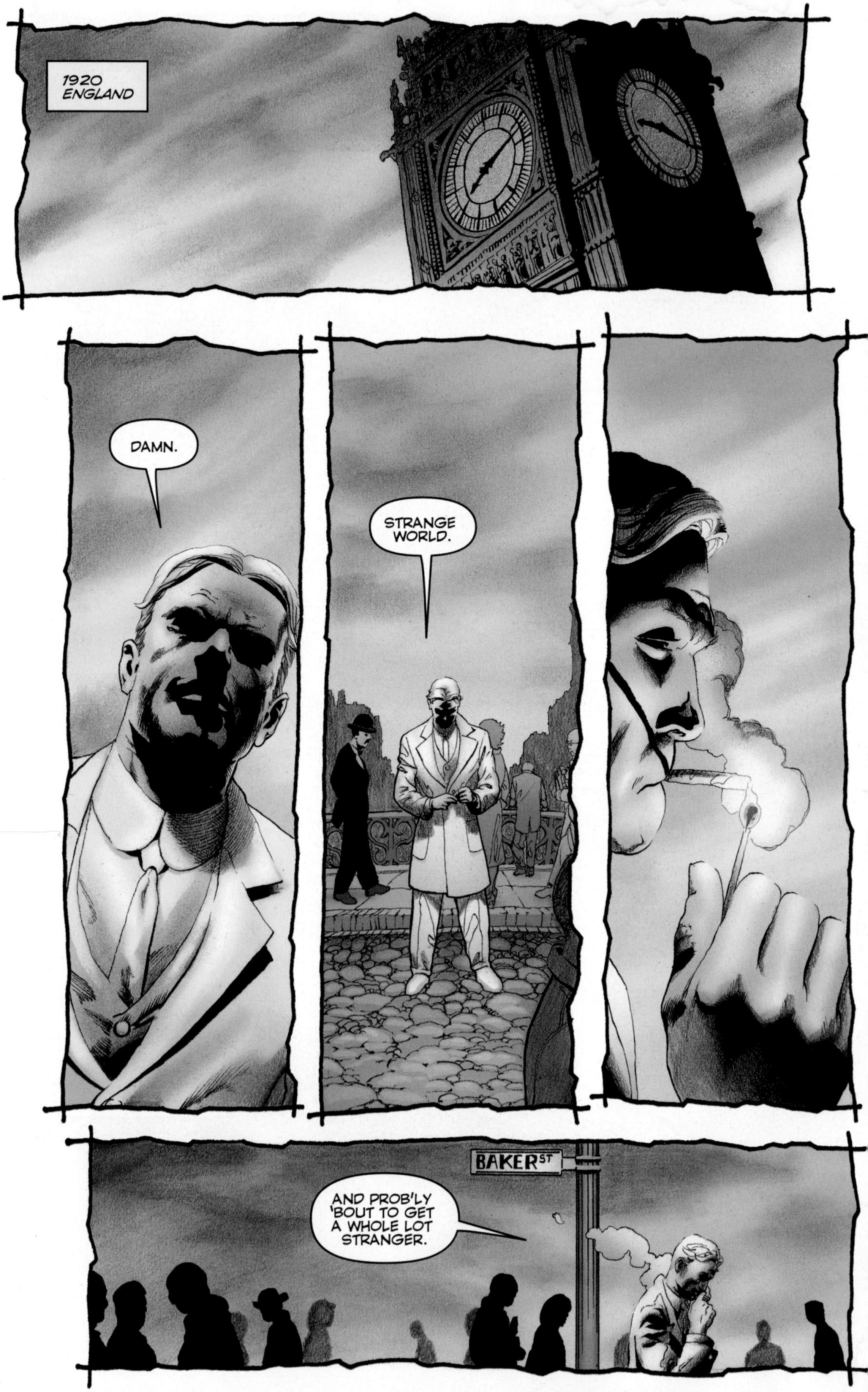
1920
ENGLAND
DAMN.
STRANGE WORLD.
AND PROB'LY 'BOUT TO GET A WHOLE LOT STRANGER.
BAKER ST

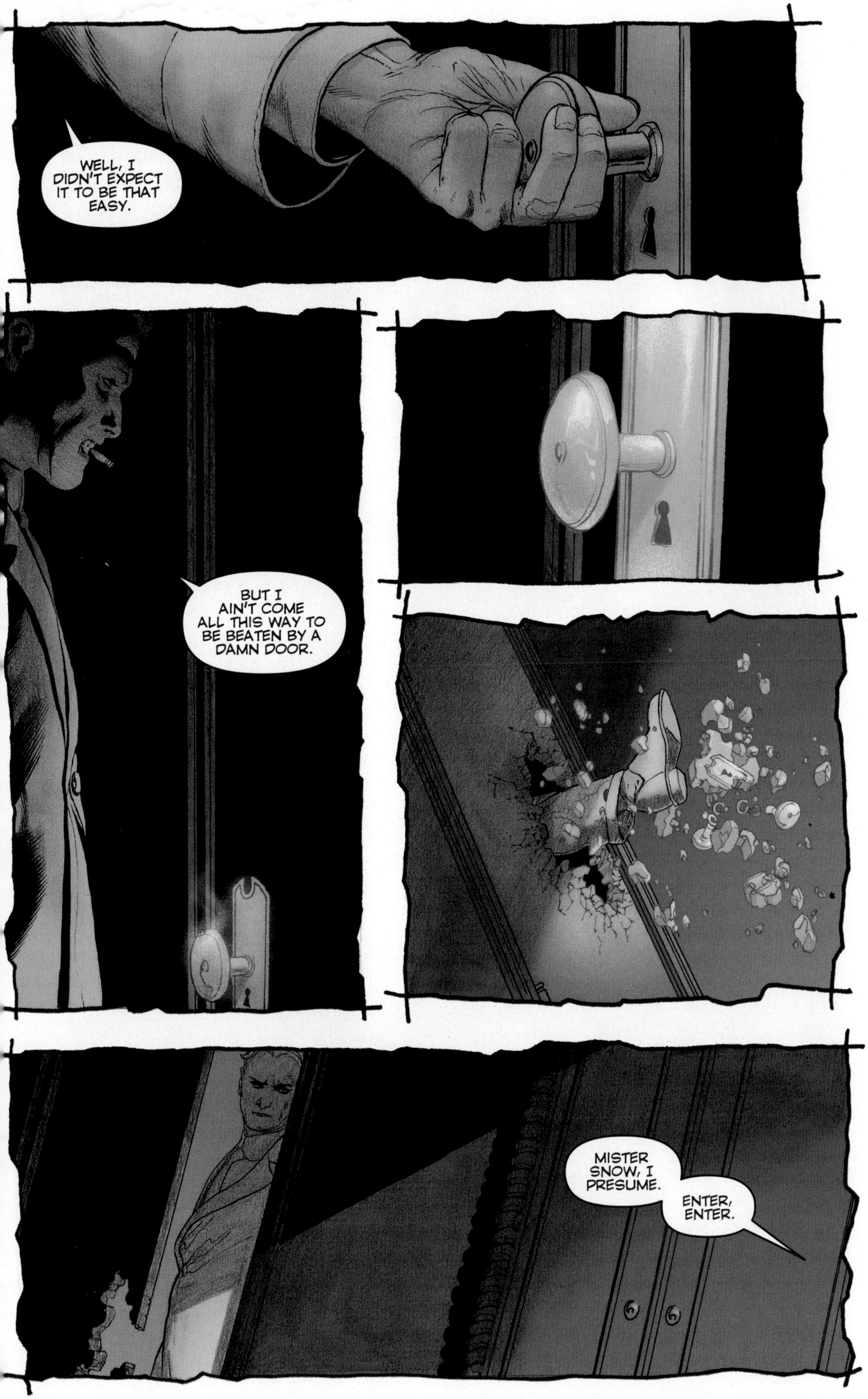
WELL, I DIDN'T EXPECT IT TO BE THAT EASY.
BUT I AIN'T COME ALL THIS WAY TO BE BEATEN BY A DAMN DOOR.
MISTER SNOW, I PRESUME.
ENTER, ENTER.

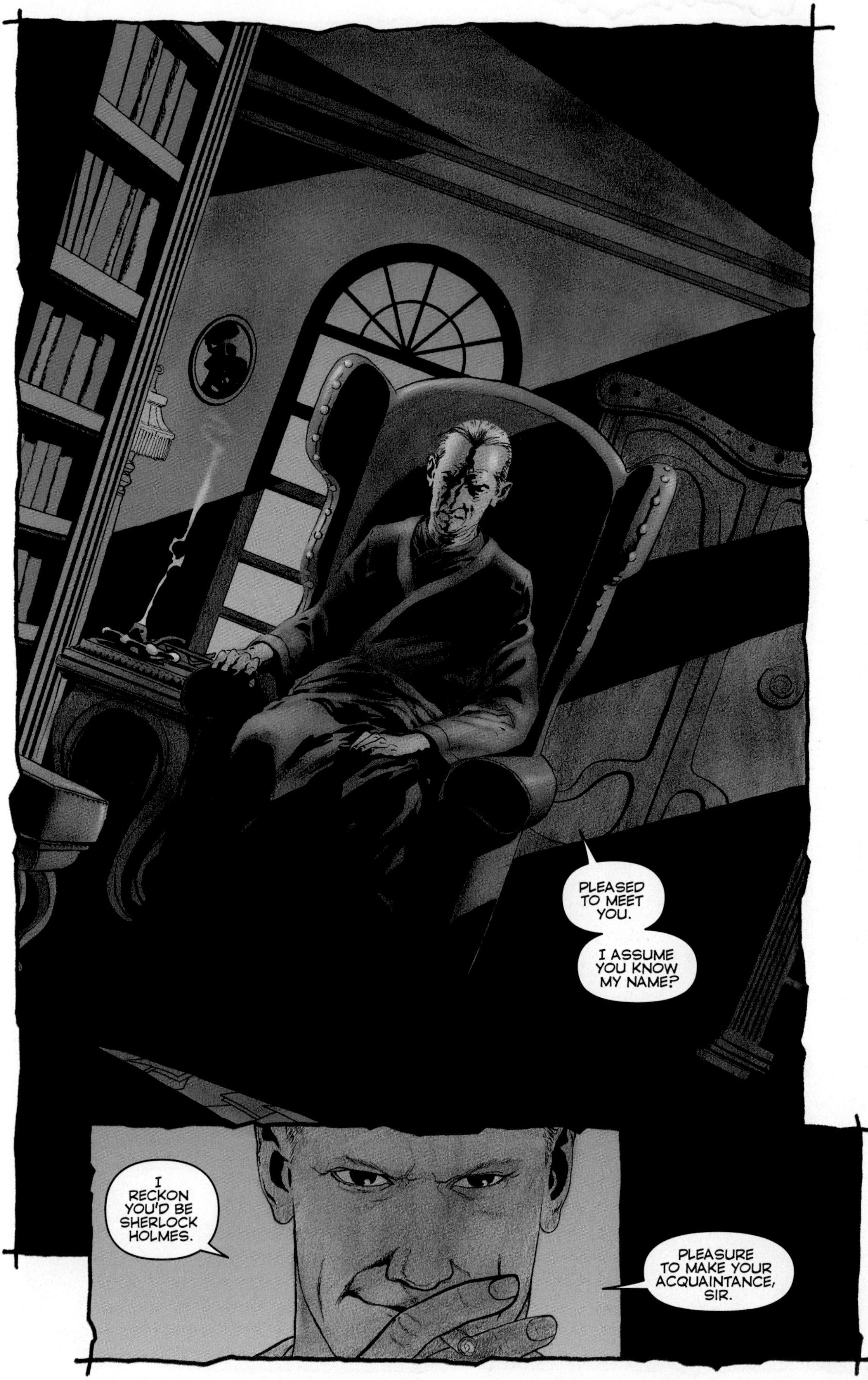
PLEASED TO MEET YOU.
I ASSUME YOU KNOW MY NAME?
I RECKON YOU'D BE SHERLOCK HOLMES.
PLEASURE TO MAKE YOUR ACQUAINTANCE, SIR.

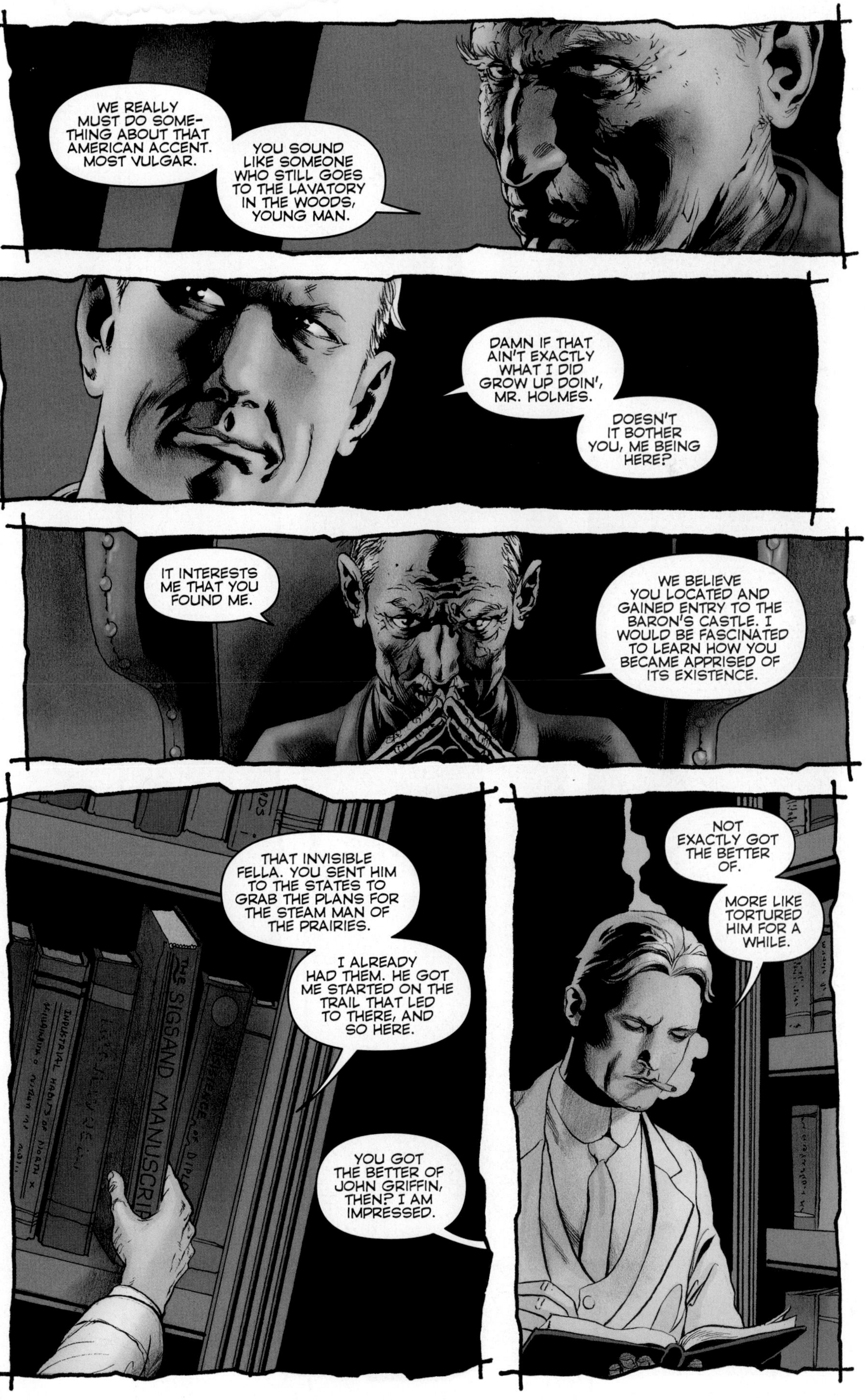

WE REALLY MUST DO SOMETHING ABOUT THAT AMERICAN ACCENT. MOST VULGAR.
YOU SOUND LIKE SOMEONE WHO STILL GOES TO THE LAVATORY IN THE WOODS, YOUNG MAN.
DAMN IF THAT AIN'T EXACTLY WHAT I DID GROW UP DOIN', MR. HOLMES.
DOESN'T IT BOTHER YOU, ME BEING HERE?
IT INTERESTS ME THAT YOU FOUND ME.
WE BELIEVE YOU LOCATED AND GAINED ENTRY TO THE BARON'S CASTLE. I WOULD BE FASCINATED TO LEARN HOW YOU BECAME APPRISED OF ITS EXISTENCE.
THAT INVISIBLE FELLA. YOU SENT HIM TO THE STATES TO GRAB THE PLANS FOR THE STEAM MAN OF THE PRAIRIES.
I ALREADY HAD THEM. HE GOT ME STARTED ON THE TRAIL THAT LED TO THERE, AND SO HERE.
YOU GOT THE BETTER OF JOHN GRIFFIN, THEN? I AM IMPRESSED.
NOT EXACTLY GOT THE BETTER OF.
MORE LIKE TORTURED HIM FOR A WHILE.

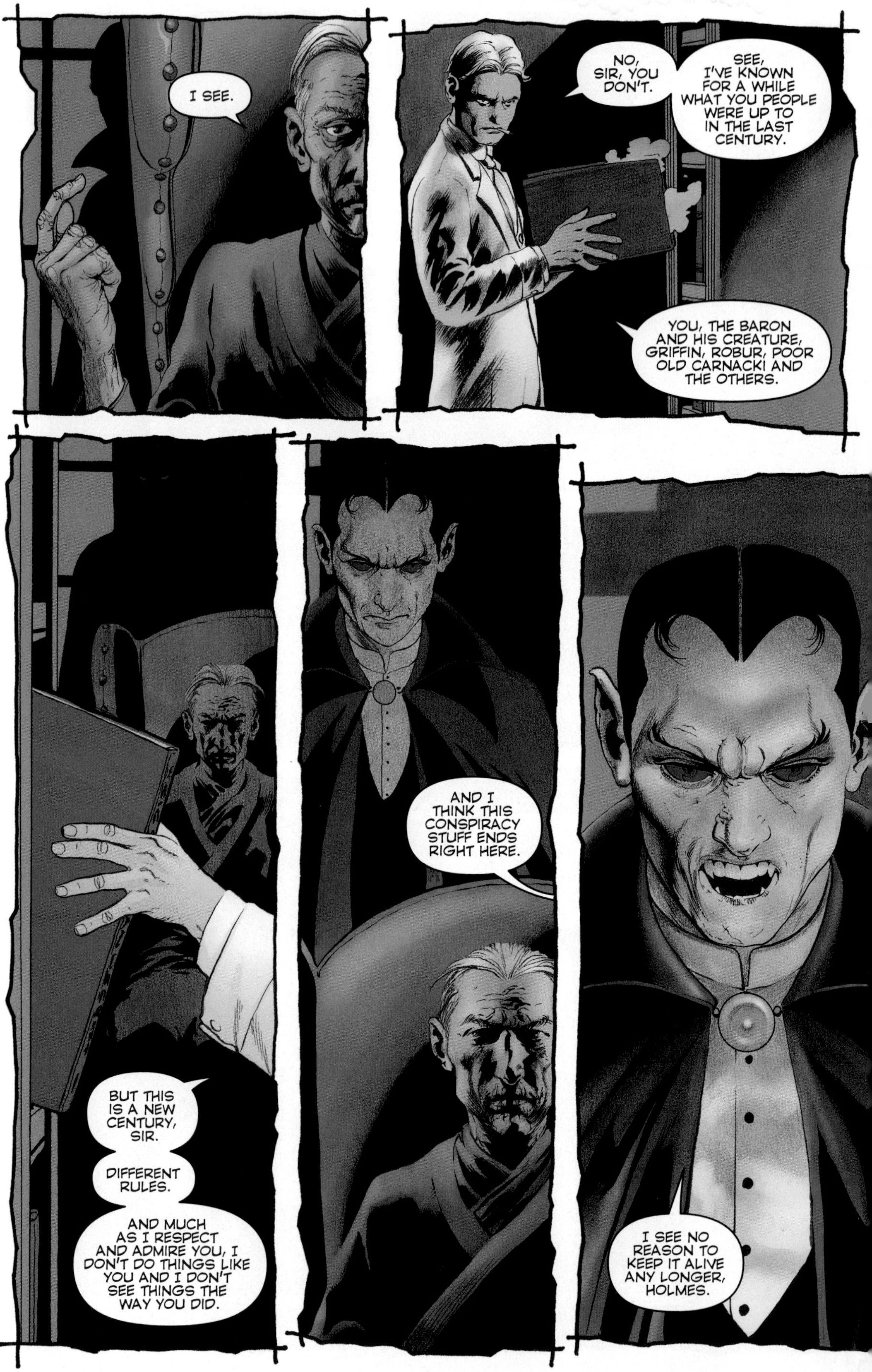
I SEE.
NO, SIR, YOU DON'T.
SEE, I'VE KNOWN FOR A WHILE WHAT YOU PEOPLE WERE UP TO IN THE LAST CENTURY.
YOU, THE BARON AND HIS CREATURE, GRIFFIN, ROBUR, POOR OLD CARNACKI AND THE OTHERS.
BUT THIS IS A NEW CENTURY, SIR.
DIFFERENT RULES.
AND MUCH AS I RESPECT AND ADMIRE YOU, I DON'T DO THINGS LIKE YOU AND I DON'T SEE THINGS THE WAY YOU DID.
AND I THINK THIS CONSPIRACY STUFF ENDS RIGHT HERE.
I SEE NO REASON TO KEEP IT ALIVE ANY LONGER, HOLMES.

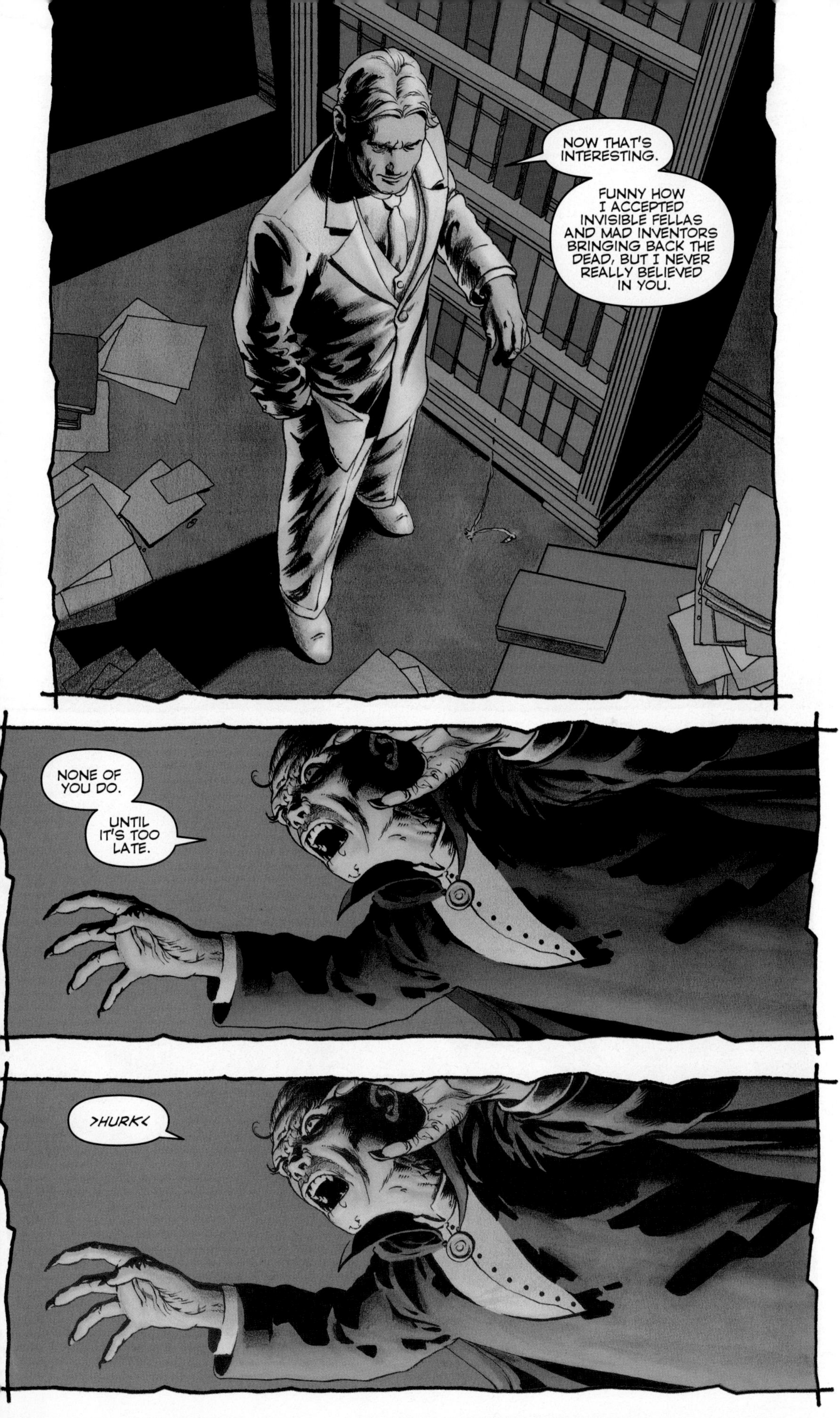
NOW THAT'S INTERESTING.
FUNNY HOW I ACCEPTED INVISIBLE FELLAS AND MAD INVENTORS BRINGING BACK THE DEAD, BUT I NEVER REALLY BELIEVED IN YOU.
NONE OF YOU DO.
UNTIL IT'S TOO LATE.
>HURK<

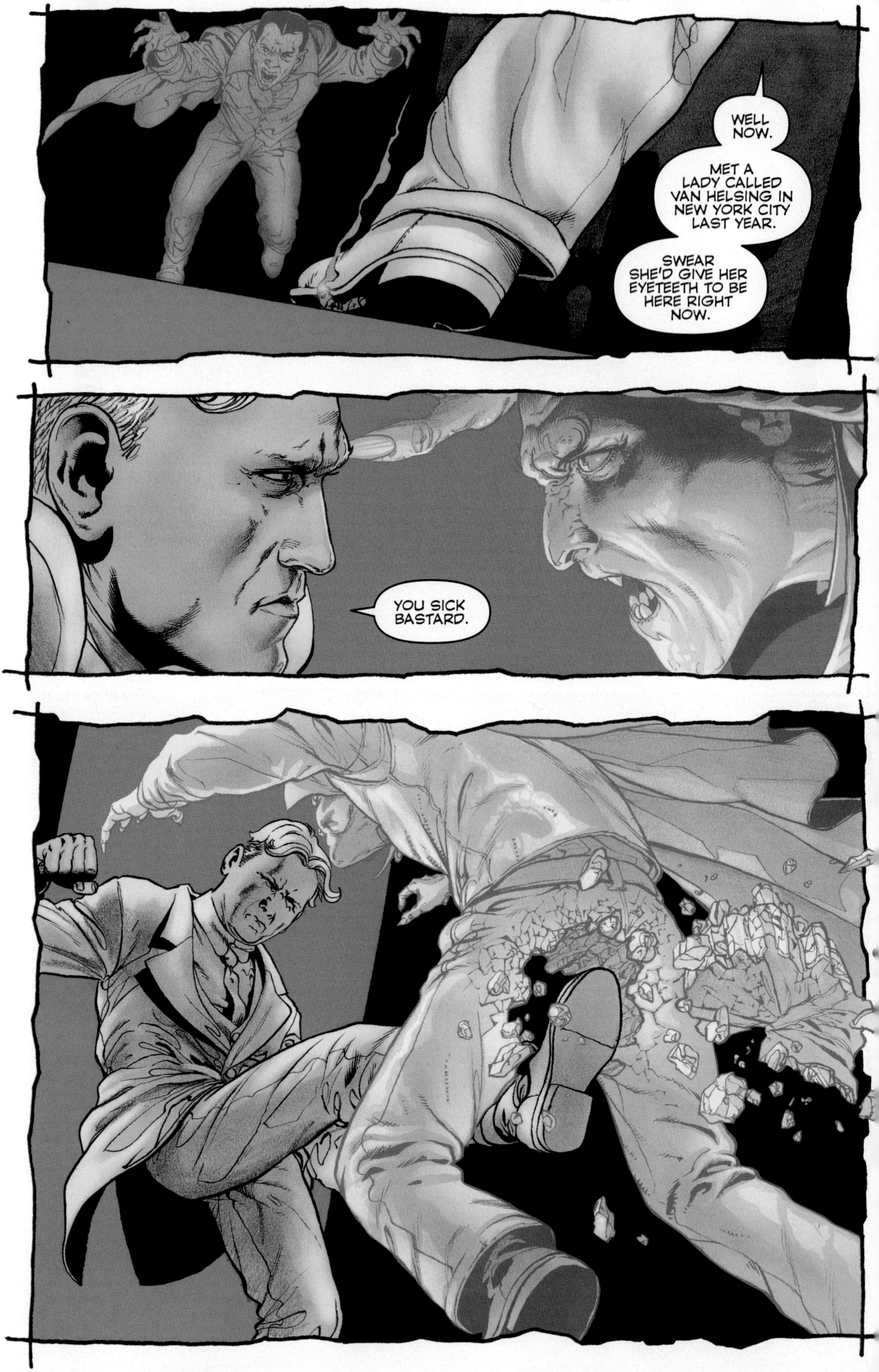
WELL NOW.
MET A LADY CALLED VAN HELSING IN NEW YORK CITY LAST YEAR.
SWEAR SHE'D GIVE HER EYETEETH TO BE HERE RIGHT NOW.
YOU SICK BASTARD.

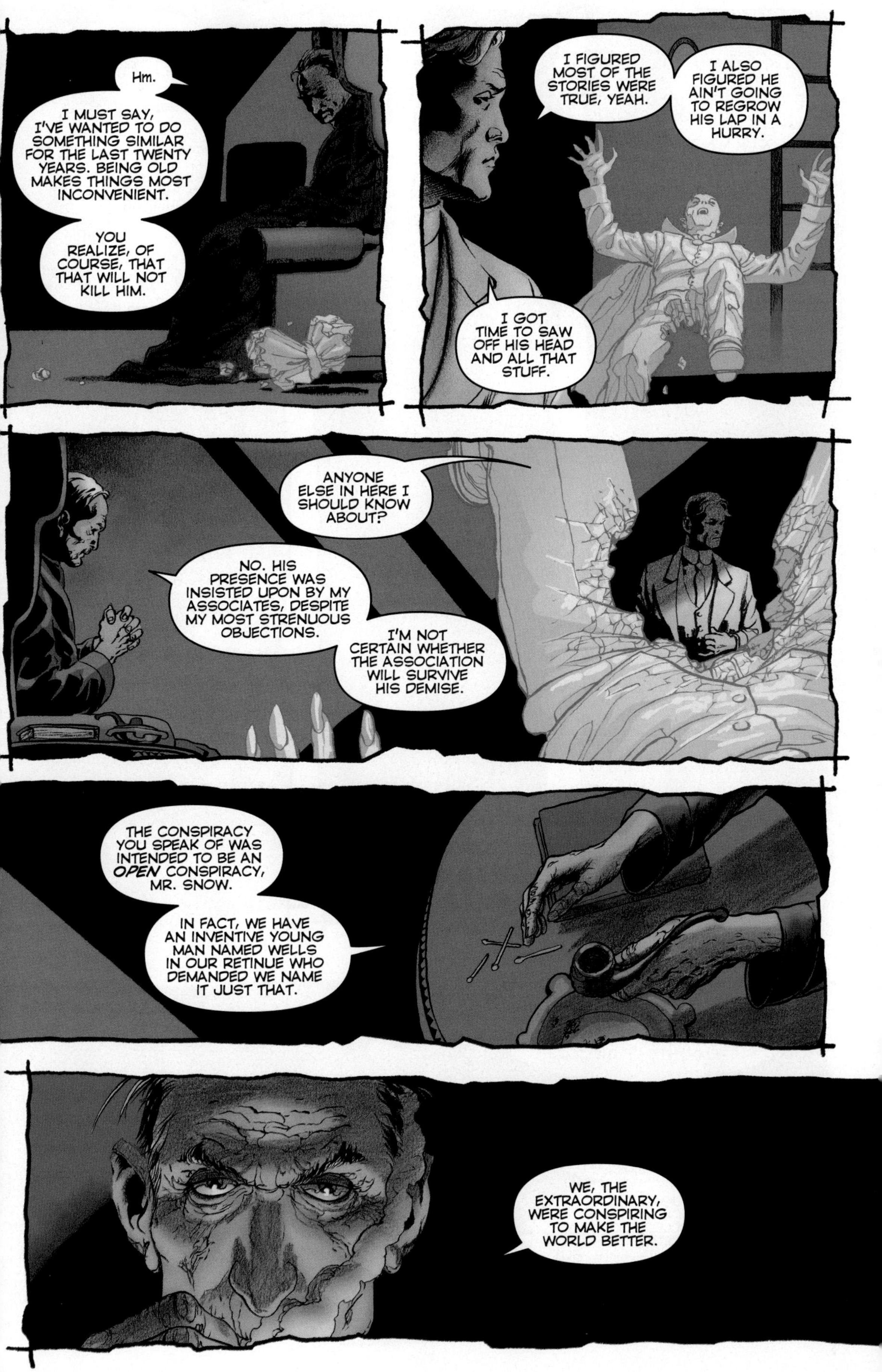
Hm.
I MUST SAY, I'VE WANTED TO DO SOMETHING SIMILAR FOR THE LAST TWENTY YEARS. BEING OLD MAKES THINGS MOST INCONVENIENT.
YOU REALIZE, OF COURSE, THAT THAT WILL NOT KILL HIM.
I FIGURED MOST OF THE STORIES WERE TRUE, YEAH.
I ALSO FIGURED HE AIN'T GOING TO REGROW HIS LAP IN A HURRY.
I GOT TIME TO SAW OFF HIS HEAD AND ALL THAT STUFF.
ANYONE ELSE IN HERE I SHOULD KNOW ABOUT?
NO. HIS PRESENCE WAS INSISTED UPON BY MY ASSOCIATES, DESPITE MY MOST STRENUOUS OBJECTIONS.
I'M NOT CERTAIN WHETHER THE ASSOCIATION WILL SURVIVE HIS DEMISE.
THE CONSPIRACY YOU SPEAK OF WAS INTENDED TO BE AN *OPEN* CONSPIRACY, MR. SNOW.
IN FACT, WE HAVE AN INVENTIVE YOUNG MAN NAMED WELLS IN OUR RETINUE WHO DEMANDED WE NAME IT JUST THAT.
WE, THE EXTRAORDINARY, WERE CONSPIRING TO MAKE THE WORLD BETTER.

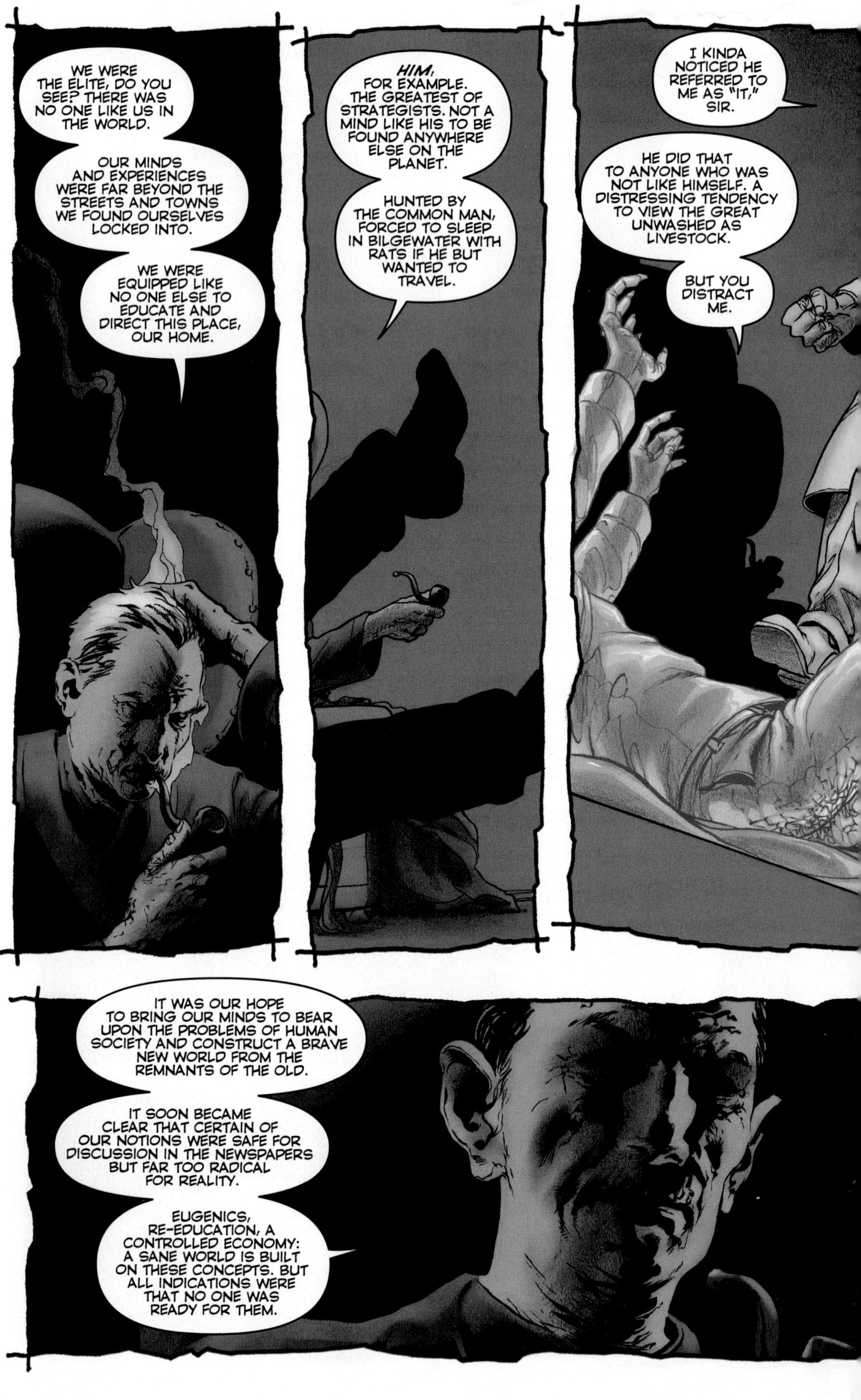
WE WERE THE ELITE, DO YOU SEE? THERE WAS NO ONE LIKE US IN THE WORLD.
OUR MINDS AND EXPERIENCES WERE FAR BEYOND THE STREETS AND TOWNS WE FOUND OURSELVES LOCKED INTO.
WE WERE EQUIPPED LIKE NO ONE ELSE TO EDUCATE AND DIRECT THIS PLACE, OUR HOME.
HIM, FOR EXAMPLE. THE GREATEST OF STRATEGISTS. NOT A MIND LIKE HIS TO BE FOUND ANYWHERE ELSE ON THE PLANET.
HUNTED BY THE COMMON MAN, FORCED TO SLEEP IN BILGEWATER WITH RATS IF HE BUT WANTED TO TRAVEL.
I KINDA NOTICED HE REFERRED TO ME AS "IT," SIR.
HE DID THAT TO ANYONE WHO WAS NOT LIKE HIMSELF. A DISTRESSING TENDENCY TO VIEW THE GREAT UNWASHED AS LIVESTOCK.
BUT YOU DISTRACT ME.
IT WAS OUR HOPE TO BRING OUR MINDS TO BEAR UPON THE PROBLEMS OF HUMAN SOCIETY AND CONSTRUCT A BRAVE NEW WORLD FROM THE REMNANTS OF THE OLD.
IT SOON BECAME CLEAR THAT CERTAIN OF OUR NOTIONS WERE SAFE FOR DISCUSSION IN THE NEWSPAPERS BUT FAR TOO RADICAL FOR REALITY.
EUGENICS, RE-EDUCATION, A CONTROLLED ECONOMY: A SANE WORLD IS BUILT ON THESE CONCEPTS. BUT ALL INDICATIONS WERE THAT NO ONE WAS READY FOR THEM.

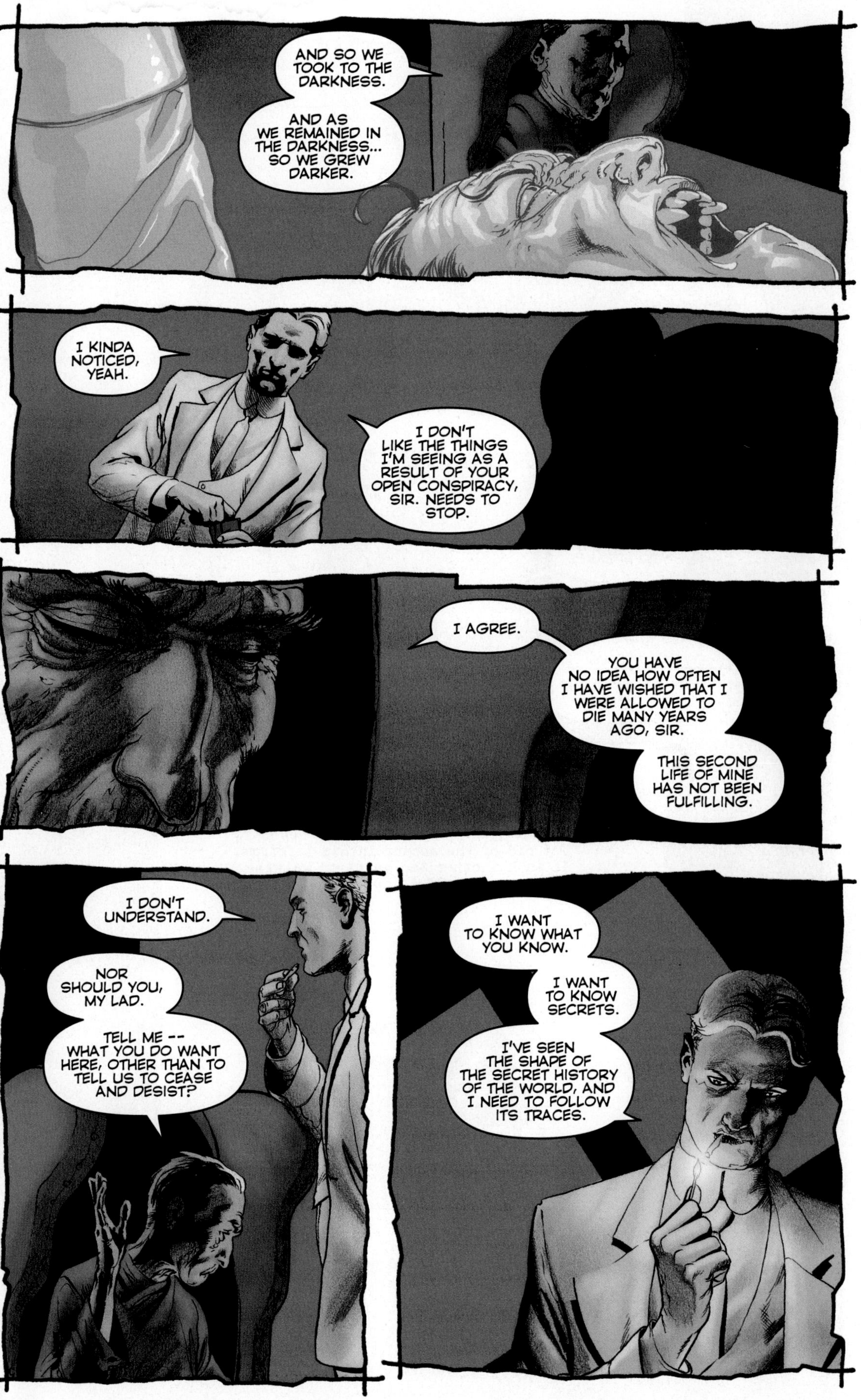
AND SO WE TOOK TO THE DARKNESS.
AND AS WE REMAINED IN THE DARKNESS... SO WE GREW DARKER.
I KINDA NOTICED, YEAH.
I DON'T LIKE THE THINGS I'M SEEING AS A RESULT OF YOUR OPEN CONSPIRACY, SIR. NEEDS TO STOP.
I AGREE.
YOU HAVE NO IDEA HOW OFTEN I HAVE WISHED THAT I WERE ALLOWED TO DIE MANY YEARS AGO, SIR.
THIS SECOND LIFE OF MINE HAS NOT BEEN FULFILLING.
I DON'T UNDERSTAND.
NOR SHOULD YOU, MY LAD.
TELL ME -- WHAT YOU DO WANT HERE, OTHER THAN TO TELL US TO CEASE AND DESIST?
I WANT TO KNOW WHAT YOU KNOW.
I WANT TO KNOW SECRETS.
I'VE SEEN THE SHAPE OF THE SECRET HISTORY OF THE WORLD, AND I NEED TO FOLLOW ITS TRACES.

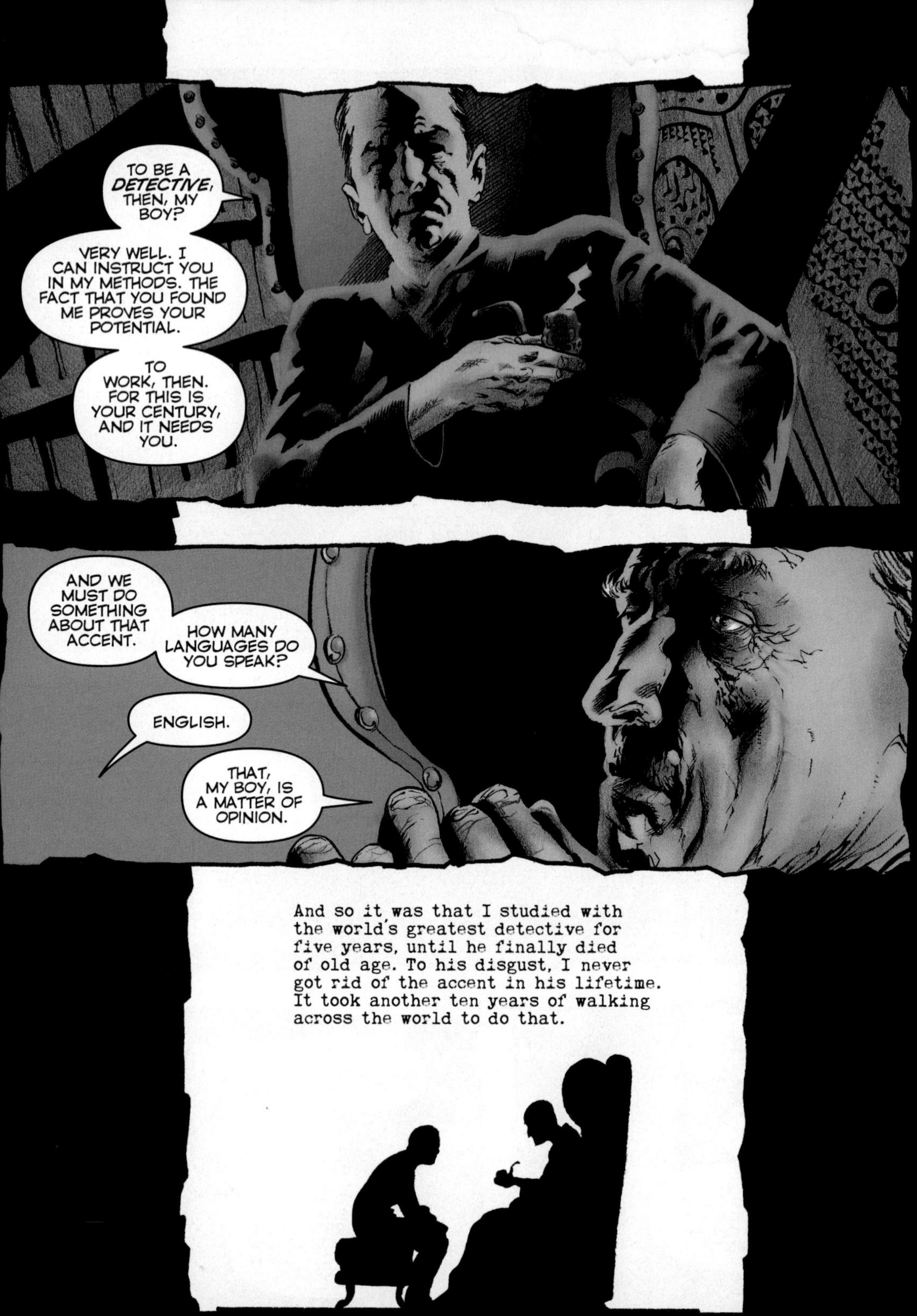
TO BE A *DETECTIVE*, THEN, MY BOY?
VERY WELL. I CAN INSTRUCT YOU IN MY METHODS. THE FACT THAT YOU FOUND ME PROVES YOUR POTENTIAL.
TO WORK, THEN. FOR THIS IS YOUR CENTURY, AND IT NEEDS YOU.
AND WE MUST DO SOMETHING ABOUT THAT ACCENT.
HOW MANY LANGUAGES DO YOU SPEAK?
ENGLISH.
THAT, MY BOY, IS A MATTER OF OPINION.
And so it was that I studied with the world's greatest detective for five years, until he finally died of old age. To his disgust, I never got rid of the accent in his lifetime. It took another ten years of walking across the world to do that.

But I never lost my love of the secrets.
And I don't think I ever will.

Century

Elllis Cassaday DePuy O'Neil Layman

Planetary created by Warren Ellis and John Cassaday

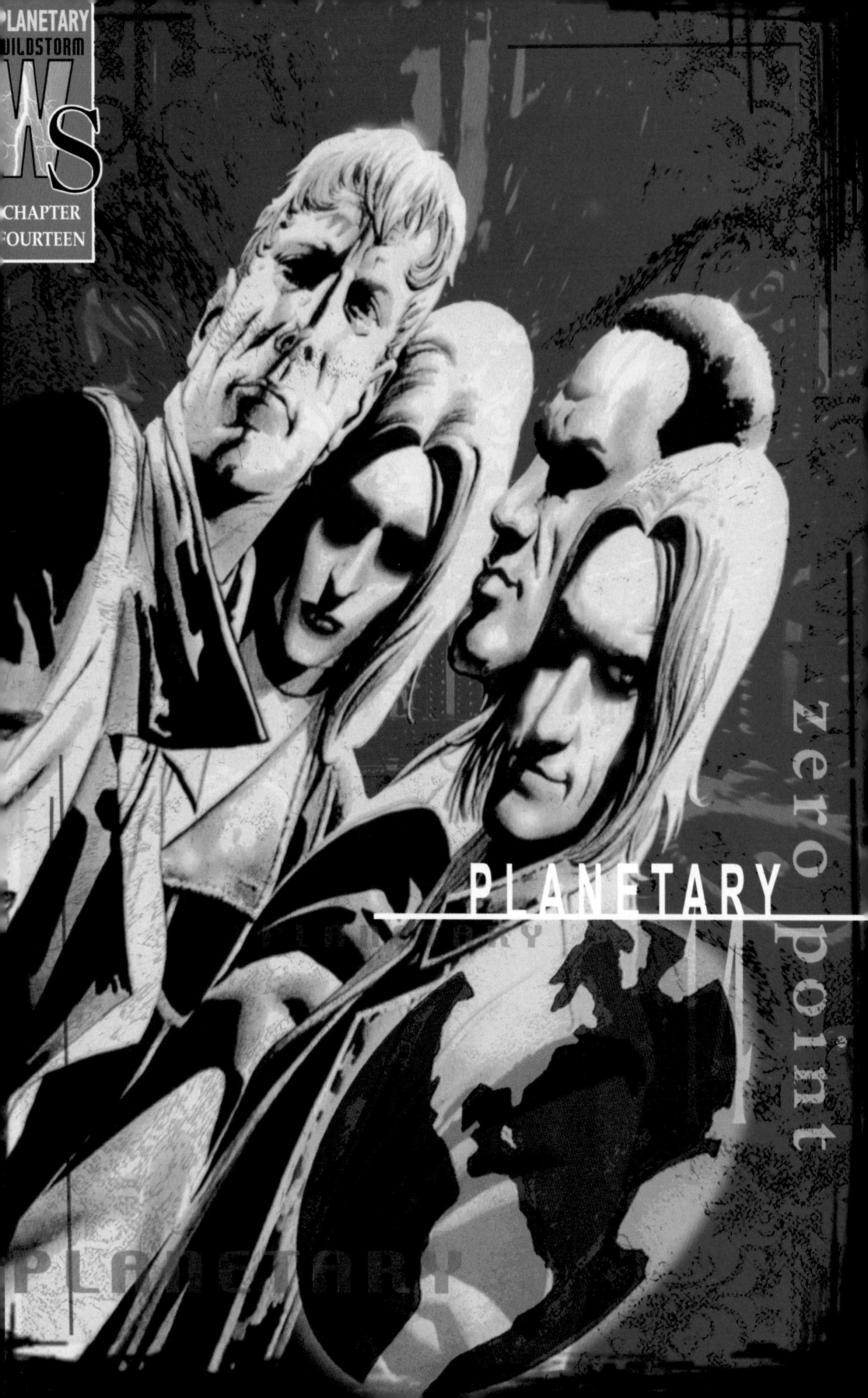
PLANETARY
WILDSTORM
WS
CHAPTER
FOURTEEN
PLANETARY
zero point
PLANETARY

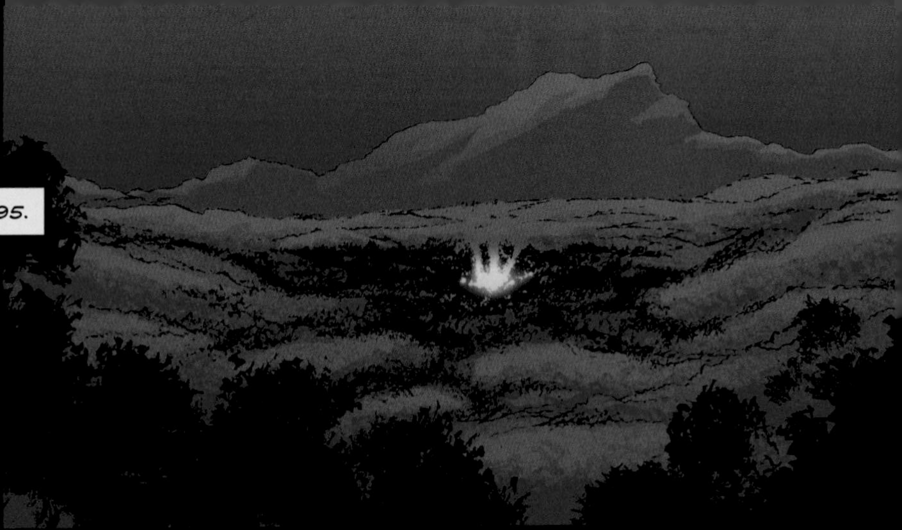
1995.

ZEROPOINT

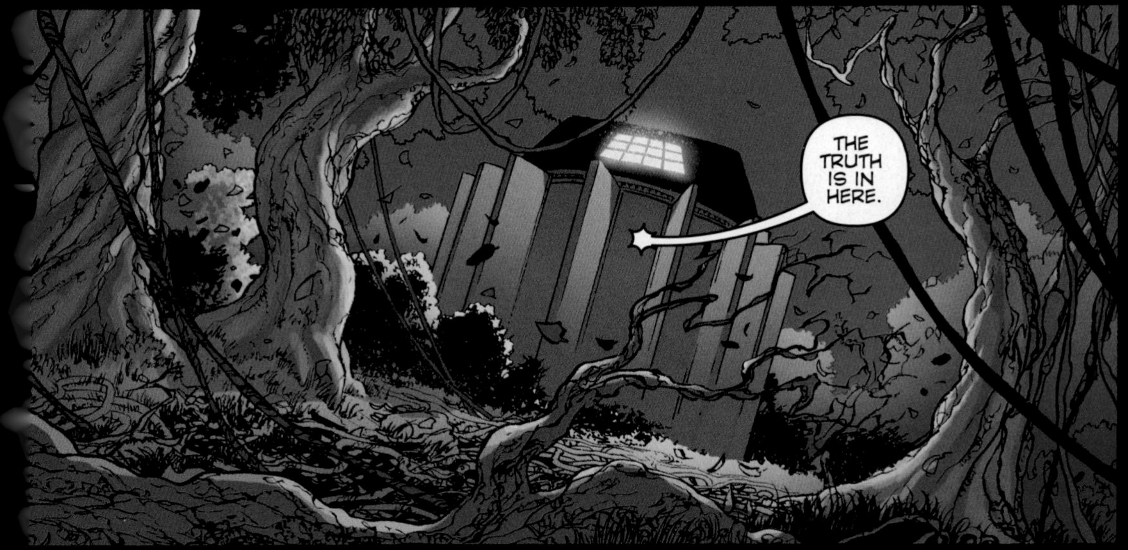
THE TRUTH IS IN HERE.

written **El**lis · drawn **Cass**aday · colored De**Puy** · lettered O'**Neil** · edited **Lay**man

Planetary created by Warren Ellis and John Cassaday

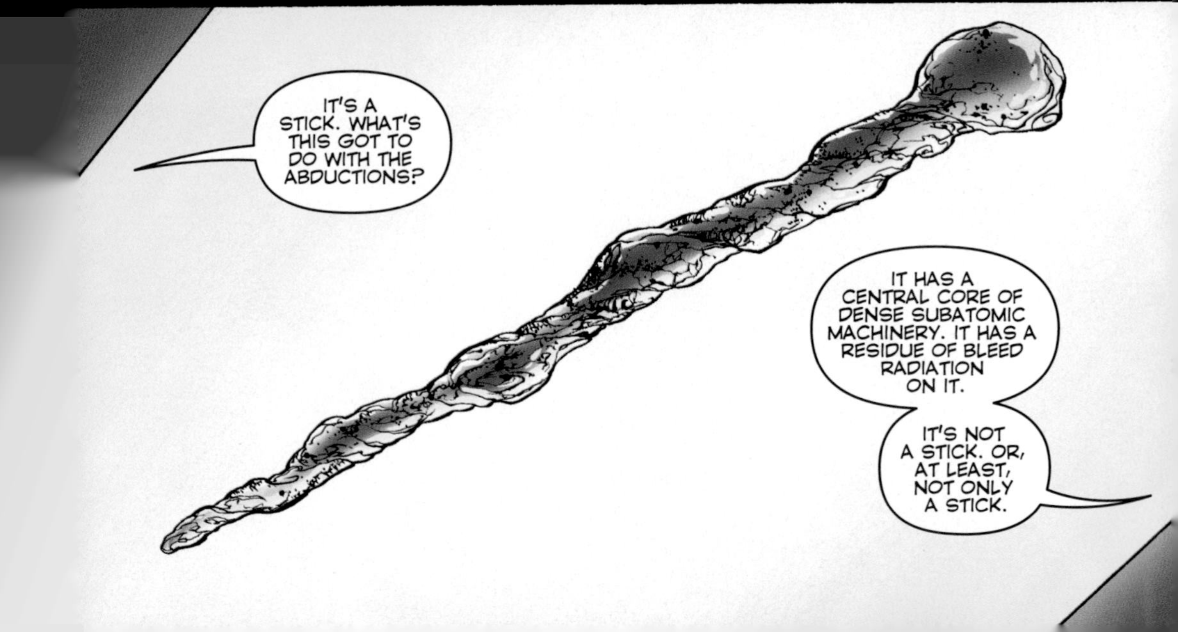
IT'S A STICK. WHAT'S THIS GOT TO DO WITH THE ABDUCTIONS?
IT HAS A CENTRAL CORE OF DENSE SUBATOMIC MACHINERY. IT HAS A RESIDUE OF BLEED RADIATION ON IT.
IT'S NOT A STICK. OR, AT LEAST, NOT ONLY A STICK.

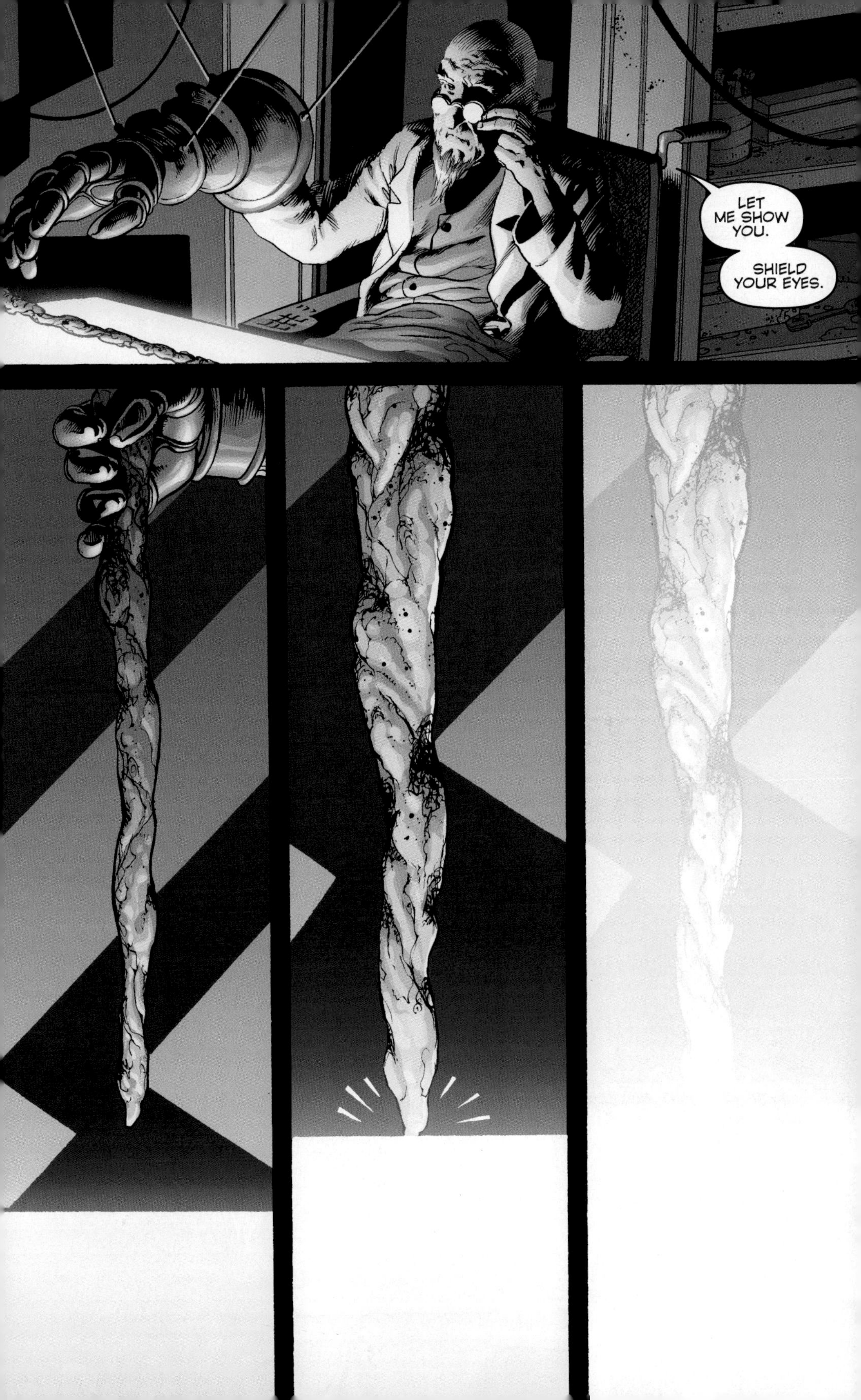
LET ME SHOW YOU.
SHIELD YOUR EYES.

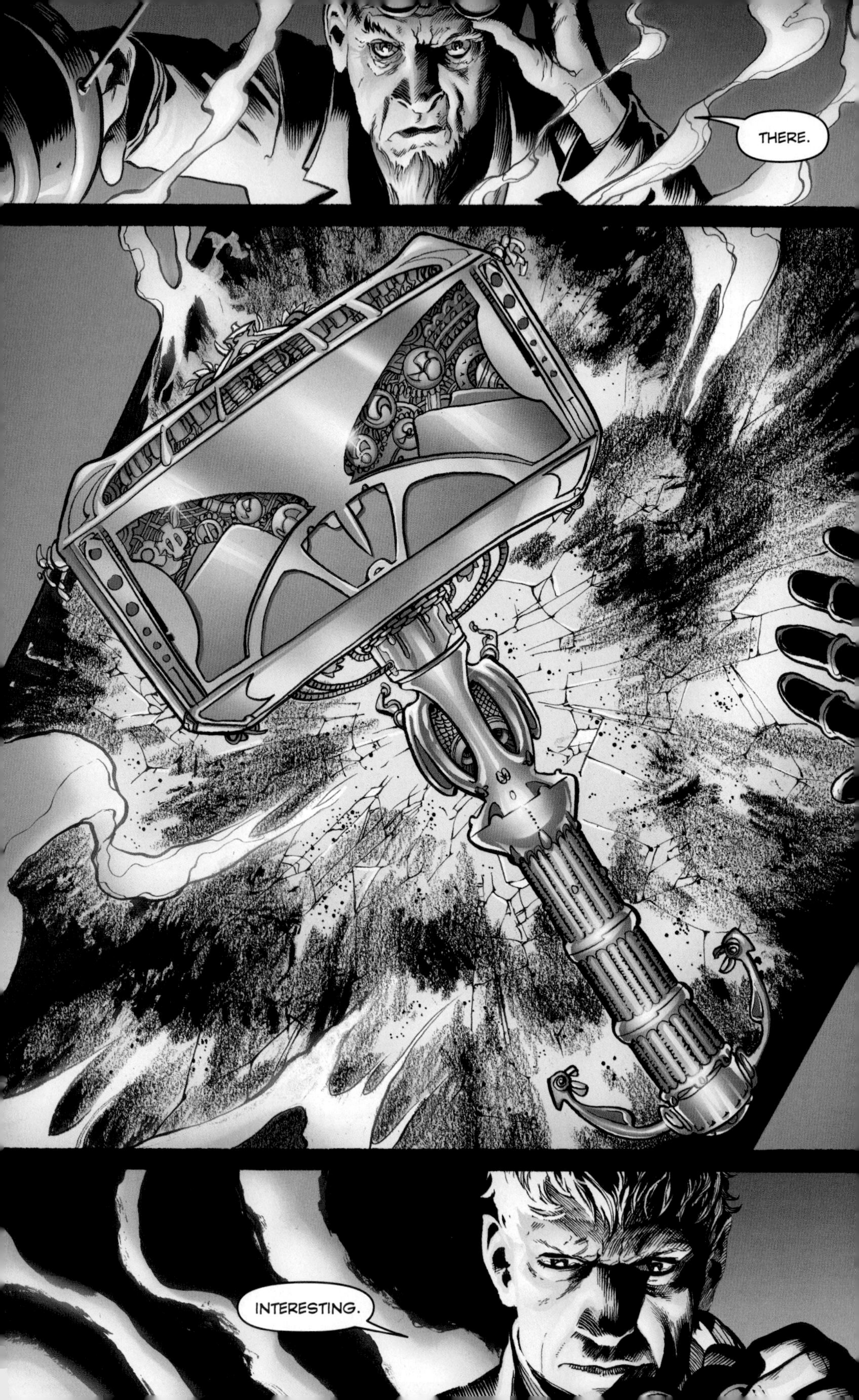
THERE.
INTERESTING.

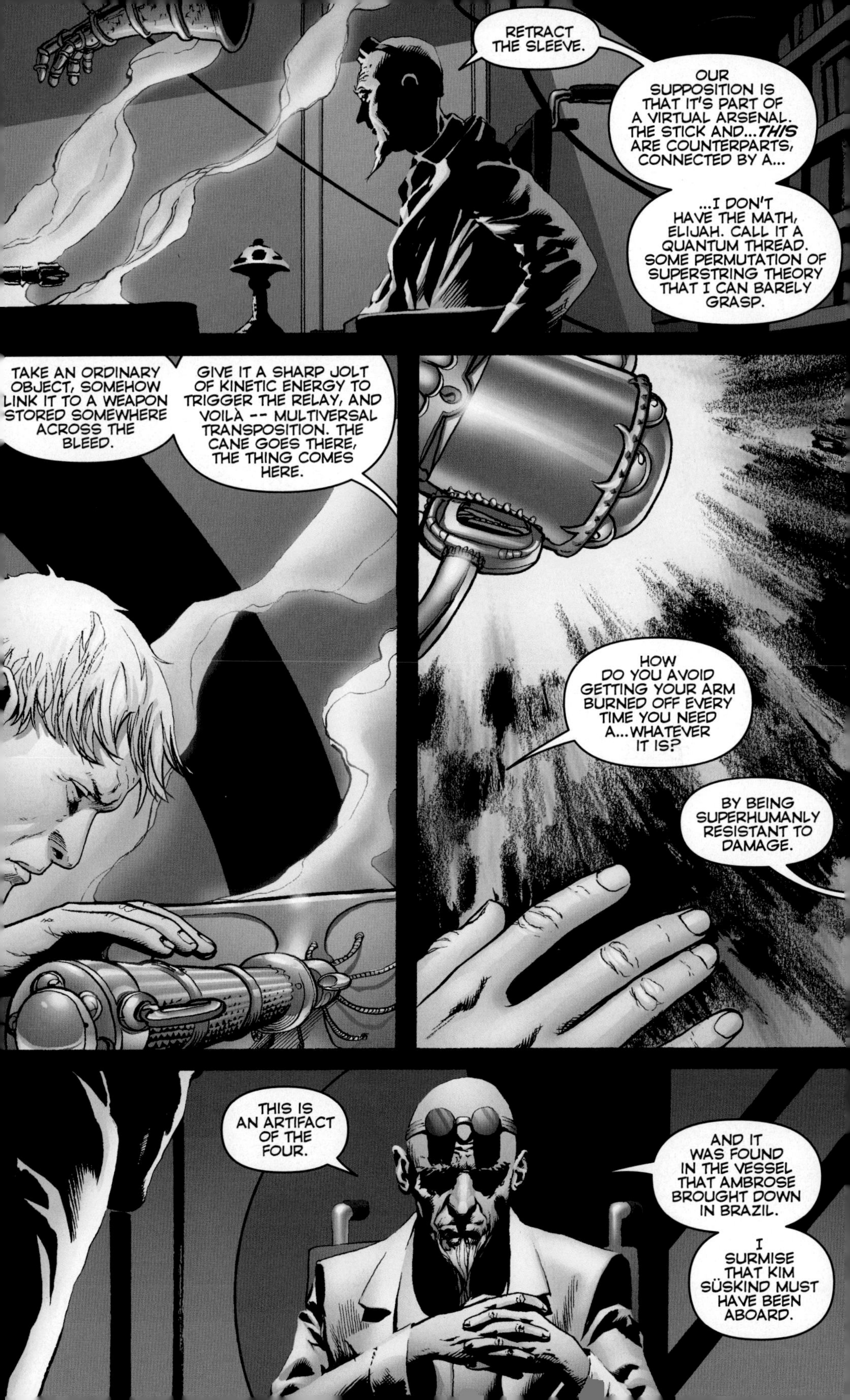
RETRACT THE SLEEVE.
OUR SUPPOSITION IS THAT IT'S PART OF A VIRTUAL ARSENAL. THE STICK AND...*THIS* ARE COUNTERPARTS, CONNECTED BY A...
...I DON'T HAVE THE MATH, ELIJAH. CALL IT A QUANTUM THREAD. SOME PERMUTATION OF SUPERSTRING THEORY THAT I CAN BARELY GRASP.
TAKE AN ORDINARY OBJECT, SOMEHOW LINK IT TO A WEAPON STORED SOMEWHERE ACROSS THE BLEED.
GIVE IT A SHARP JOLT OF KINETIC ENERGY TO TRIGGER THE RELAY, AND VOILÀ -- MULTIVERSAL TRANSPOSITION. THE CANE GOES THERE, THE THING COMES HERE.
HOW DO YOU AVOID GETTING YOUR ARM BURNED OFF EVERY TIME YOU NEED A...WHATEVER IT IS?
BY BEING SUPERHUMANLY RESISTANT TO DAMAGE.
THIS IS AN ARTIFACT OF THE FOUR.
AND IT WAS FOUND IN THE VESSEL THAT AMBROSE BROUGHT DOWN IN BRAZIL.
I SURMISE THAT KIM SÜSKIND MUST HAVE BEEN ABOARD.

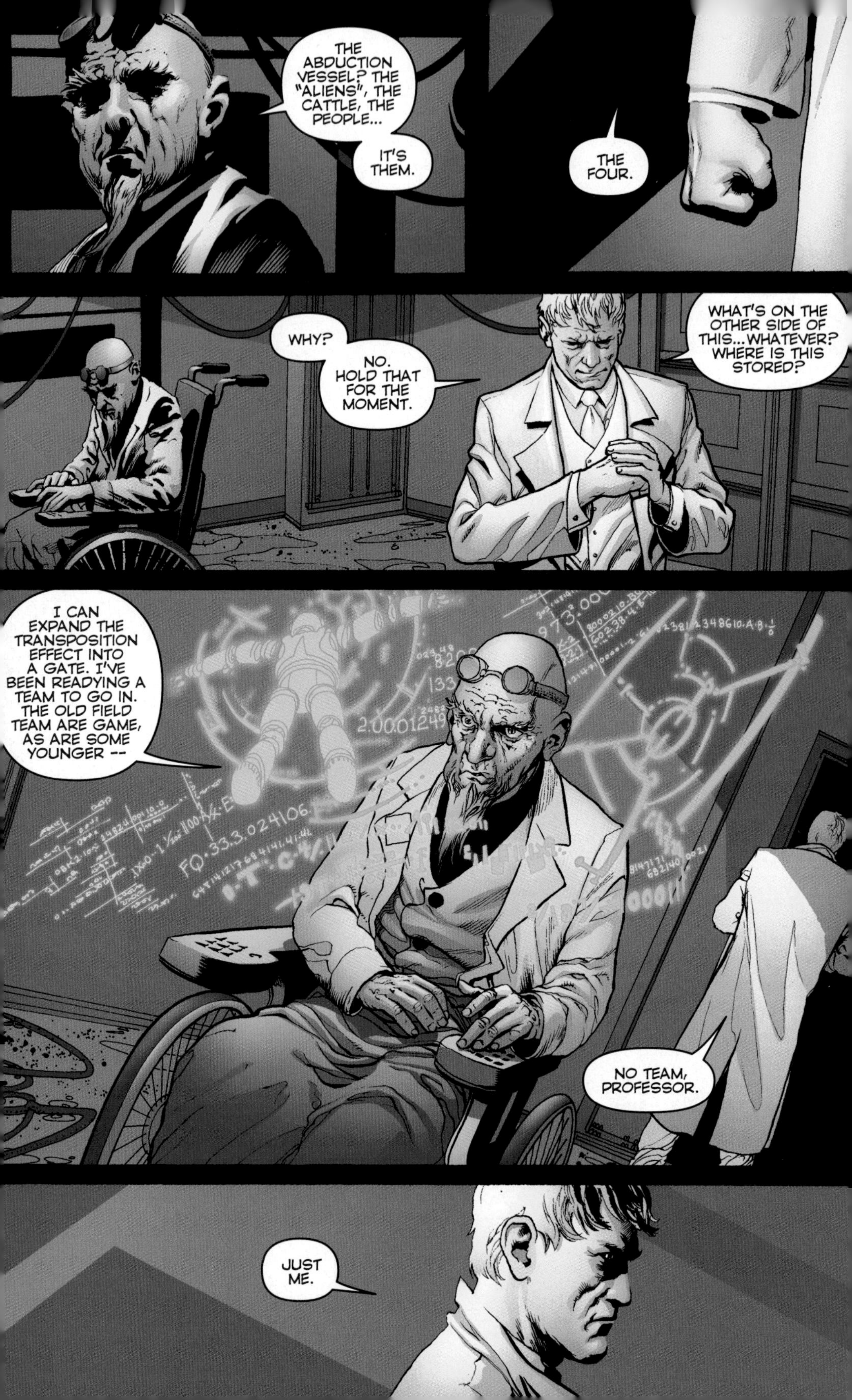
THE ABDUCTION VESSEL? THE "ALIENS", THE CATTLE, THE PEOPLE...
IT'S THEM.
THE FOUR.
WHY?
NO. HOLD THAT FOR THE MOMENT.
WHAT'S ON THE OTHER SIDE OF THIS...WHATEVER? WHERE IS THIS STORED?
I CAN EXPAND THE TRANSPOSITION EFFECT INTO A GATE. I'VE BEEN READYING A TEAM TO GO IN. THE OLD FIELD TEAM ARE GAME, AS ARE SOME YOUNGER --
NO TEAM, PROFESSOR.
JUST ME.

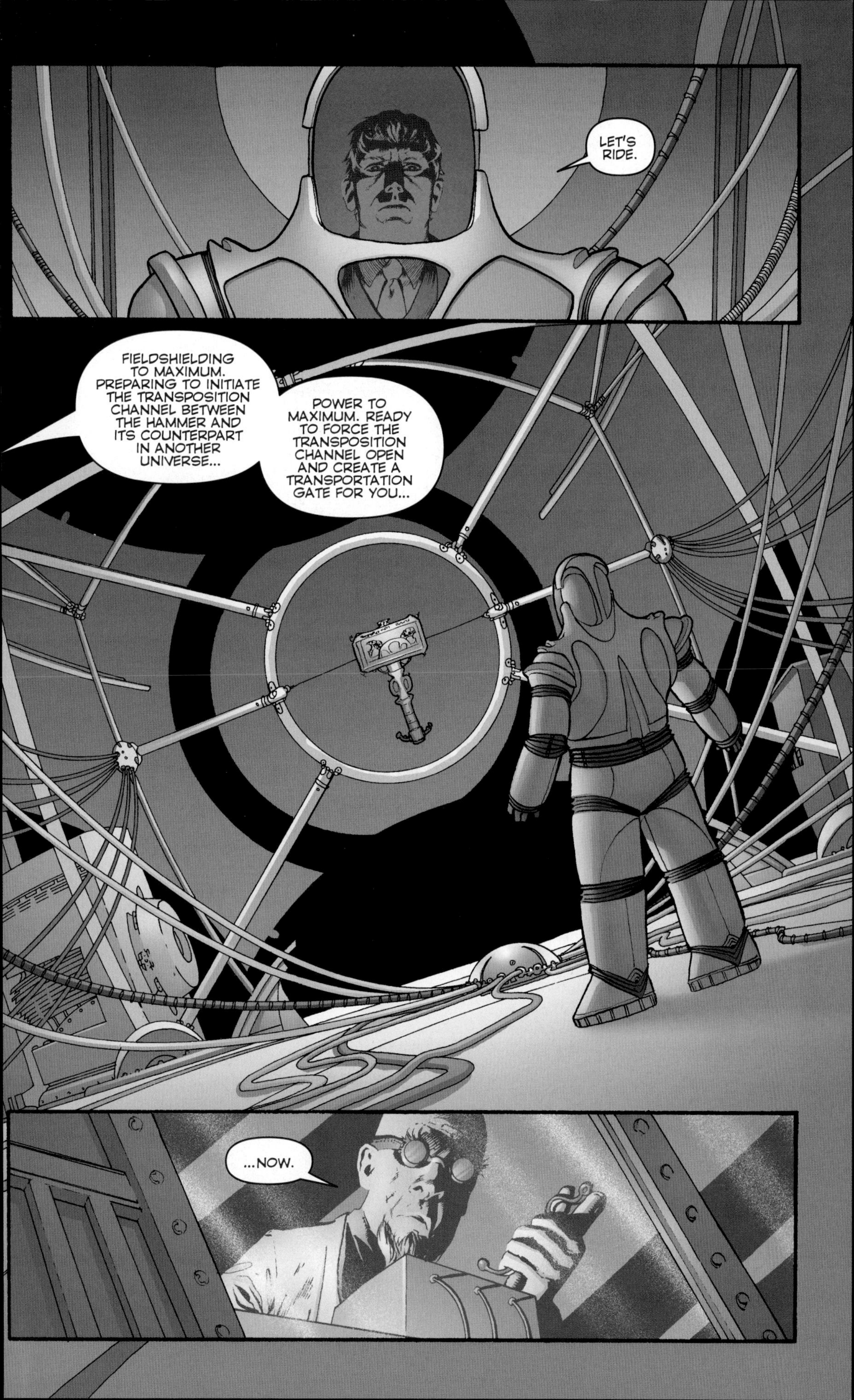
LET'S RIDE.
FIELDSHIELDING TO MAXIMUM. PREPARING TO INITIATE THE TRANSPOSITION CHANNEL BETWEEN THE HAMMER AND ITS COUNTERPART IN ANOTHER UNIVERSE...
POWER TO MAXIMUM. READY TO FORCE THE TRANSPOSITION CHANNEL OPEN AND CREATE A TRANSPORTATION GATE FOR YOU...
...NOW.

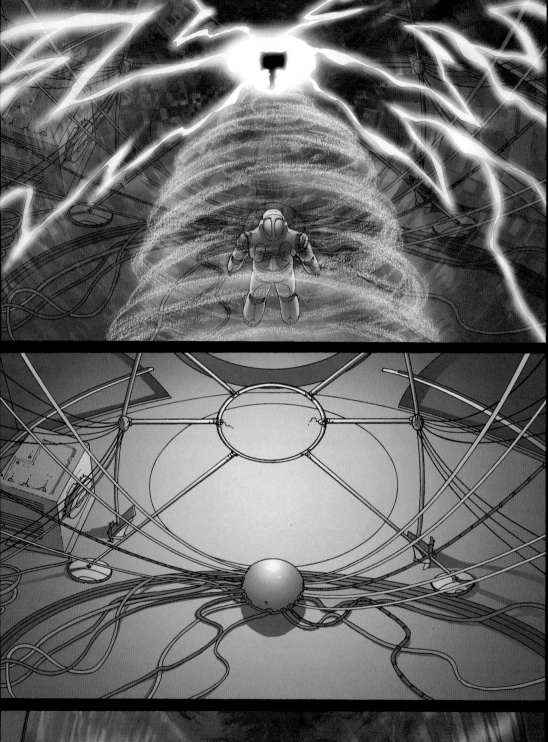

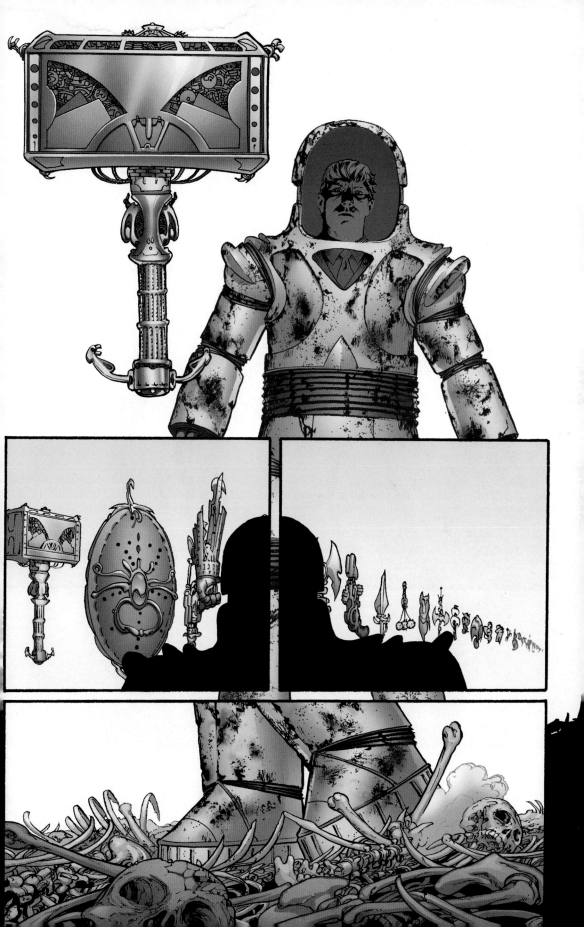

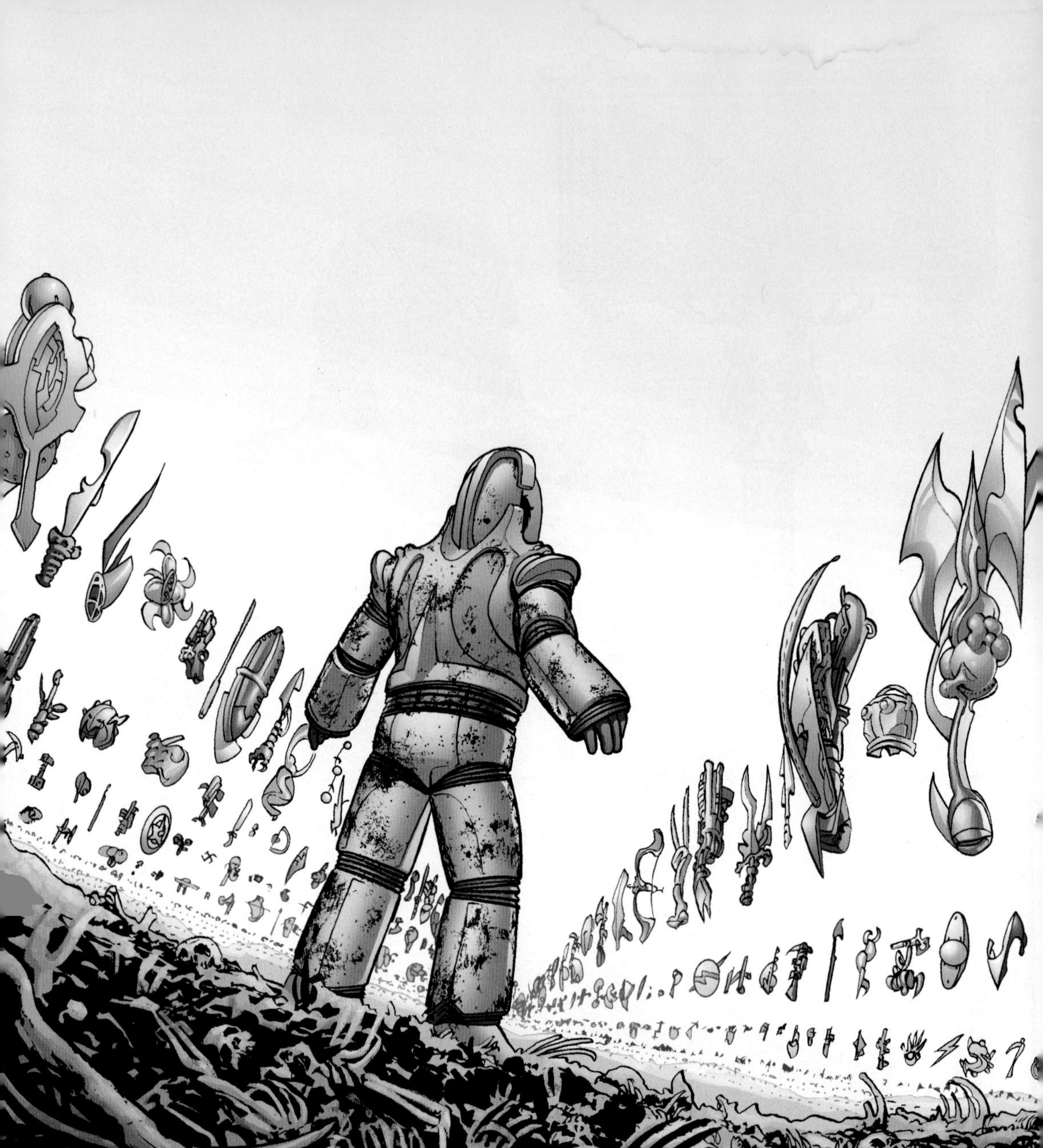

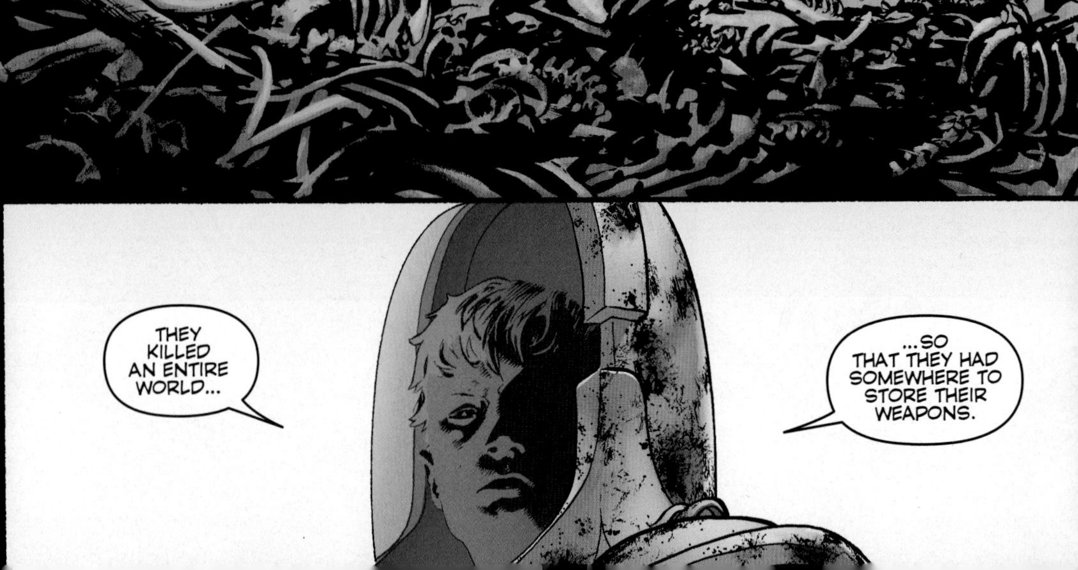
THEY KILLED AN ENTIRE WORLD...
...SO THAT THEY HAD SOMEWHERE TO STORE THEIR WEAPONS.

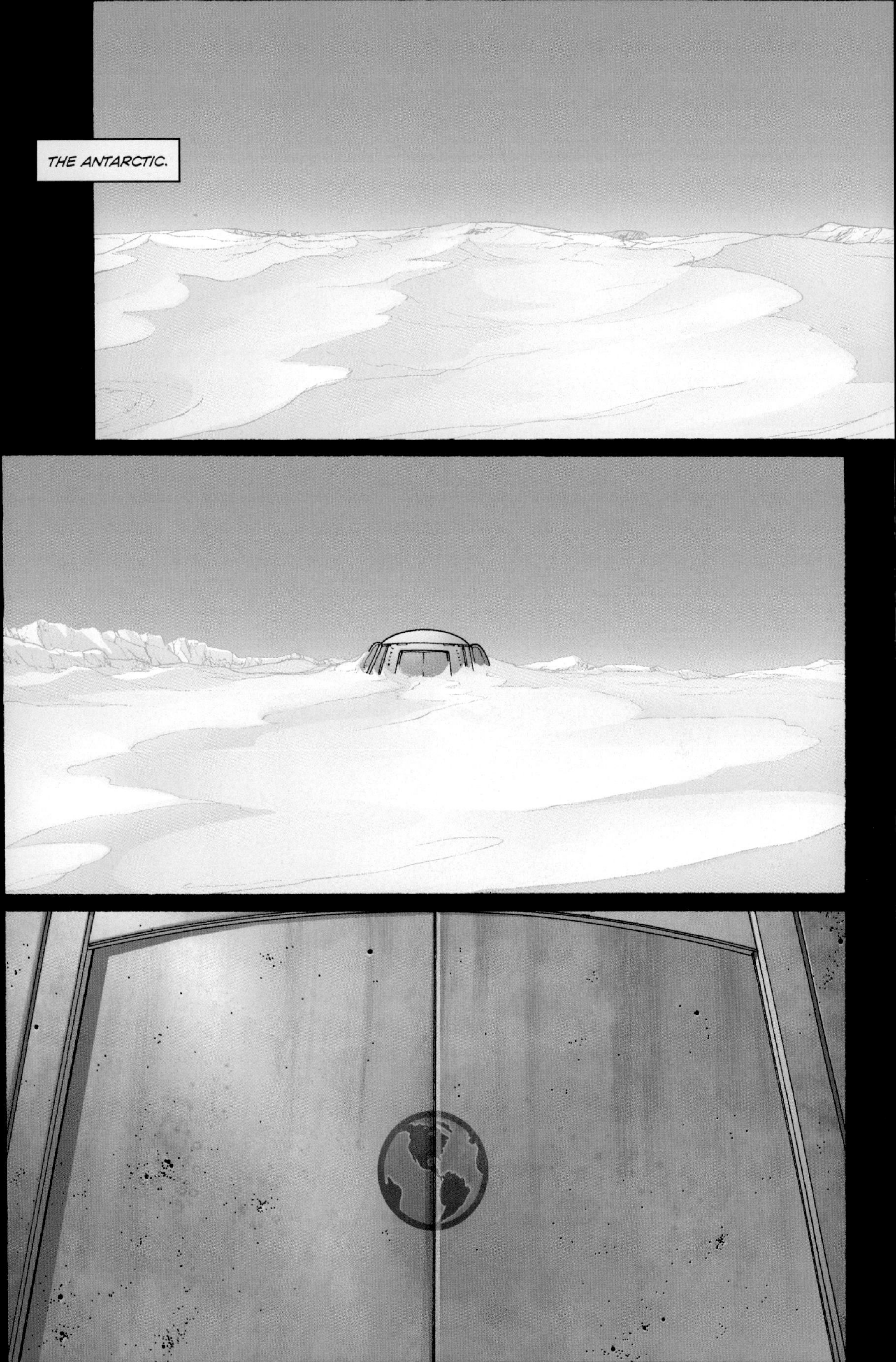
THE ANTARCTIC.

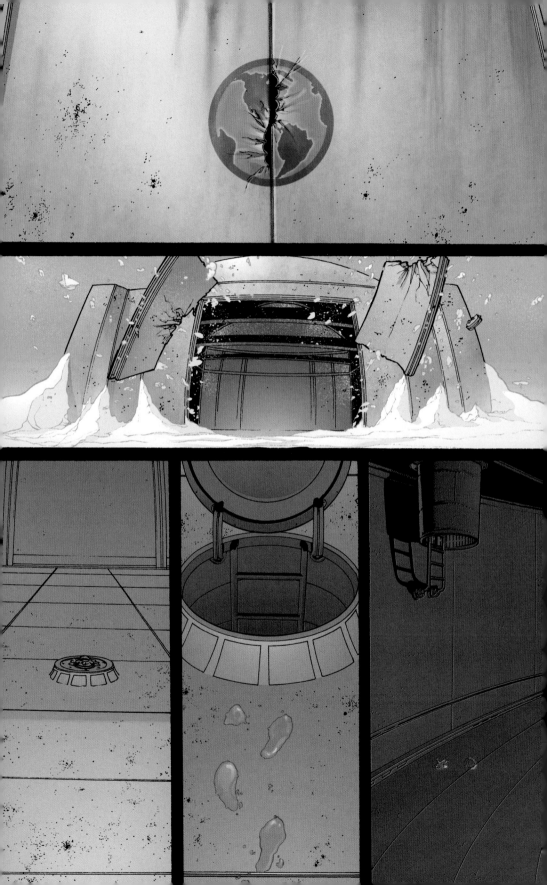

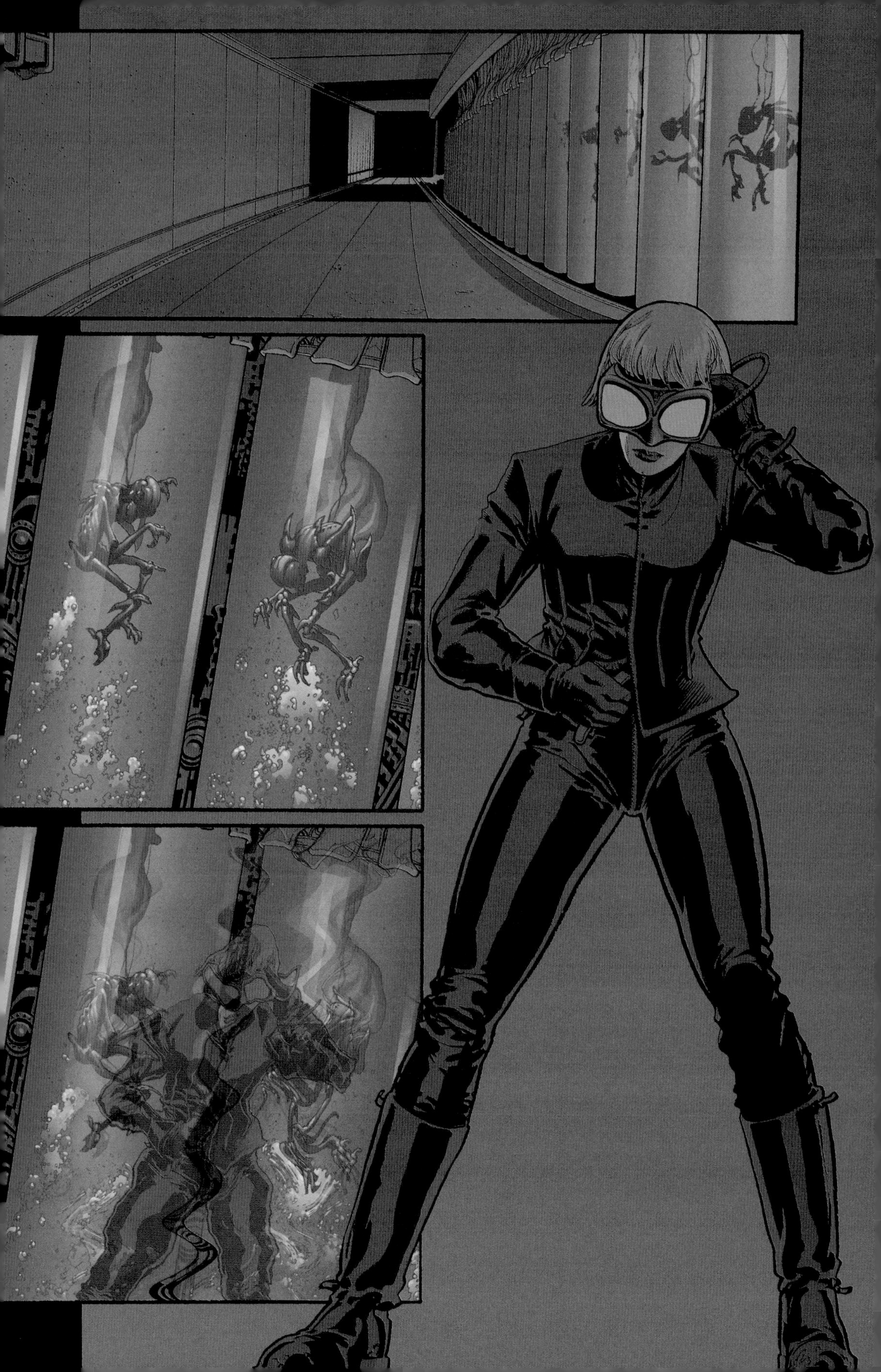

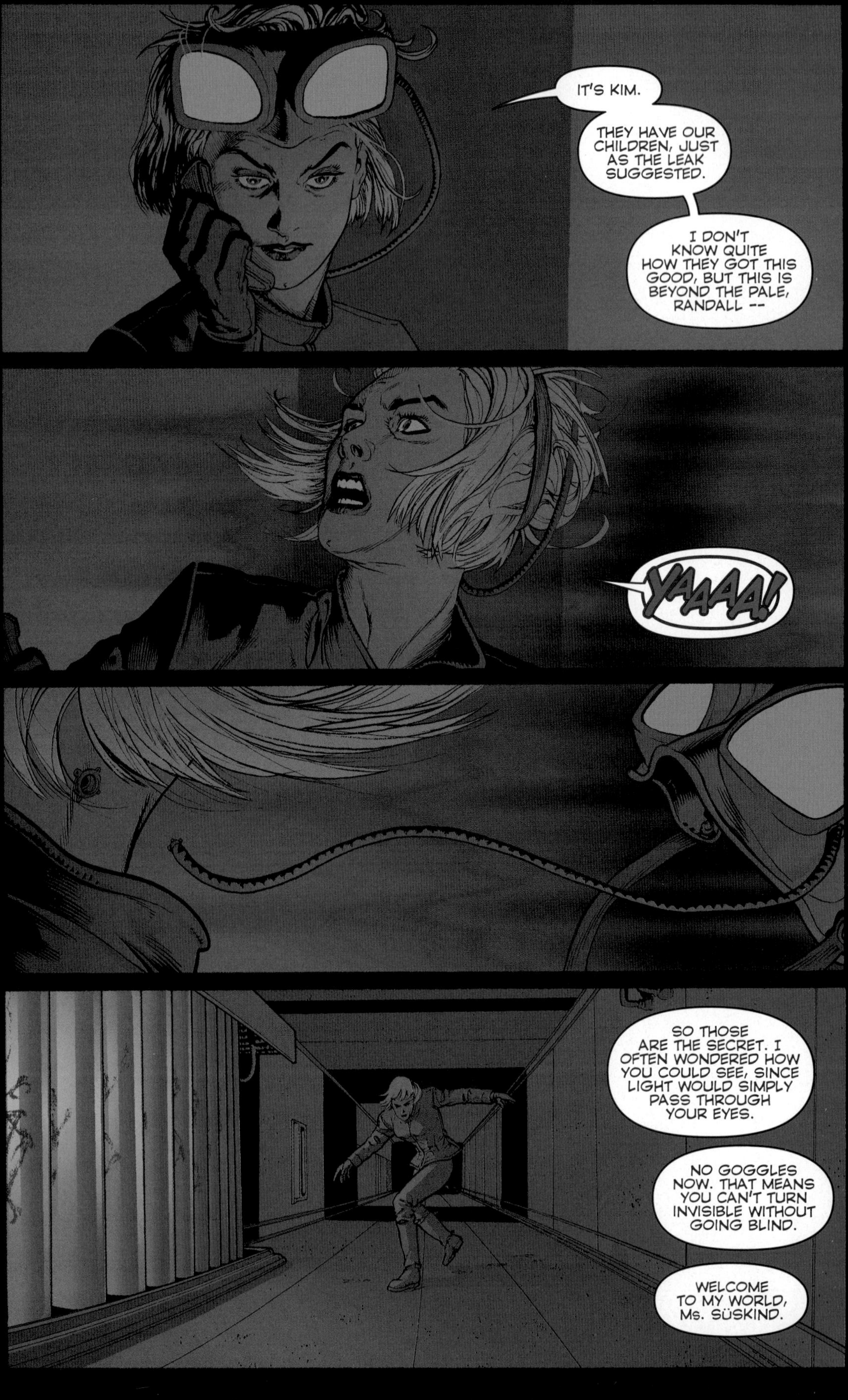
IT'S KIM.
THEY HAVE OUR CHILDREN, JUST AS THE LEAK SUGGESTED.
I DON'T KNOW QUITE HOW THEY GOT THIS GOOD, BUT THIS IS BEYOND THE PALE, RANDALL --
YAAAA!
SO THOSE ARE THE SECRET. I OFTEN WONDERED HOW YOU COULD SEE, SINCE LIGHT WOULD SIMPLY PASS THROUGH YOUR EYES.
NO GOGGLES NOW. THAT MEANS YOU CAN'T TURN INVISIBLE WITHOUT GOING BLIND.
WELCOME TO MY WORLD, Ms. SÜSKIND.

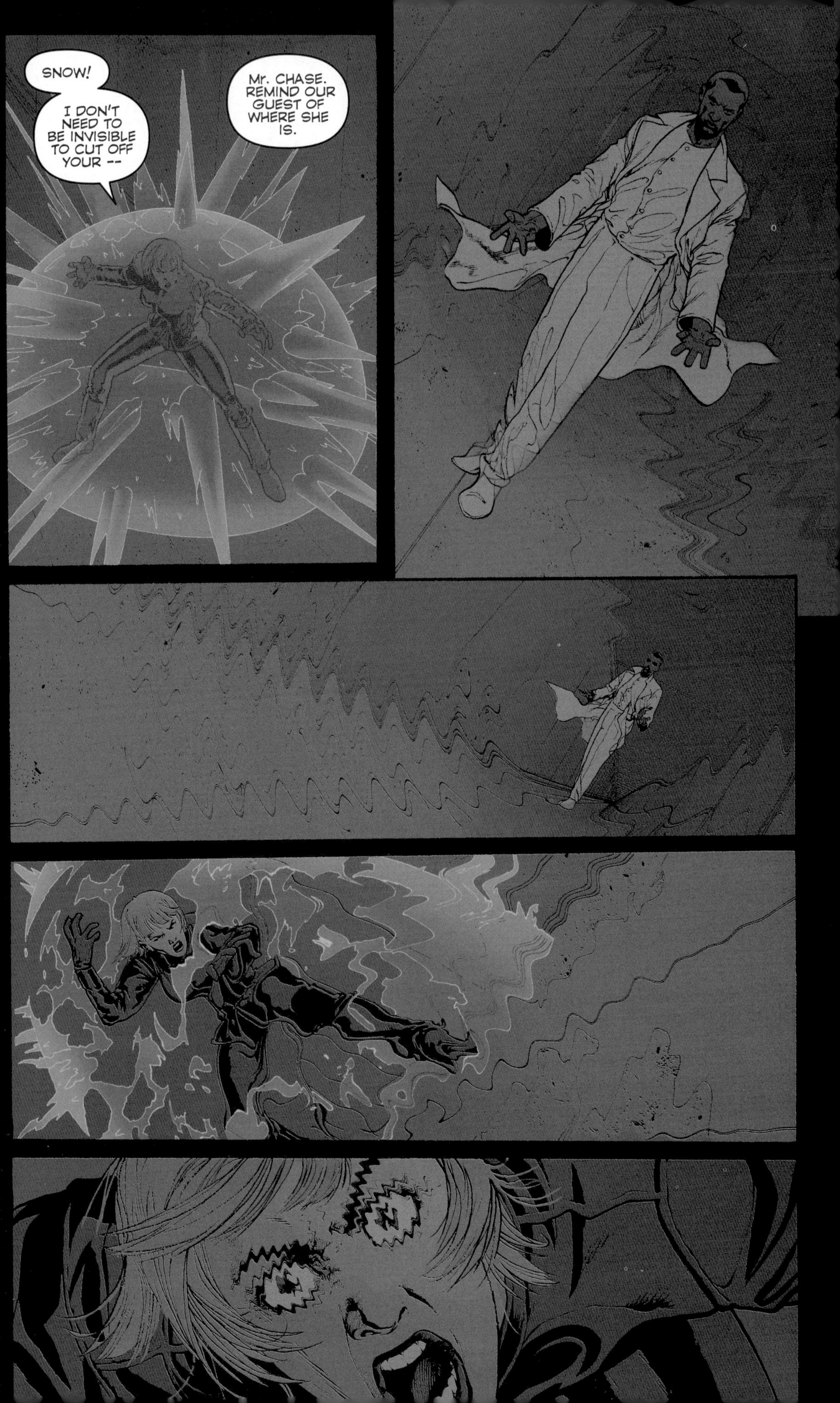
SNOW!
I DON'T NEED TO BE INVISIBLE TO CUT OFF YOUR --
Mr. CHASE. REMIND OUR GUEST OF WHERE SHE IS.

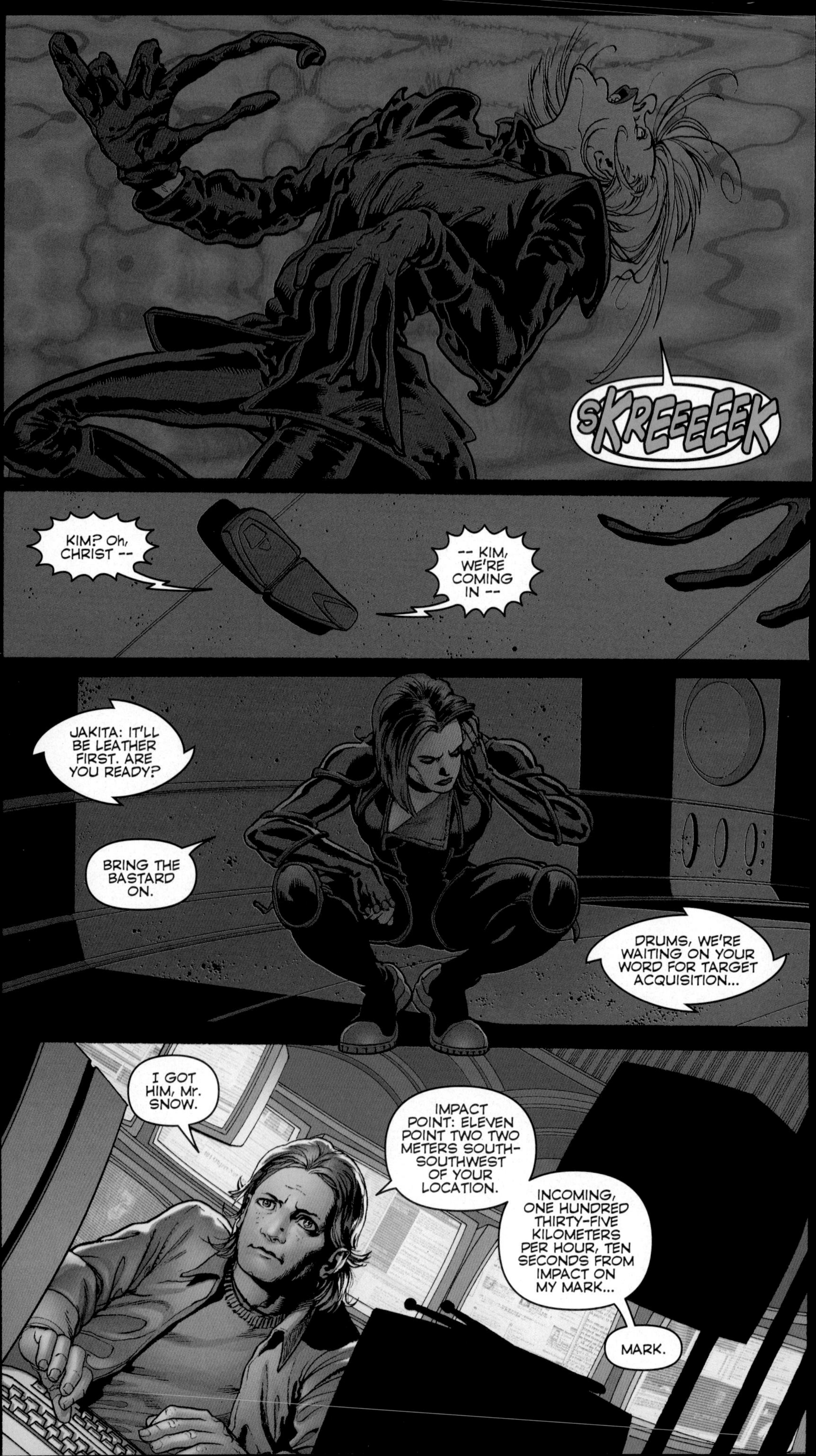
SKREEEEEK
KIM? Oh, CHRIST --
-- KIM, WE'RE COMING IN --
JAKITA: IT'LL BE LEATHER FIRST. ARE YOU READY?
BRING THE BASTARD ON.
DRUMS, WE'RE WAITING ON YOUR WORD FOR TARGET ACQUISITION...
I GOT HIM, Mr. SNOW.
IMPACT POINT: ELEVEN POINT TWO TWO METERS SOUTH-SOUTHWEST OF YOUR LOCATION.
INCOMING, ONE HUNDRED THIRTY-FIVE KILOMETERS PER HOUR, TEN SECONDS FROM IMPACT ON MY MARK...
MARK.

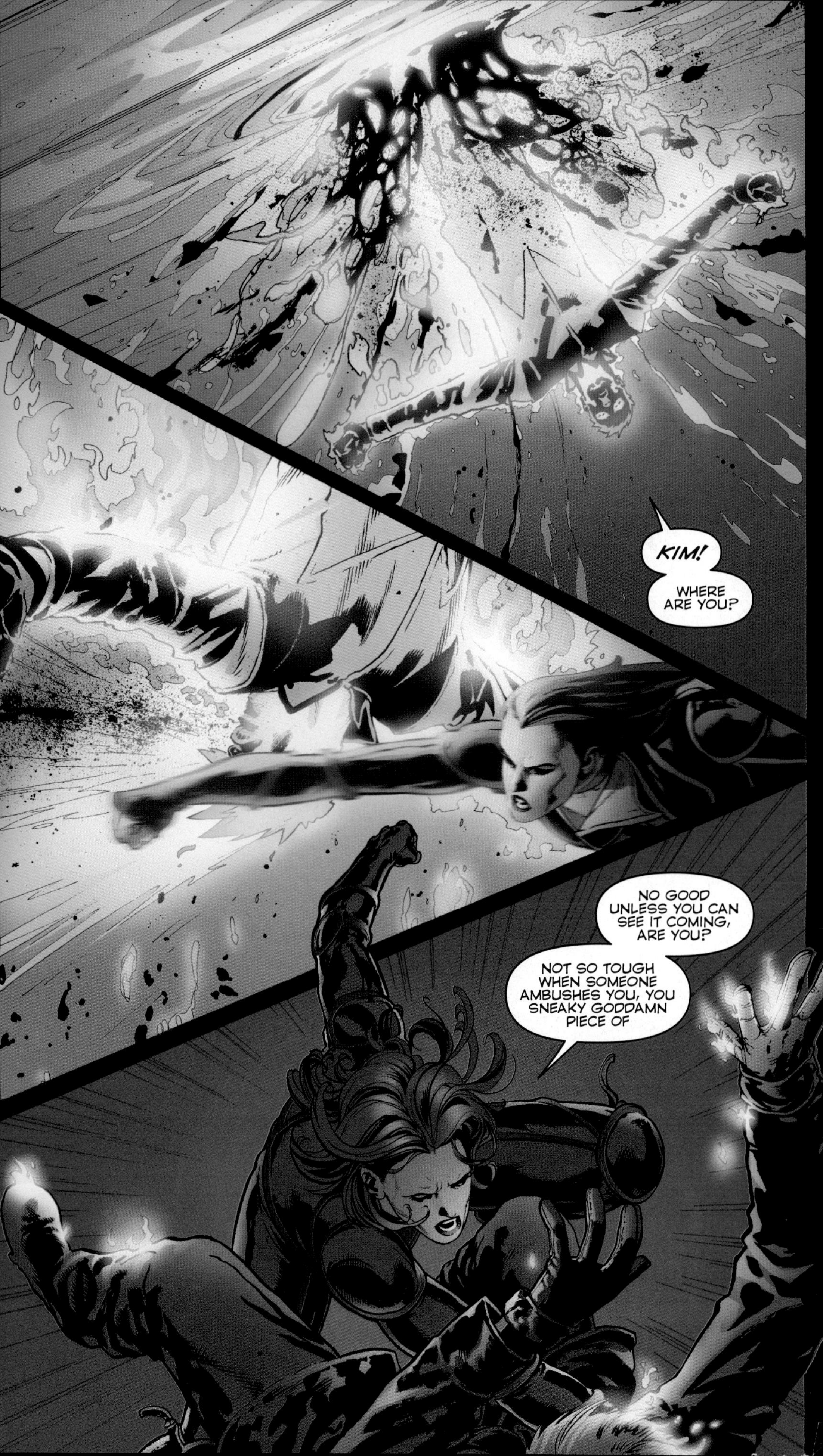
KIM!
WHERE ARE YOU?
NO GOOD UNLESS YOU CAN SEE IT COMING, ARE YOU?
NOT SO TOUGH WHEN SOMEONE AMBUSHES YOU, YOU SNEAKY GODDAMN PIECE OF

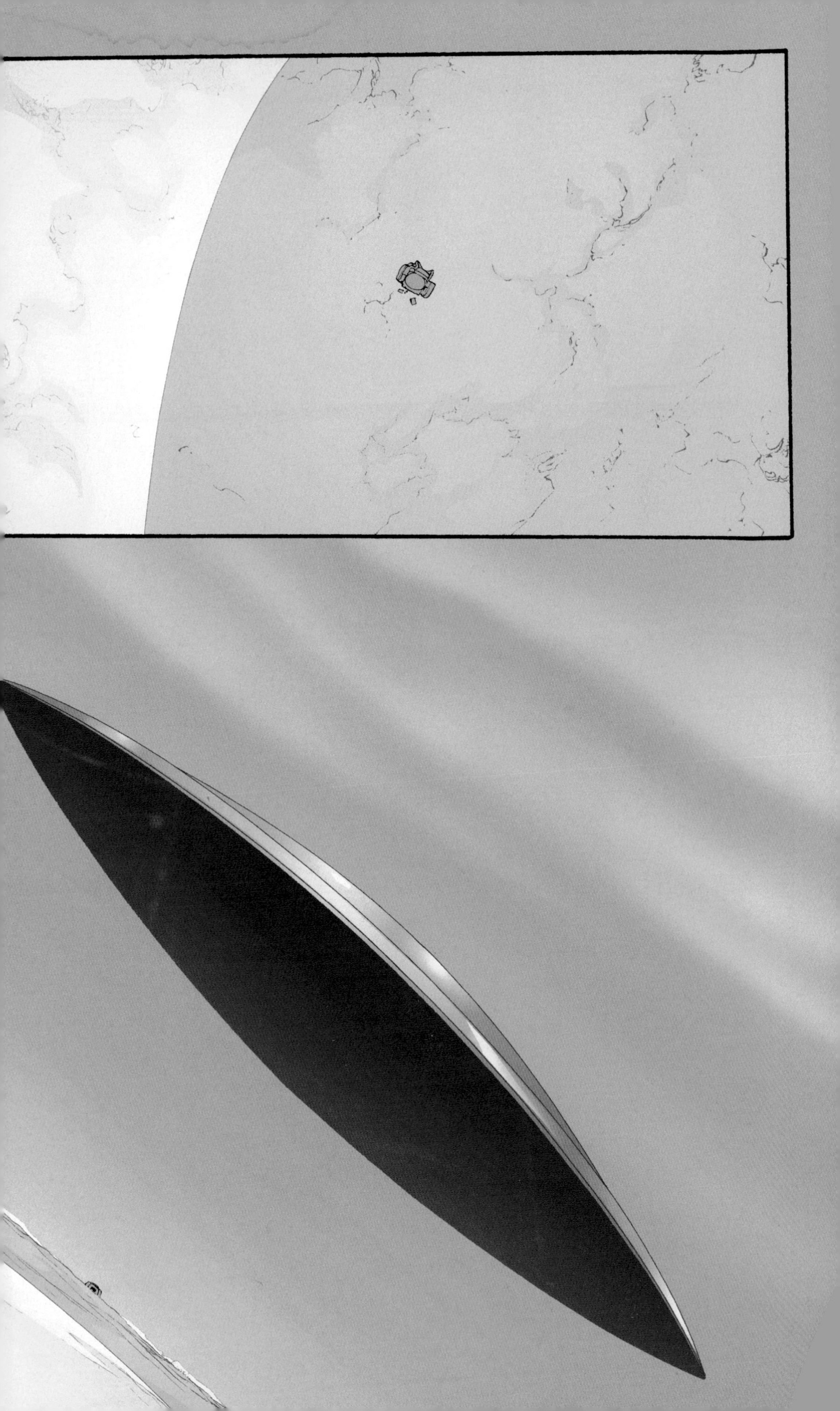

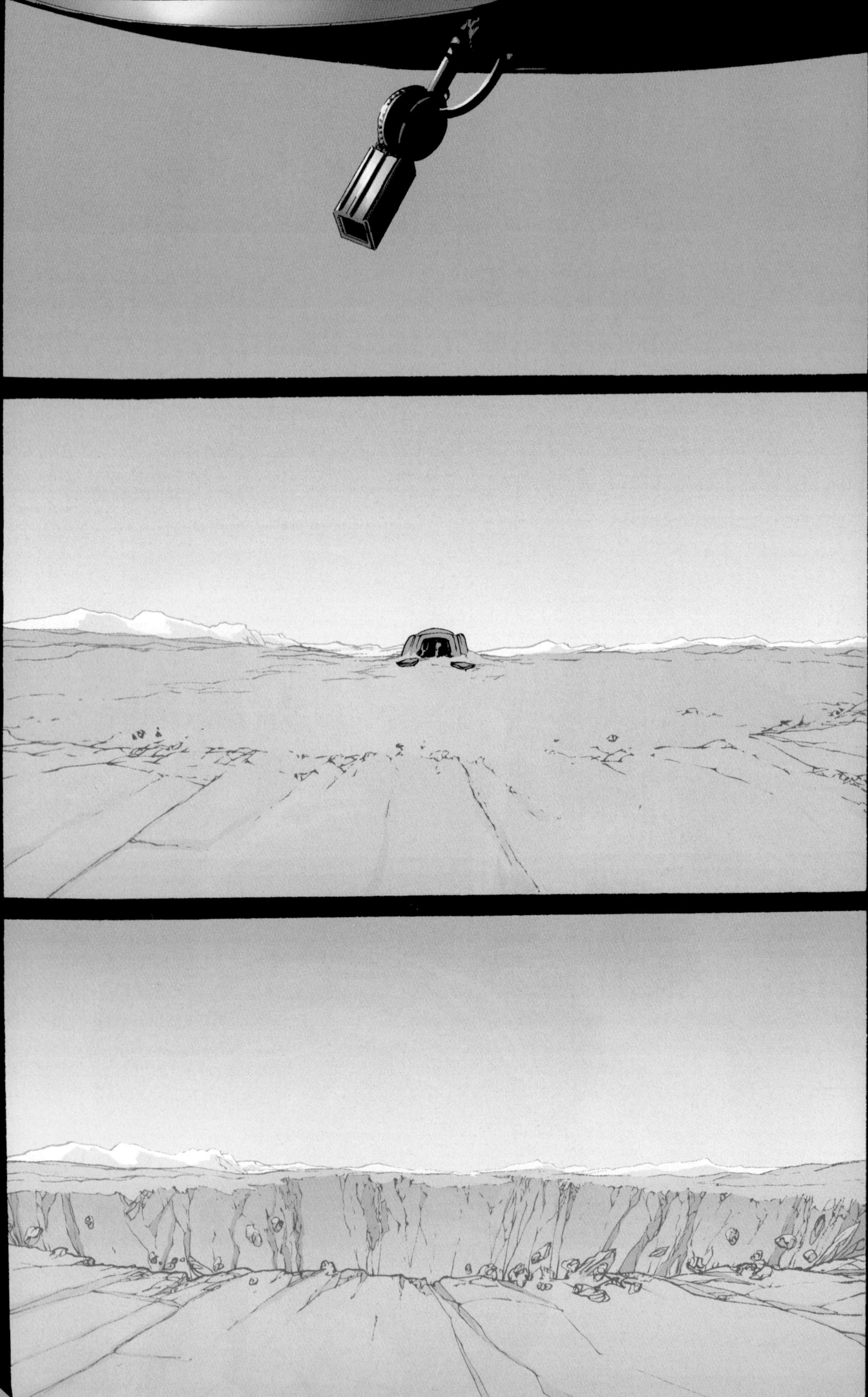

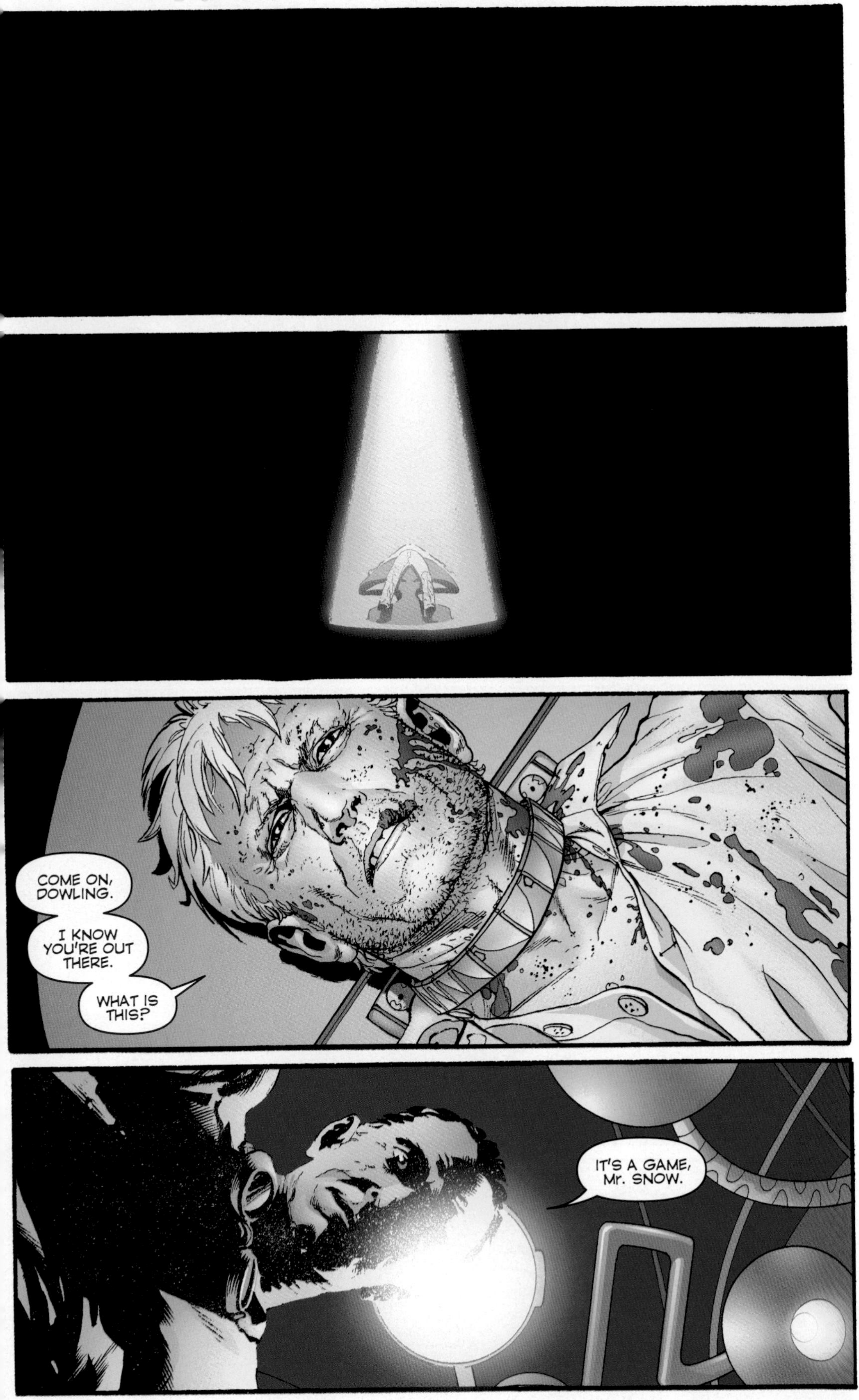
COME ON, DOWLING.
I KNOW YOU'RE OUT THERE.
WHAT IS THIS?
IT'S A GAME, Mr. SNOW.

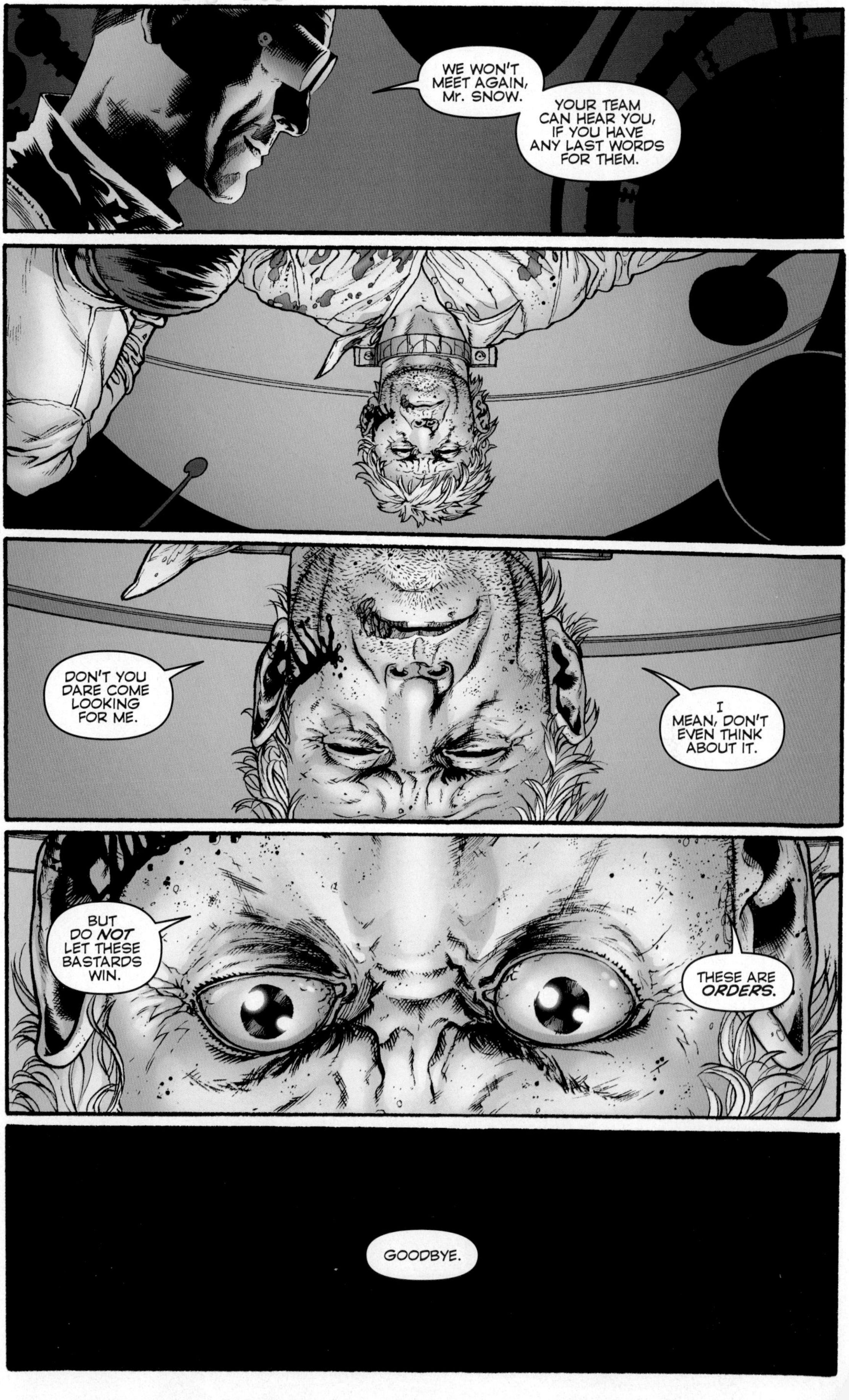
WE WON'T MEET AGAIN, Mr. SNOW.
YOUR TEAM CAN HEAR YOU, IF YOU HAVE ANY LAST WORDS FOR THEM.
DON'T YOU DARE COME LOOKING FOR ME.
I MEAN, DON'T EVEN THINK ABOUT IT.
BUT DO *NOT* LET THESE BASTARDS WIN.
THESE ARE *ORDERS*.
GOODBYE.

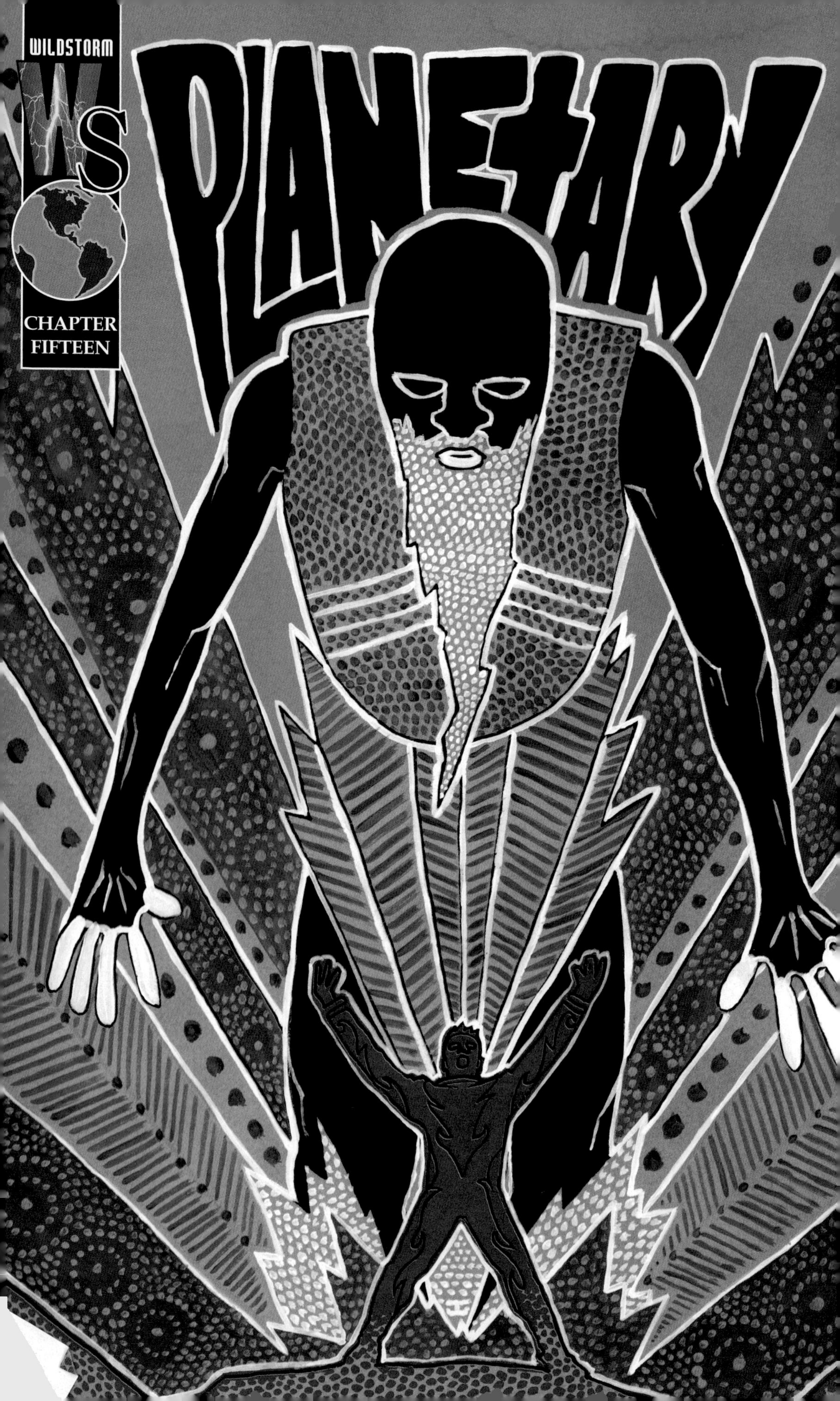
WILDSTORM
WS
PLANETARY
CHAPTER FIFTEEN

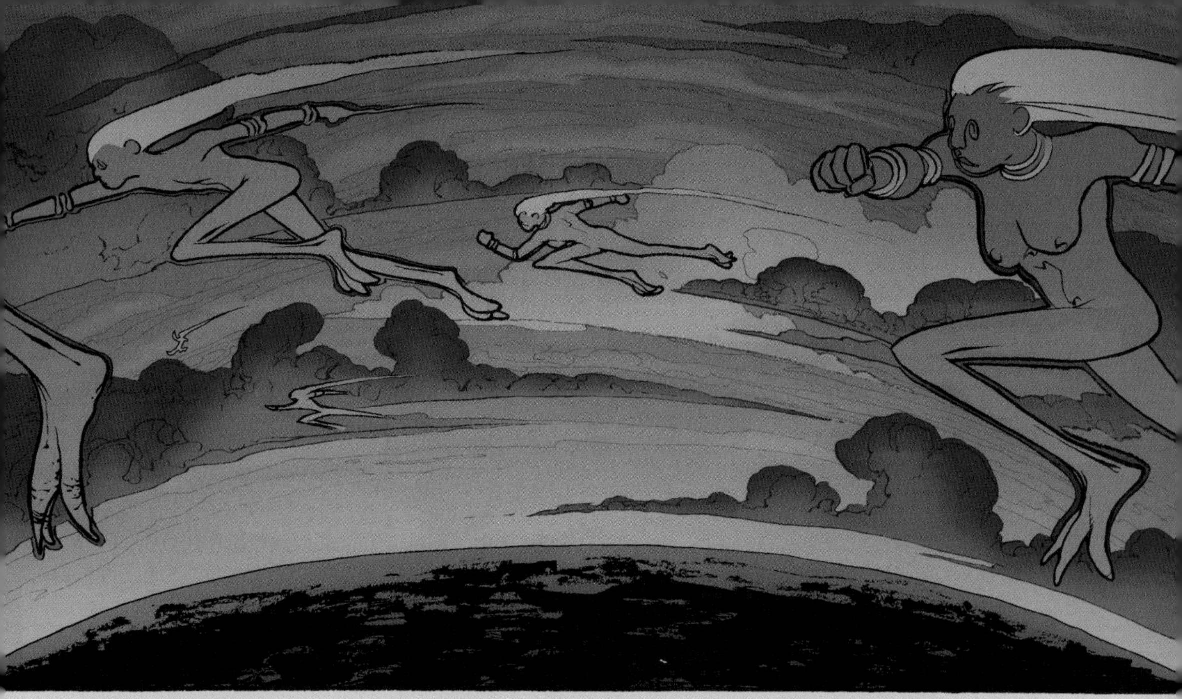

In the Beginning

The Earth was an infinite dark plain, separated from the sky and from the murky sea and enveloped in shadowy twilight.

There were no stars, no sun or moon.

In the sky, there were Sky-dwellers, running beyond the Western Clouds, ageless and sparkling.

On the earth, under the shallow ditches that in the future would become waterholes, laid The Ancients, so old they could do nothing but sleep. Like the ditches, they were pregnant with potential, for each contained the merest breath of aspirational life.

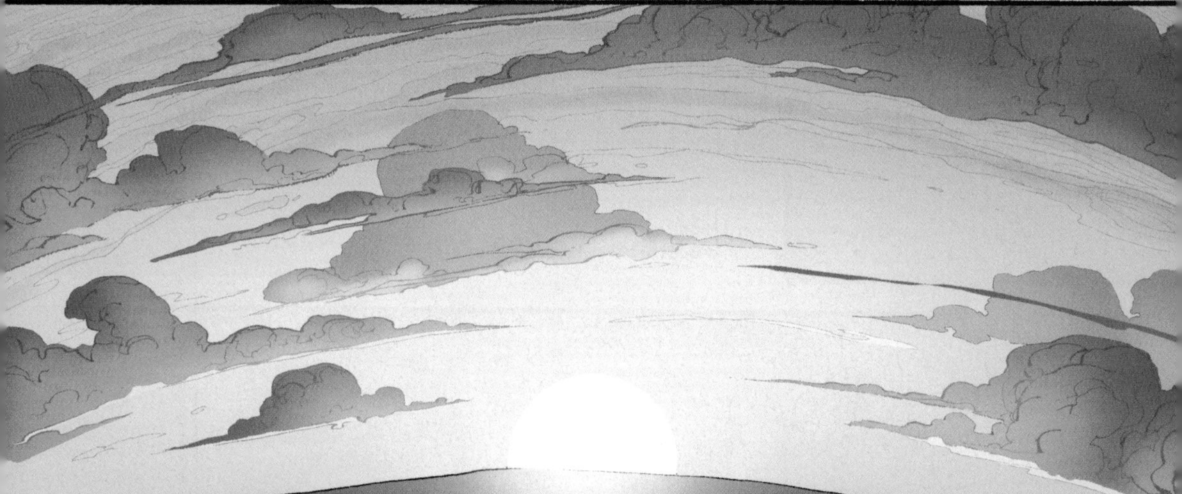

Under the plain were all the constellations, the burning sun, the shining moon. Waiting.

On the morning of the First Day, the Sun finally wanted to be born. It exploded through the surface and up into the sky, casting light and heat all about.

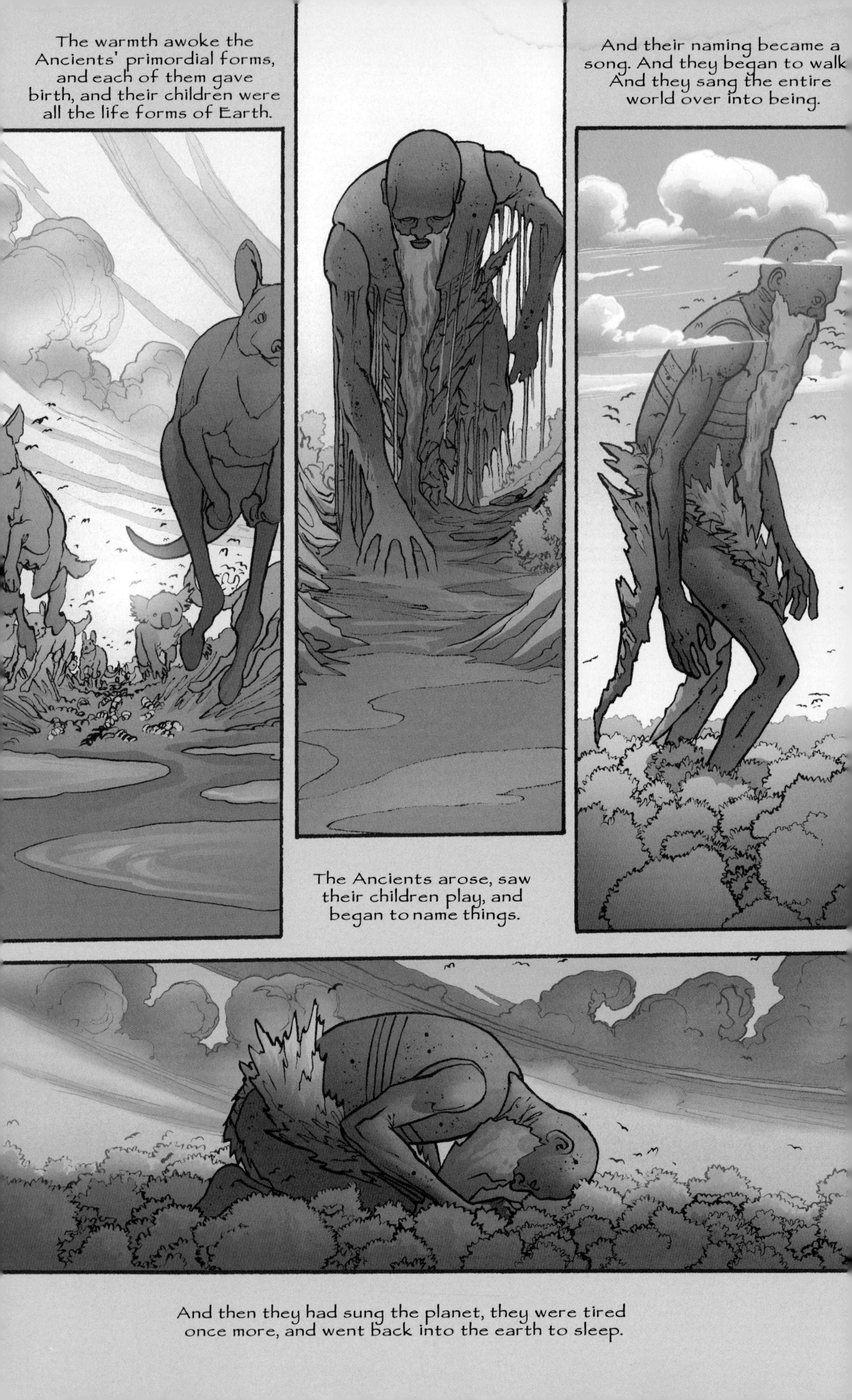
The warmth awoke the Ancients' primordial forms, and each of them gave birth, and their children were all the life forms of Earth.
The Ancients arose, saw their children play, and began to name things.
And their naming became a song. And they began to walk And they sang the entire world over into being.
And then they had sung the planet, they were tired once more, and went back into the earth to sleep.

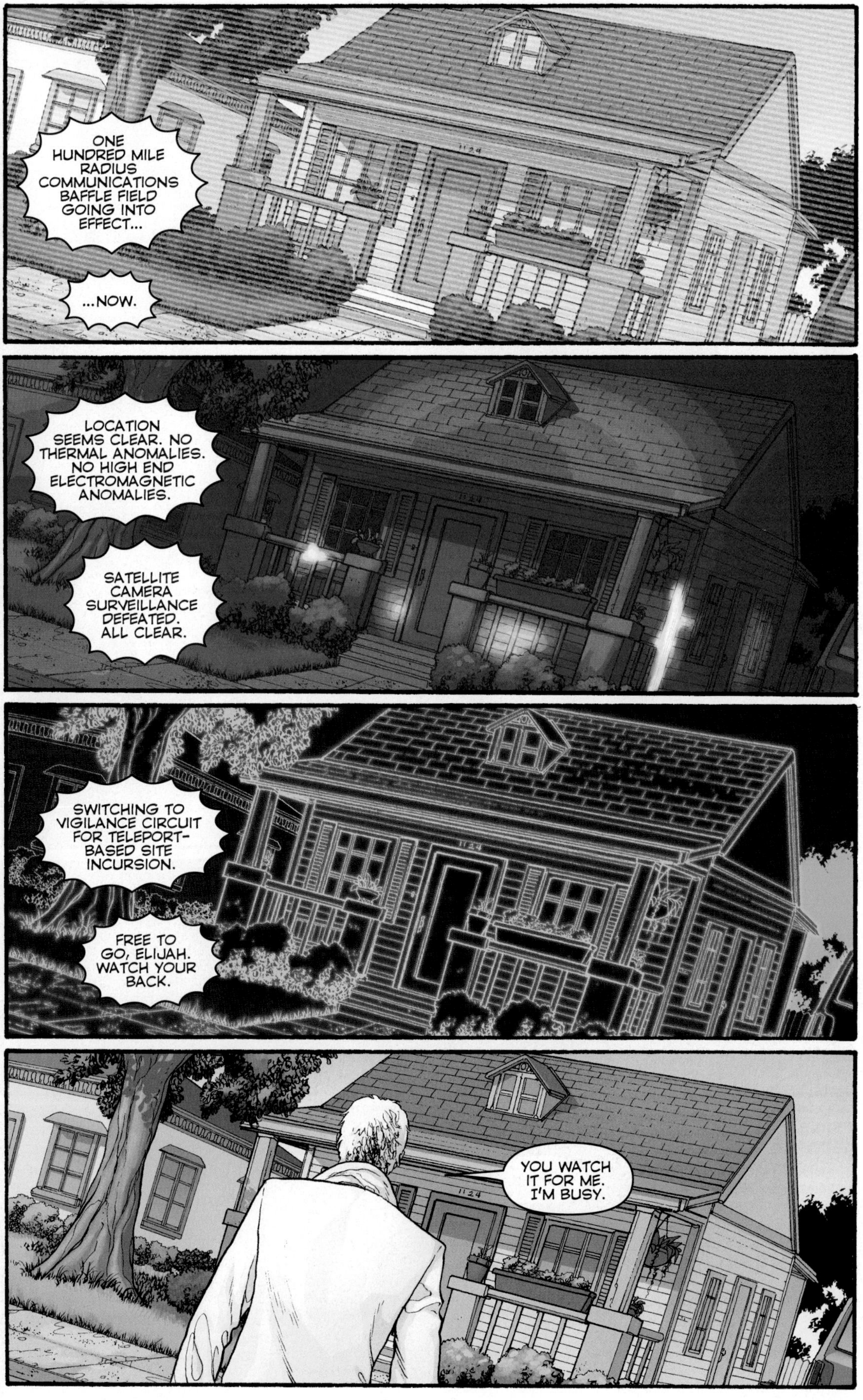

ONE HUNDRED MILE RADIUS COMMUNICATIONS BAFFLE FIELD GOING INTO EFFECT...
...NOW.
LOCATION SEEMS CLEAR. NO THERMAL ANOMALIES. NO HIGH END ELECTROMAGNETIC ANOMALIES.
SATELLITE CAMERA SURVEILLANCE DEFEATED. ALL CLEAR.
SWITCHING TO VIGILANCE CIRCUIT FOR TELEPORT-BASED SITE INCURSION.
FREE TO GO, ELIJAH. WATCH YOUR BACK.
YOU WATCH IT FOR ME. I'M BUSY.

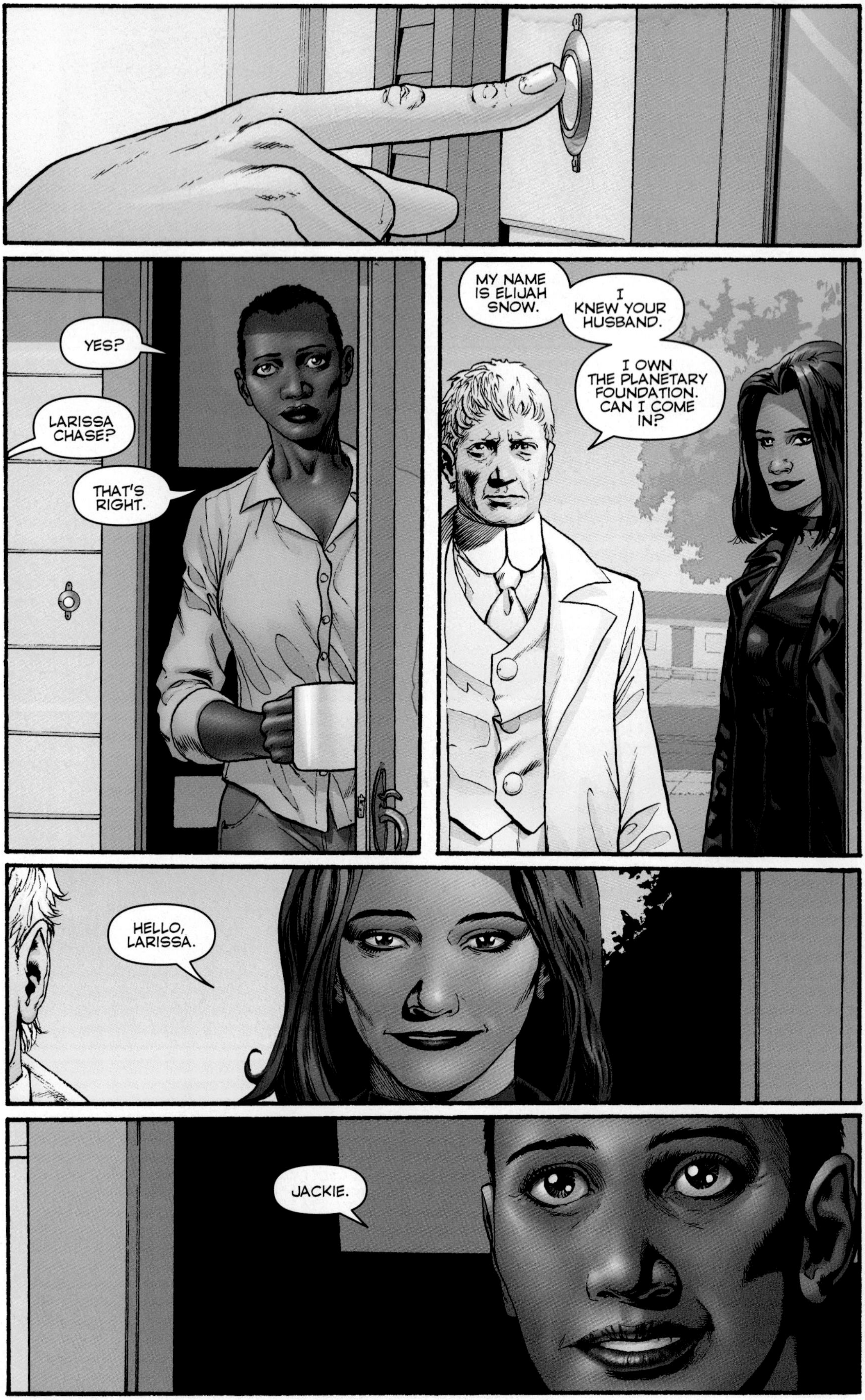
YES?
LARISSA CHASE?
THAT'S RIGHT.
MY NAME IS ELIJAH SNOW.
I KNEW YOUR HUSBAND.
I OWN THE PLANETARY FOUNDATION. CAN I COME IN?
HELLO, LARISSA.
JACKIE.

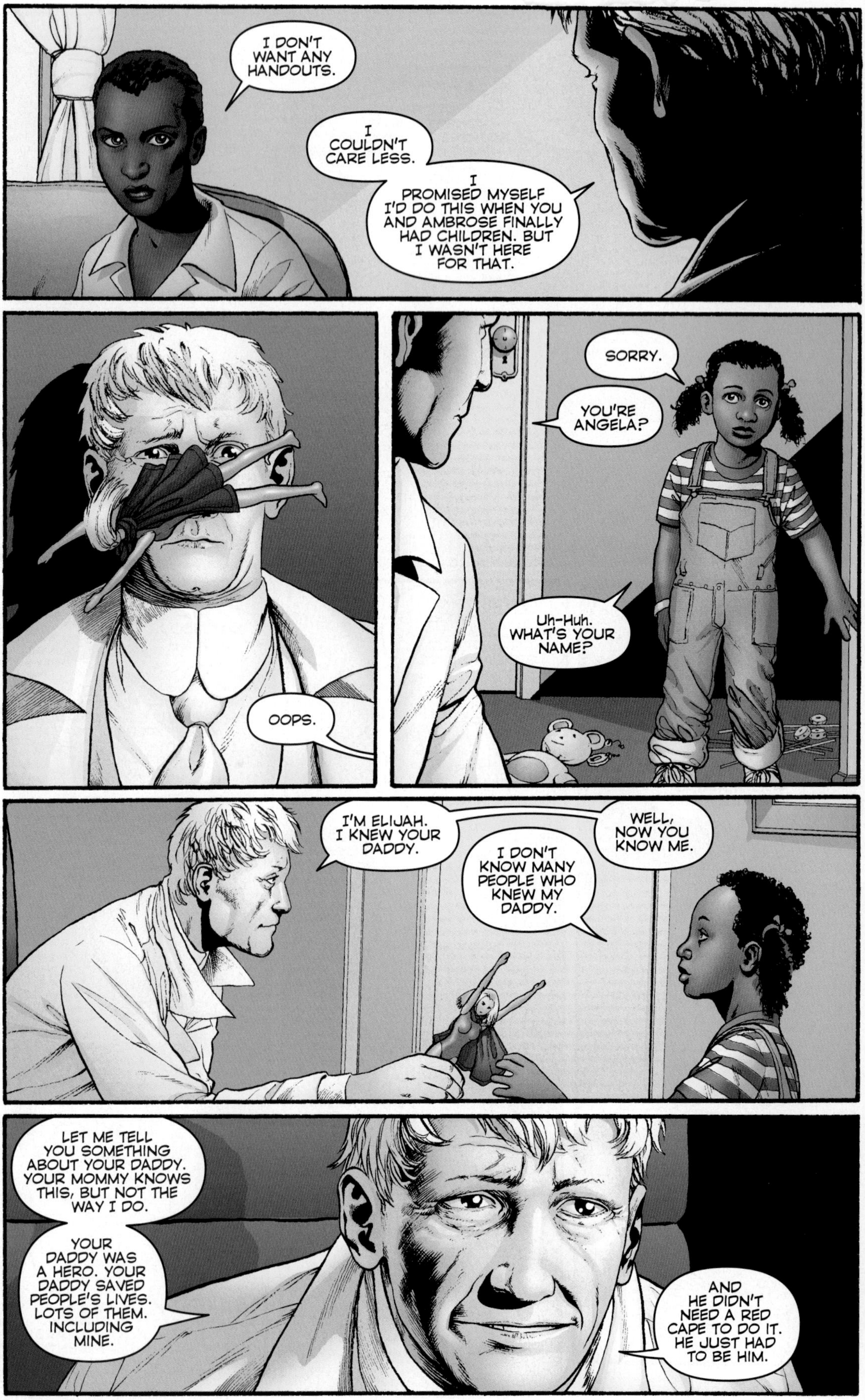
I DON'T WANT ANY HANDOUTS.
I COULDN'T CARE LESS.
I PROMISED MYSELF I'D DO THIS WHEN YOU AND AMBROSE FINALLY HAD CHILDREN. BUT I WASN'T HERE FOR THAT.
OOPS.
SORRY.
YOU'RE ANGELA?
Uh-Huh. WHAT'S YOUR NAME?
I'M ELIJAH. I KNEW YOUR DADDY.
I DON'T KNOW MANY PEOPLE WHO KNEW MY DADDY.
WELL, NOW YOU KNOW ME.
LET ME TELL YOU SOMETHING ABOUT YOUR DADDY. YOUR MOMMY KNOWS THIS, BUT NOT THE WAY I DO.
YOUR DADDY WAS A HERO. YOUR DADDY SAVED PEOPLE'S LIVES. LOTS OF THEM. INCLUDING MINE.
AND HE DIDN'T NEED A RED CAPE TO DO IT. HE JUST HAD TO BE HIM.

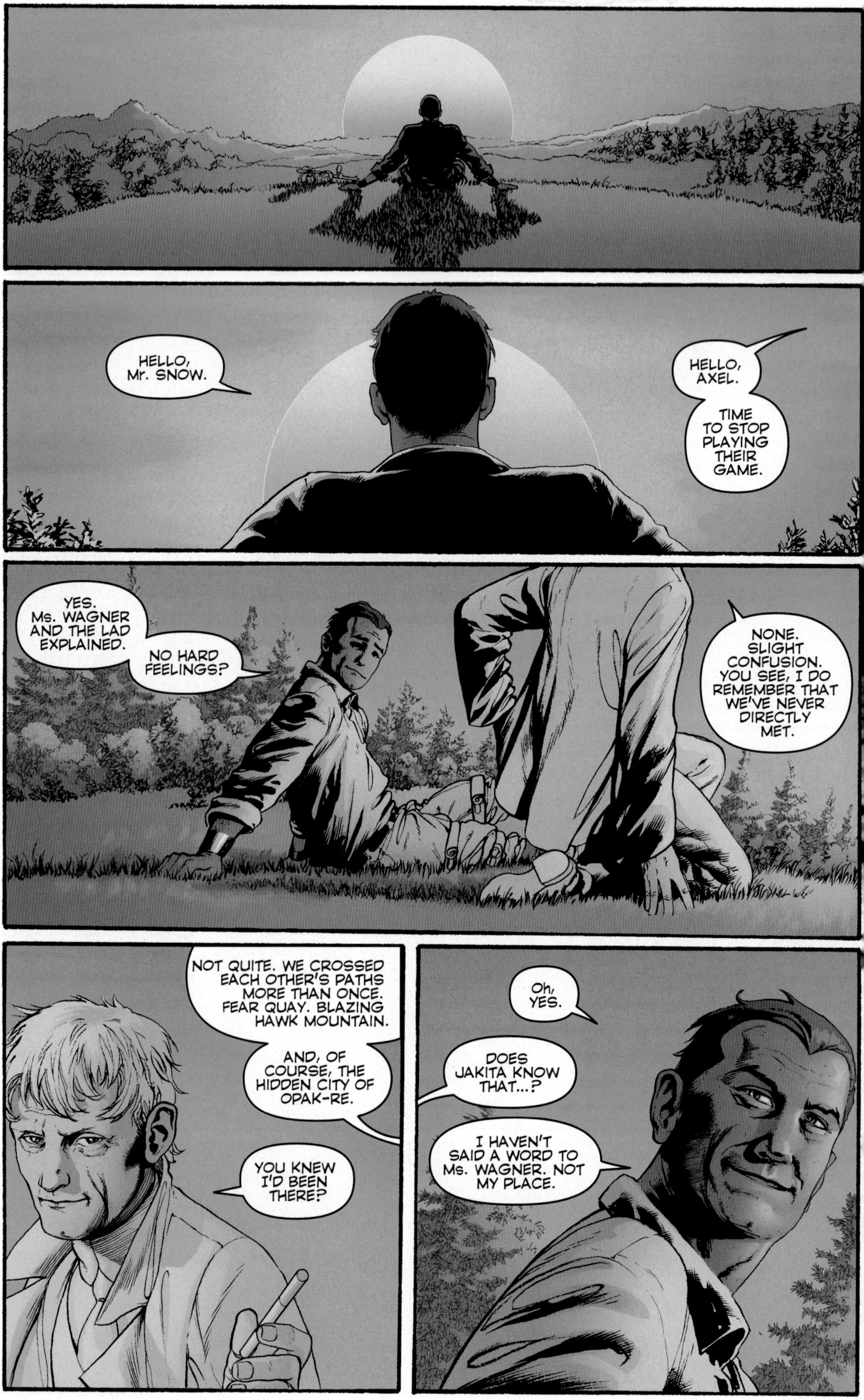
HELLO, Mr. SNOW.
HELLO, AXEL.
TIME TO STOP PLAYING THEIR GAME.
YES. Ms. WAGNER AND THE LAD EXPLAINED.
NO HARD FEELINGS?
NONE. SLIGHT CONFUSION. YOU SEE, I DO REMEMBER THAT WE'VE NEVER DIRECTLY MET.
NOT QUITE. WE CROSSED EACH OTHER'S PATHS MORE THAN ONCE. FEAR QUAY. BLAZING HAWK MOUNTAIN.
AND, OF COURSE, THE HIDDEN CITY OF OPAK-RE.
YOU KNEW I'D BEEN THERE?
Oh, YES.
DOES JAKITA KNOW THAT...?
I HAVEN'T SAID A WORD TO Ms. WAGNER. NOT MY PLACE.

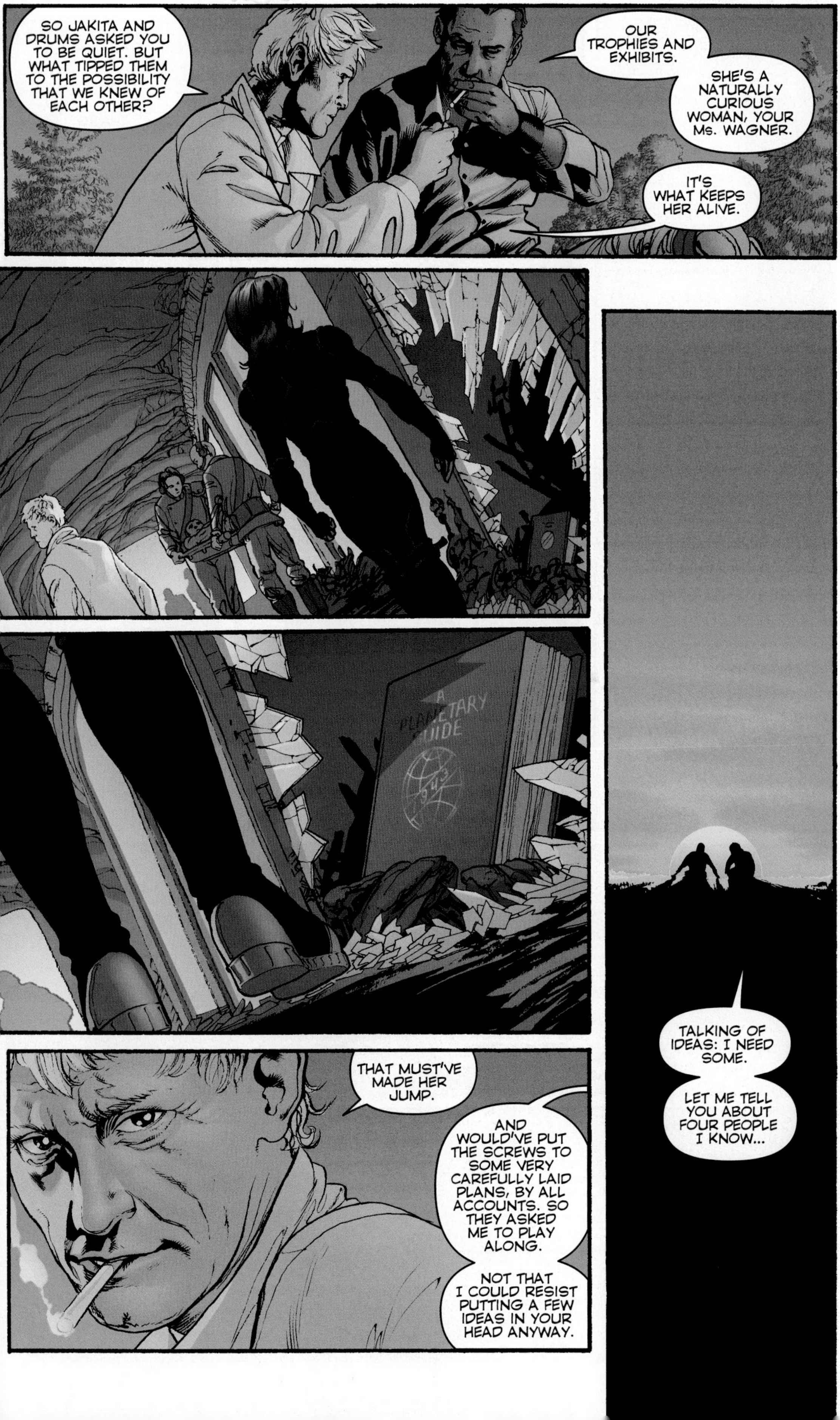
SO JAKITA AND DRUMS ASKED YOU TO BE QUIET. BUT WHAT TIPPED THEM TO THE POSSIBILITY THAT WE KNEW OF EACH OTHER?
OUR TROPHIES AND EXHIBITS.
SHE'S A NATURALLY CURIOUS WOMAN, YOUR Ms. WAGNER.
IT'S WHAT KEEPS HER ALIVE.
A PLANETARY GUIDE
THAT MUST'VE MADE HER JUMP.
AND WOULD'VE PUT THE SCREWS TO SOME VERY CAREFULLY LAID PLANS, BY ALL ACCOUNTS. SO THEY ASKED ME TO PLAY ALONG.
NOT THAT I COULD RESIST PUTTING A FEW IDEAS IN YOUR HEAD ANYWAY.
TALKING OF IDEAS: I NEED SOME.
LET ME TELL YOU ABOUT FOUR PEOPLE I KNOW...

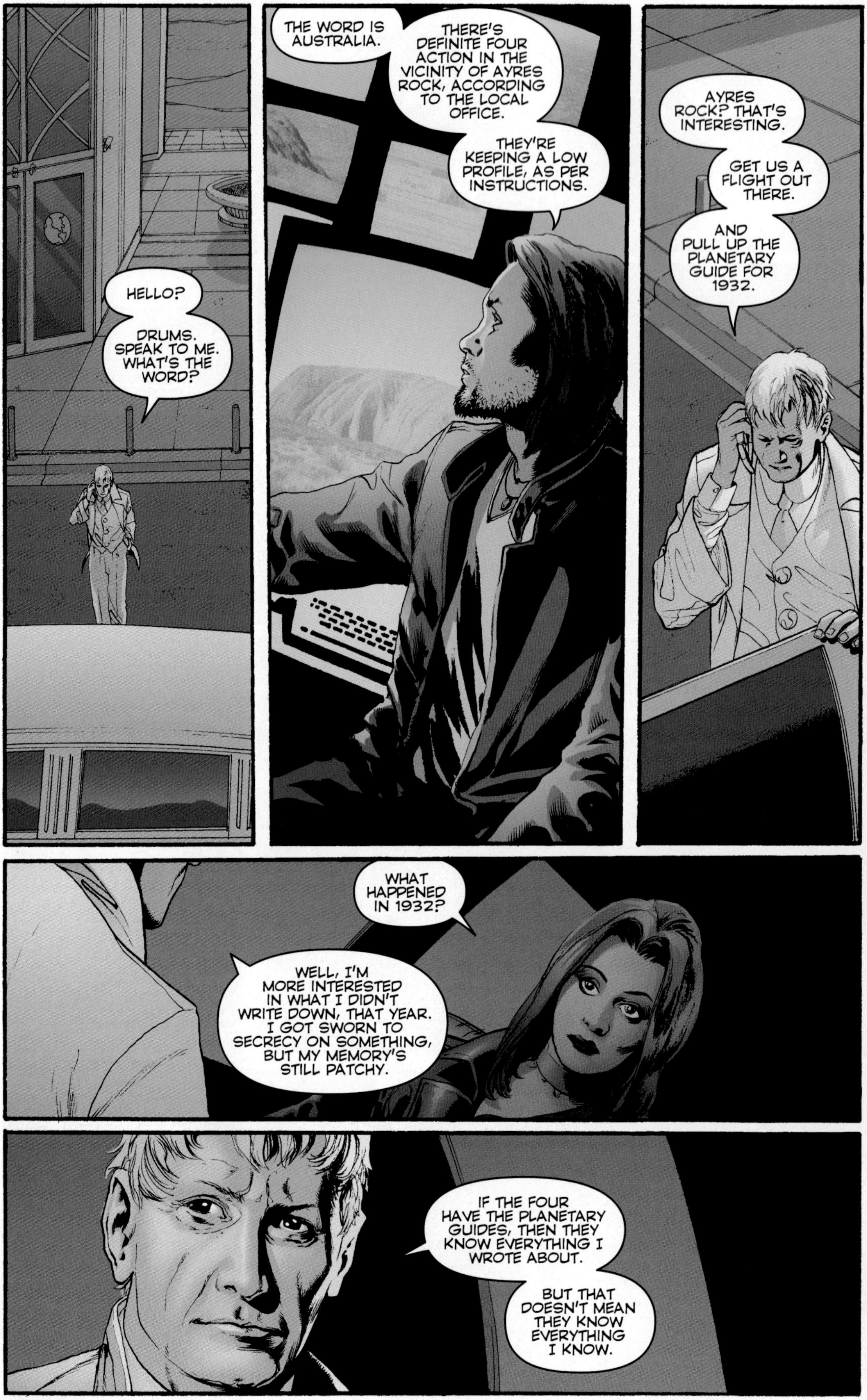
HELLO?
DRUMS. SPEAK TO ME. WHAT'S THE WORD?
THE WORD IS AUSTRALIA.
THERE'S DEFINITE FOUR ACTION IN THE VICINITY OF AYRES ROCK, ACCORDING TO THE LOCAL OFFICE.
THEY'RE KEEPING A LOW PROFILE, AS PER INSTRUCTIONS.
AYRES ROCK? THAT'S INTERESTING.
GET US A FLIGHT OUT THERE.
AND PULL UP THE PLANETARY GUIDE FOR 1932.
WHAT HAPPENED IN 1932?
WELL, I'M MORE INTERESTED IN WHAT I DIDN'T WRITE DOWN, THAT YEAR. I GOT SWORN TO SECRECY ON SOMETHING, BUT MY MEMORY'S STILL PATCHY.
IF THE FOUR HAVE THE PLANETARY GUIDES, THEN THEY KNOW EVERYTHING I WROTE ABOUT.
BUT THAT DOESN'T MEAN THEY KNOW EVERYTHING I KNOW.

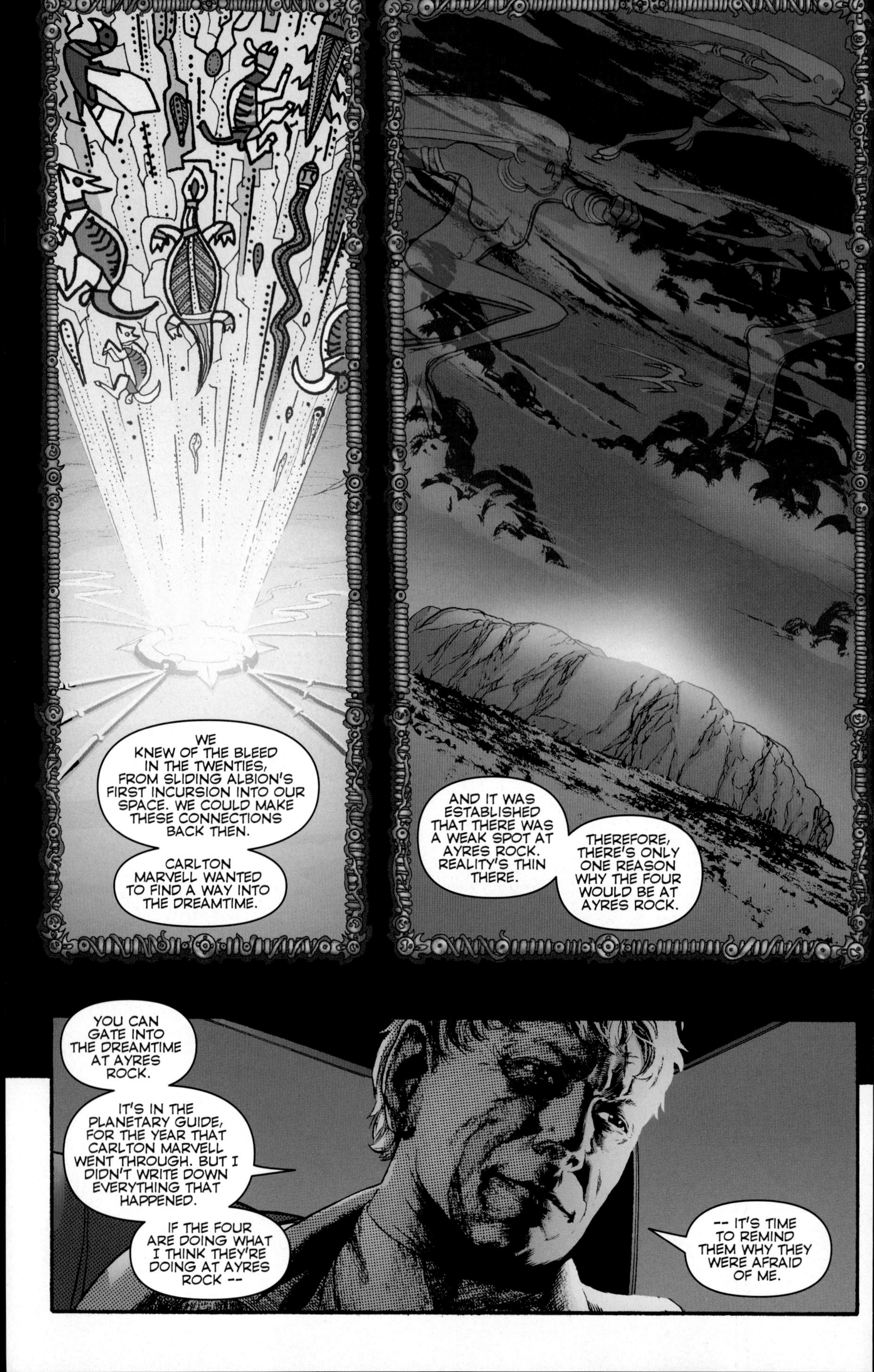
WE KNEW OF THE BLEED IN THE TWENTIES, FROM SLIDING ALBION'S FIRST INCURSION INTO OUR SPACE. WE COULD MAKE THESE CONNECTIONS BACK THEN.
CARLTON MARVELL WANTED TO FIND A WAY INTO THE DREAMTIME.
AND IT WAS ESTABLISHED THAT THERE WAS A WEAK SPOT AT AYRES ROCK. REALITY'S THIN THERE.
THEREFORE, THERE'S ONLY ONE REASON WHY THE FOUR WOULD BE AT AYRES ROCK.
YOU CAN GATE INTO THE DREAMTIME AT AYRES ROCK.
IT'S IN THE PLANETARY GUIDE, FOR THE YEAR THAT CARLTON MARVELL WENT THROUGH. BUT I DIDN'T WRITE DOWN EVERYTHING THAT HAPPENED.
IF THE FOUR ARE DOING WHAT I THINK THEY'RE DOING AT AYRES ROCK --
-- IT'S TIME TO REMIND THEM WHY THEY WERE AFRAID OF ME.

CREATION SONGS

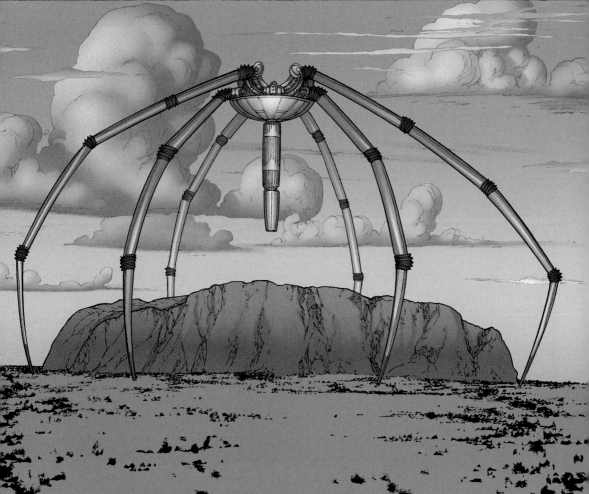

BY WARREN ELLIS AND JOHN CASSADAY

WITH LAURA DEPUY

LETTERING - BILL O'NEIL   EDITOR - JOHN LAYMAN

Planetary created by Warren Ellis and John Cassaday

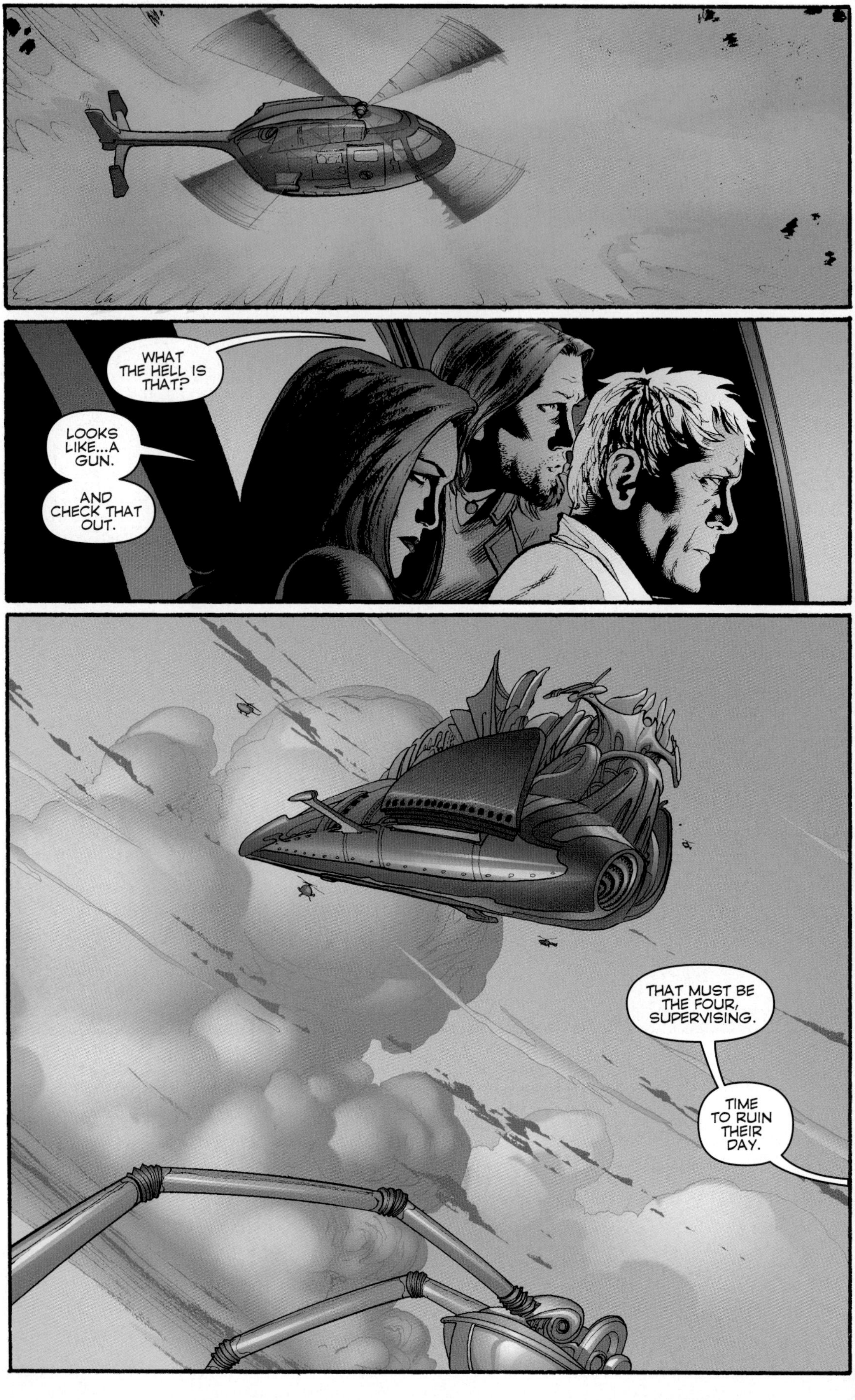
WHAT THE HELL IS THAT?
LOOKS LIKE...A GUN.
AND CHECK THAT OUT.
THAT MUST BE THE FOUR, SUPERVISING.
TIME TO RUIN THEIR DAY.

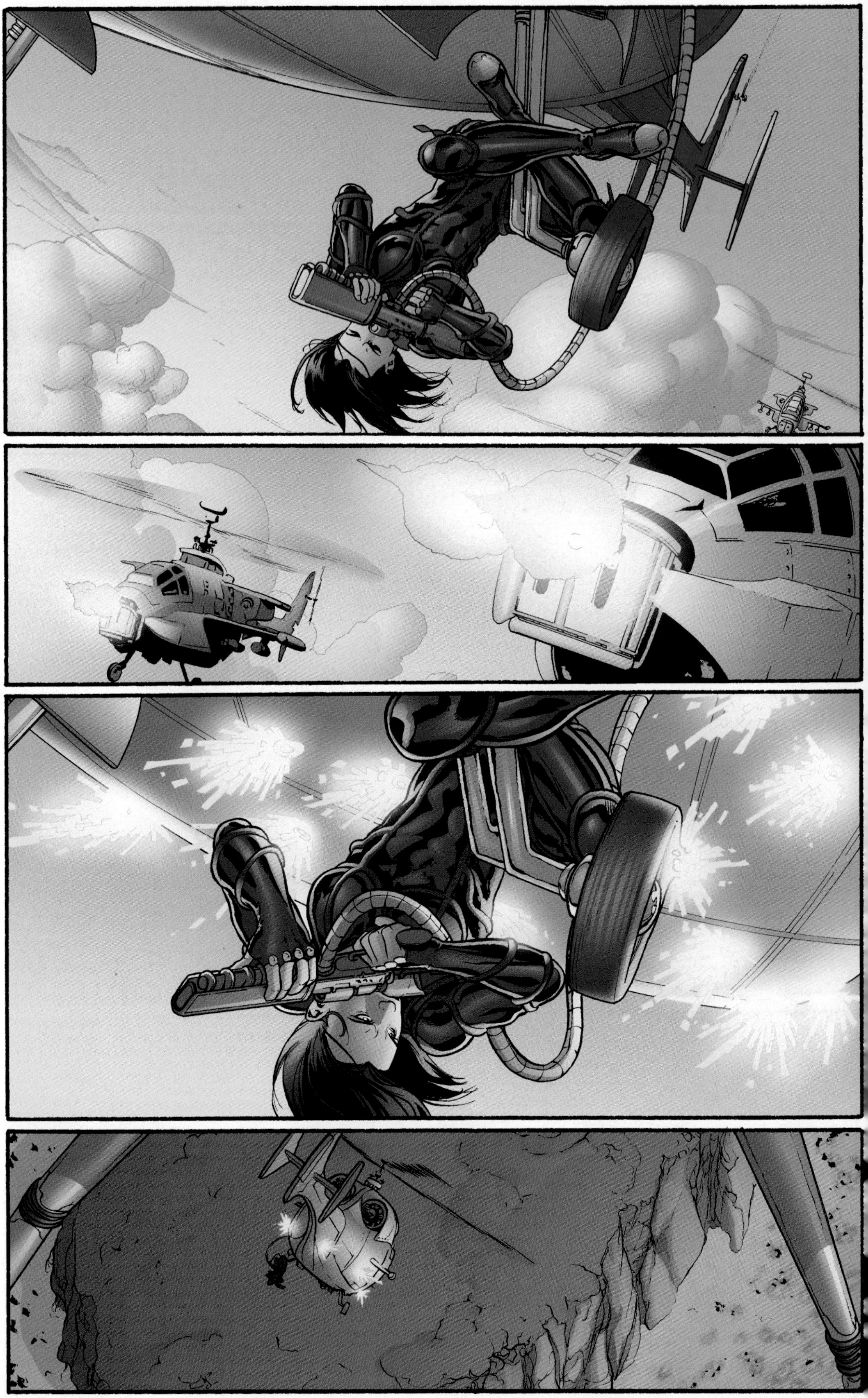

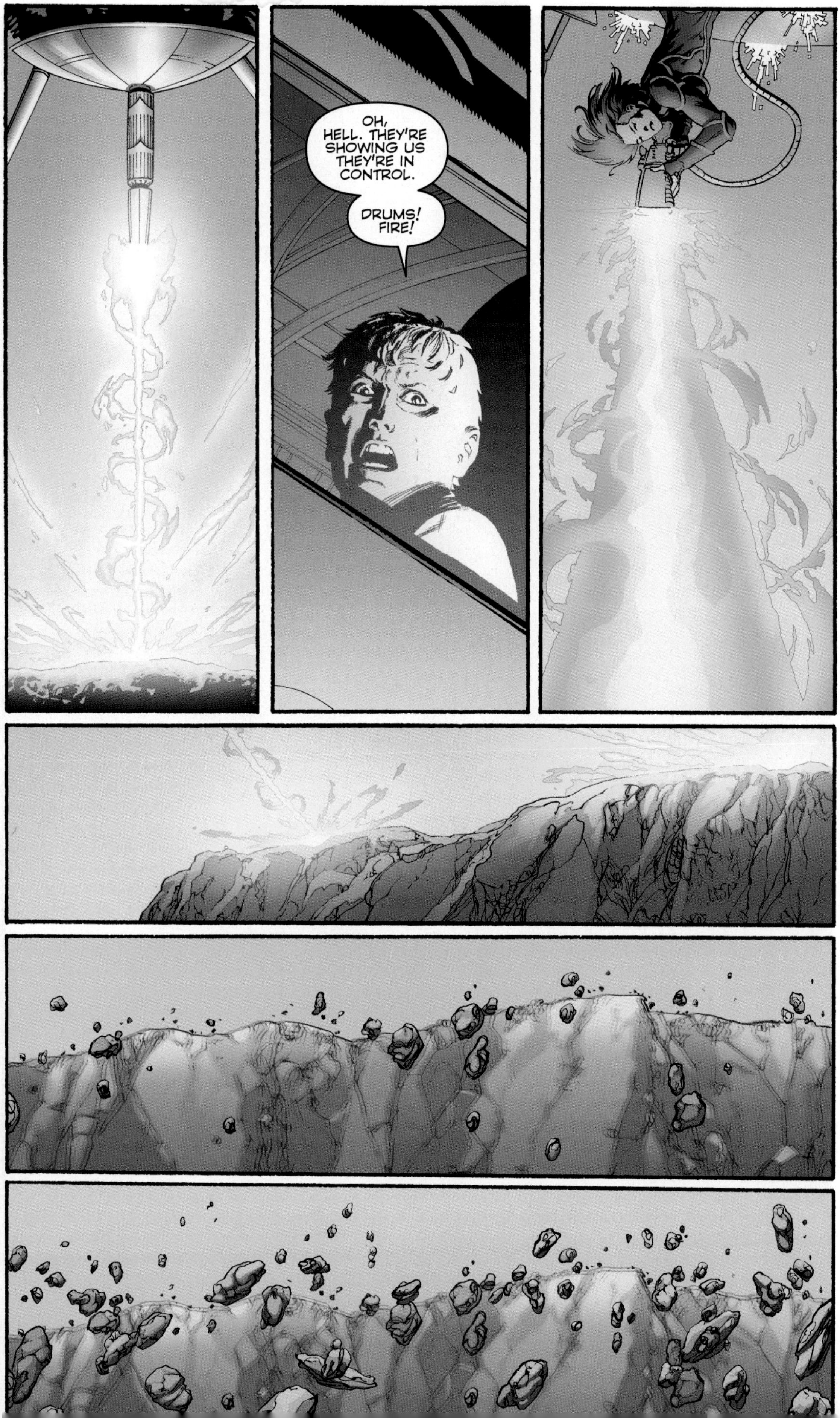
OH, HELL. THEY'RE SHOWING US THEY'RE IN CONTROL.
DRUMS! FIRE!

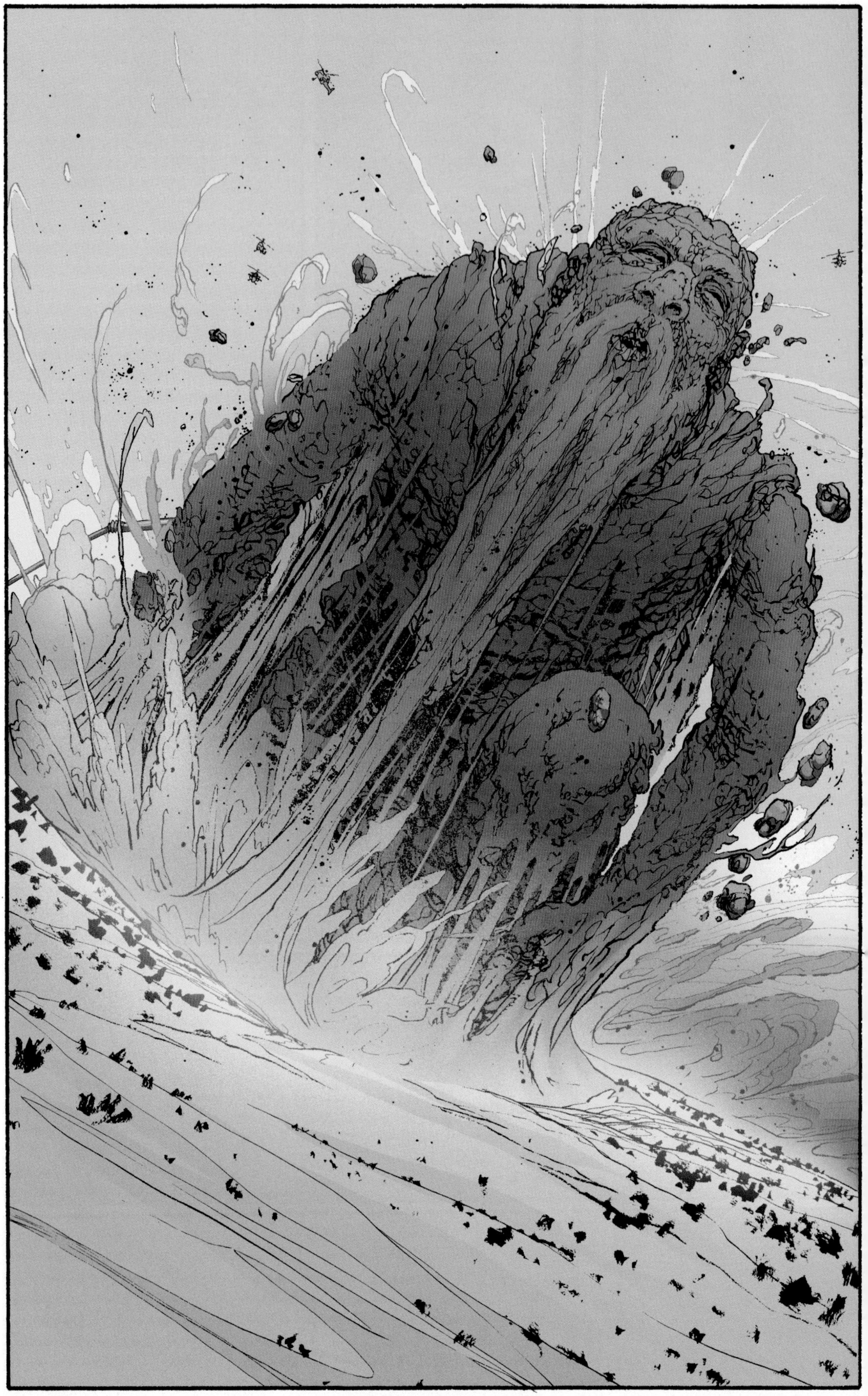

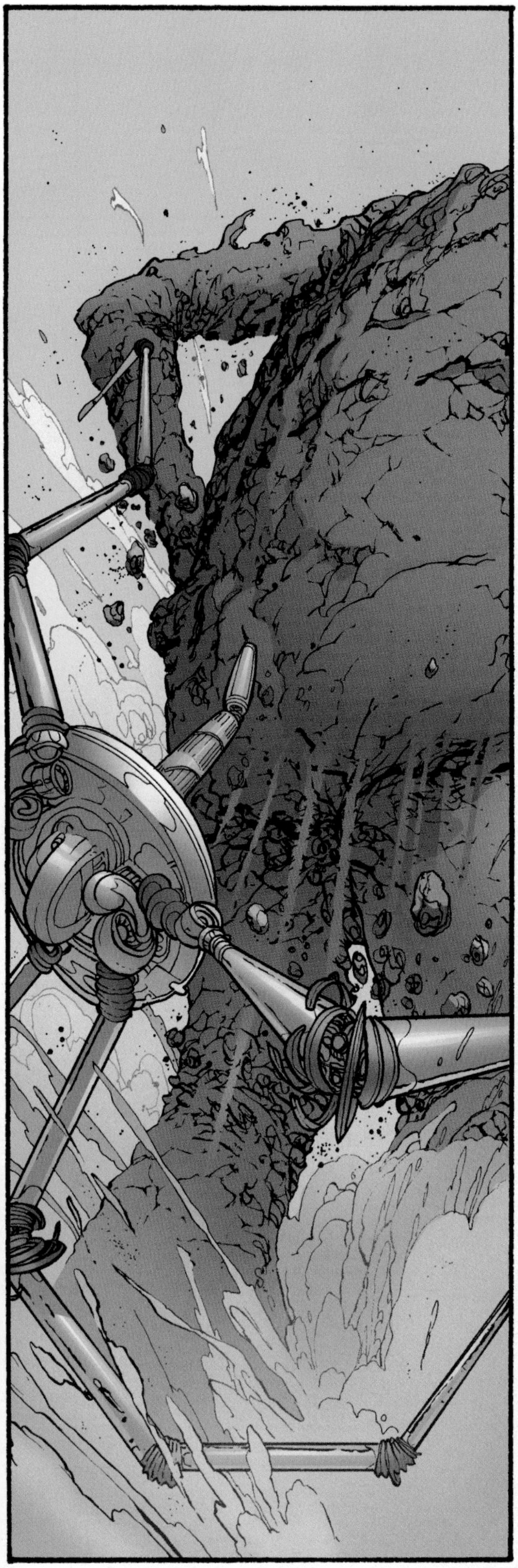
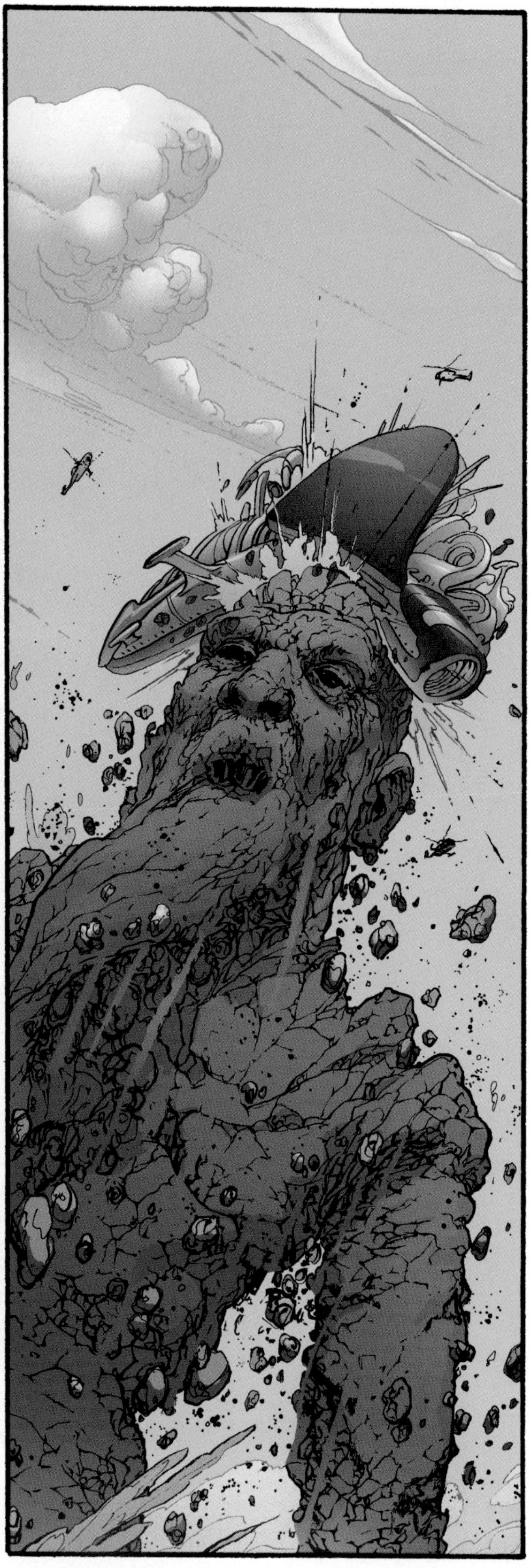

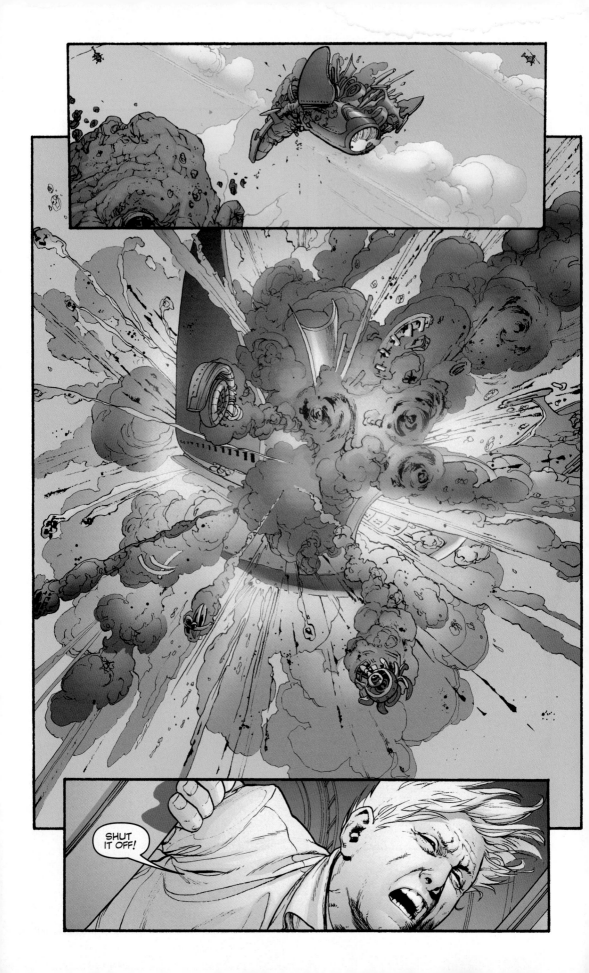

SHUT IT OFF!

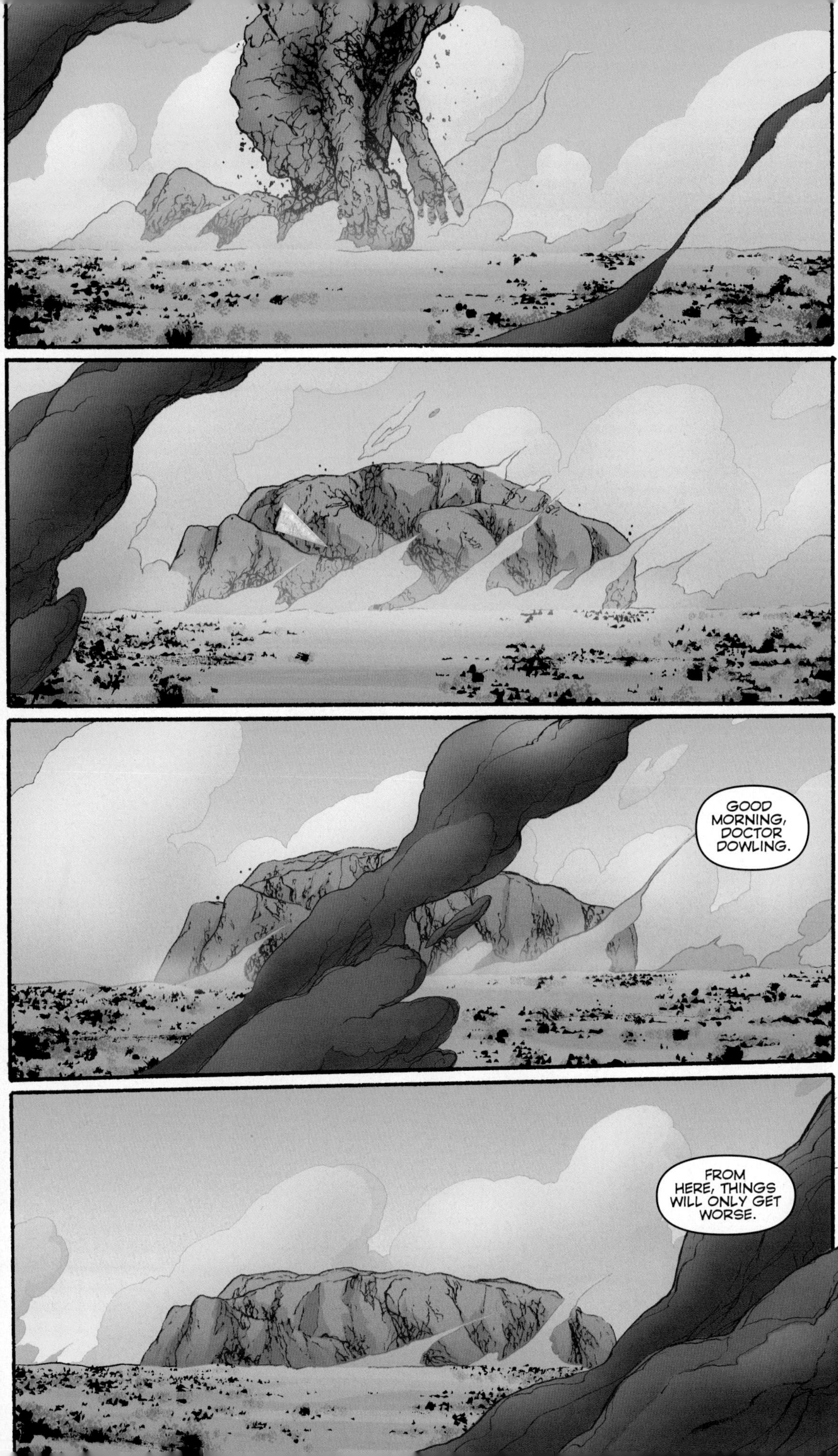
GOOD MORNING, DOCTOR DOWLING.
FROM HERE, THINGS WILL ONLY GET WORSE.

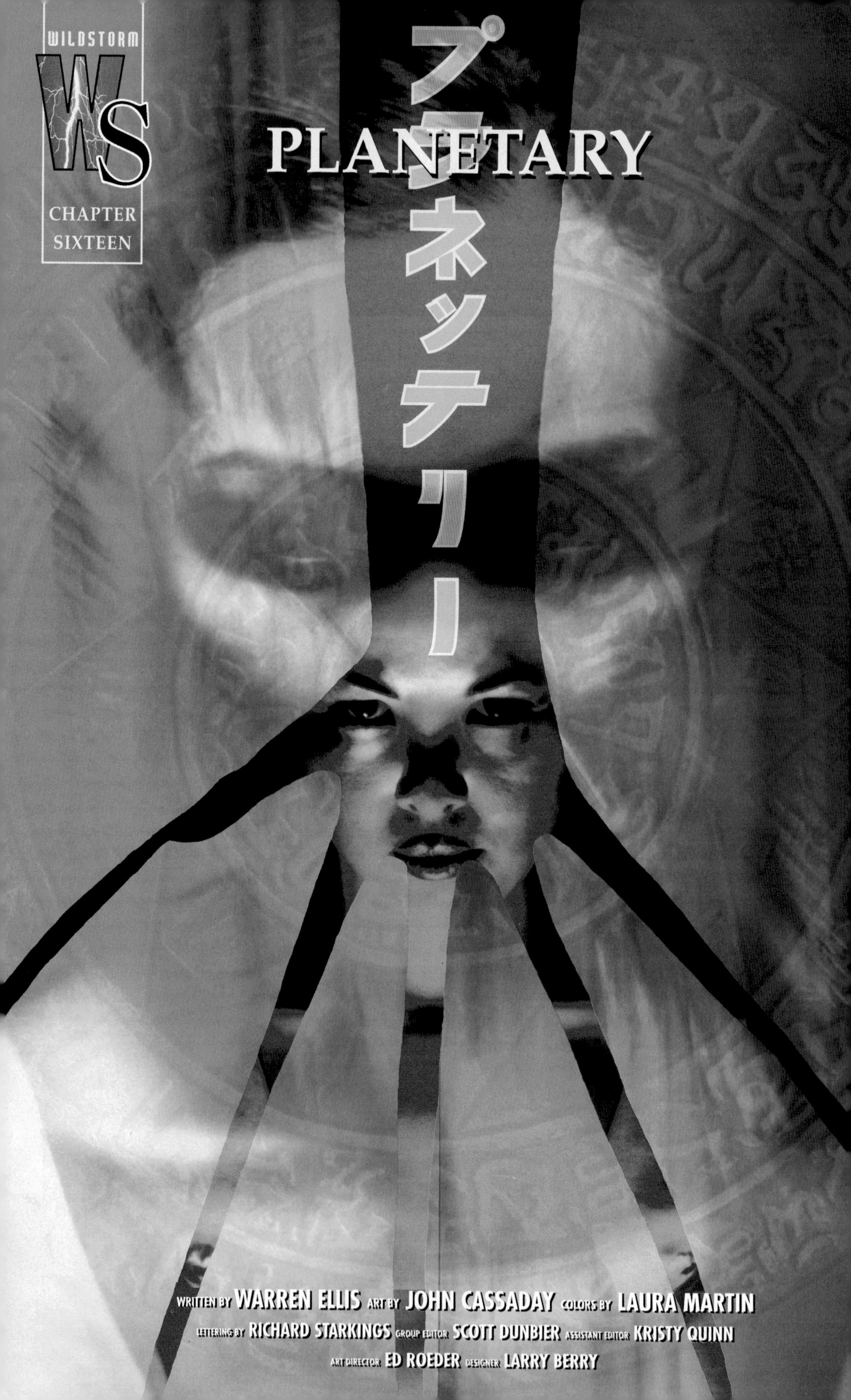
WILDSTORM
WS
CHAPTER SIXTEEN
プラネッテリー
PLANETARY
WRITTEN BY WARREN ELLIS ART BY JOHN CASSADAY COLORS BY LAURA MARTIN
LETTERING BY RICHARD STARKINGS GROUP EDITOR SCOTT DUNBIER ASSISTANT EDITOR KRISTY QUINN
ART DIRECTOR ED ROEDER DESIGNER LARRY BERRY

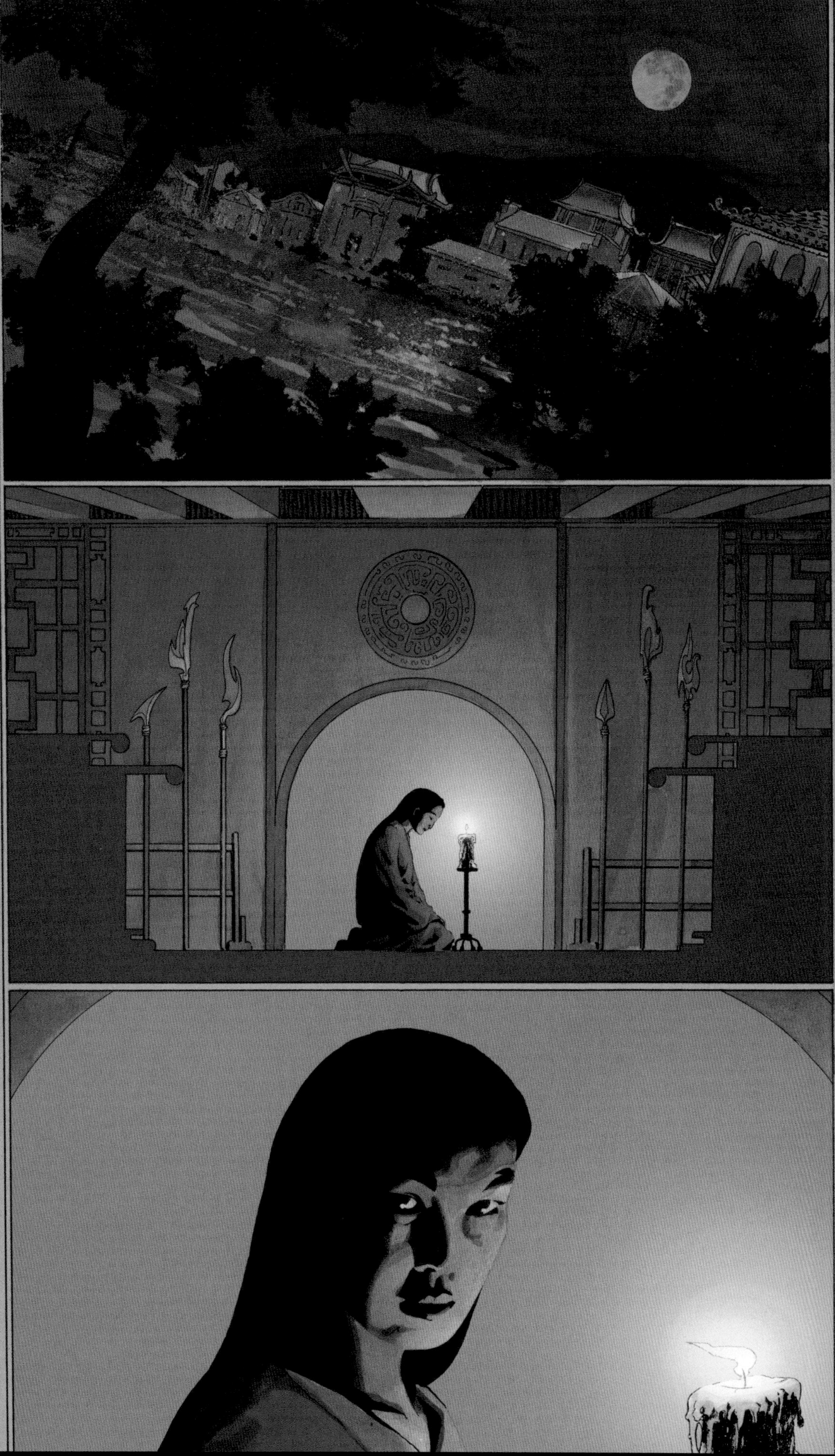

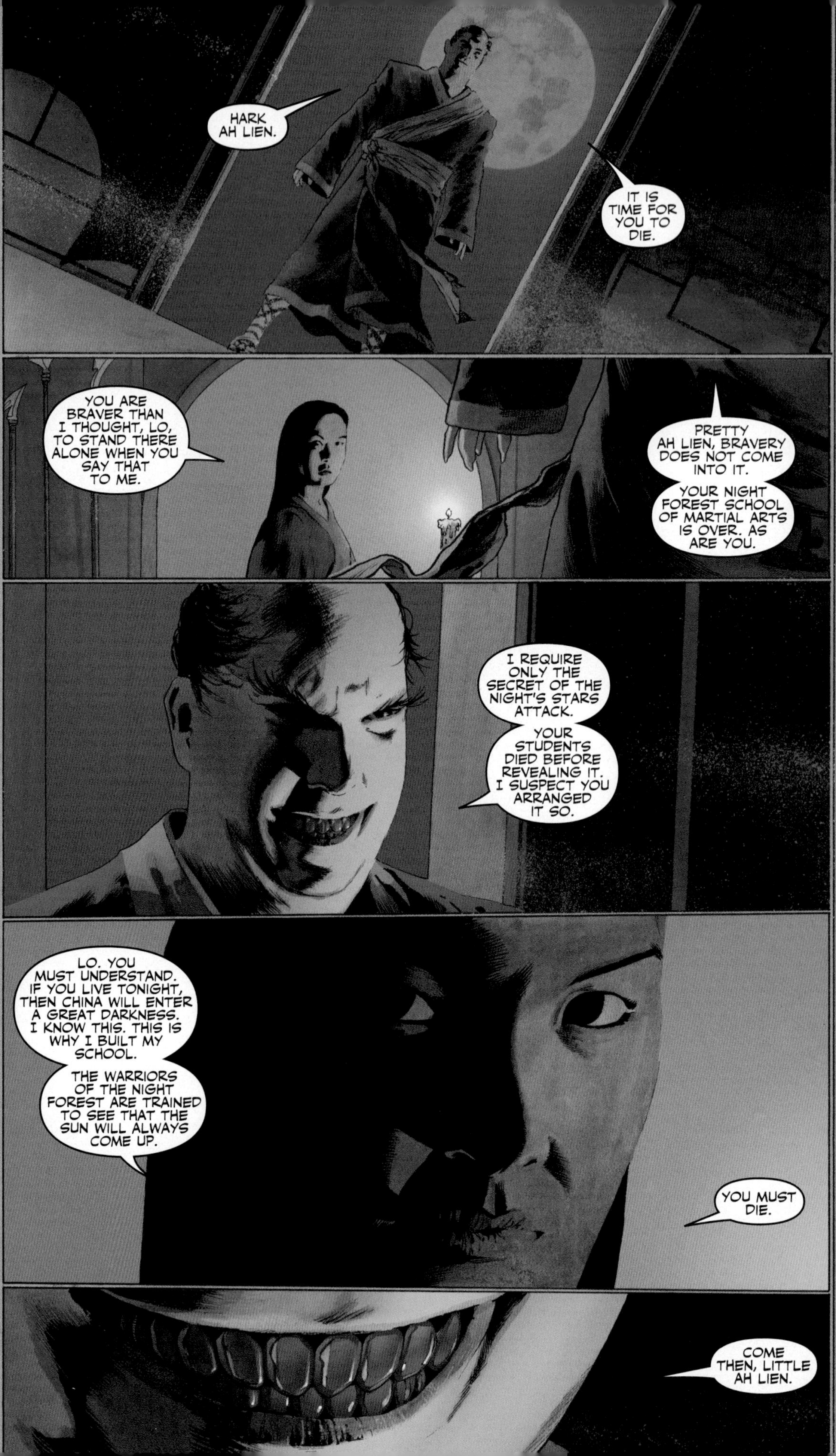
HARK AH LIEN.
IT IS TIME FOR YOU TO DIE.
YOU ARE BRAVER THAN I THOUGHT, LO, TO STAND THERE ALONE WHEN YOU SAY THAT TO ME.
PRETTY AH LIEN, BRAVERY DOES NOT COME INTO IT.
YOUR NIGHT FOREST SCHOOL OF MARTIAL ARTS IS OVER. AS ARE YOU.
I REQUIRE ONLY THE SECRET OF THE NIGHT'S STARS ATTACK.
YOUR STUDENTS DIED BEFORE REVEALING IT. I SUSPECT YOU ARRANGED IT SO.
LO. YOU MUST UNDERSTAND. IF YOU LIVE TONIGHT, THEN CHINA WILL ENTER A GREAT DARKNESS. I KNOW THIS. THIS IS WHY I BUILT MY SCHOOL.
THE WARRIORS OF THE NIGHT FOREST ARE TRAINED TO SEE THAT THE SUN WILL ALWAYS COME UP.
YOU MUST DIE.
COME THEN, LITTLE AH LIEN.

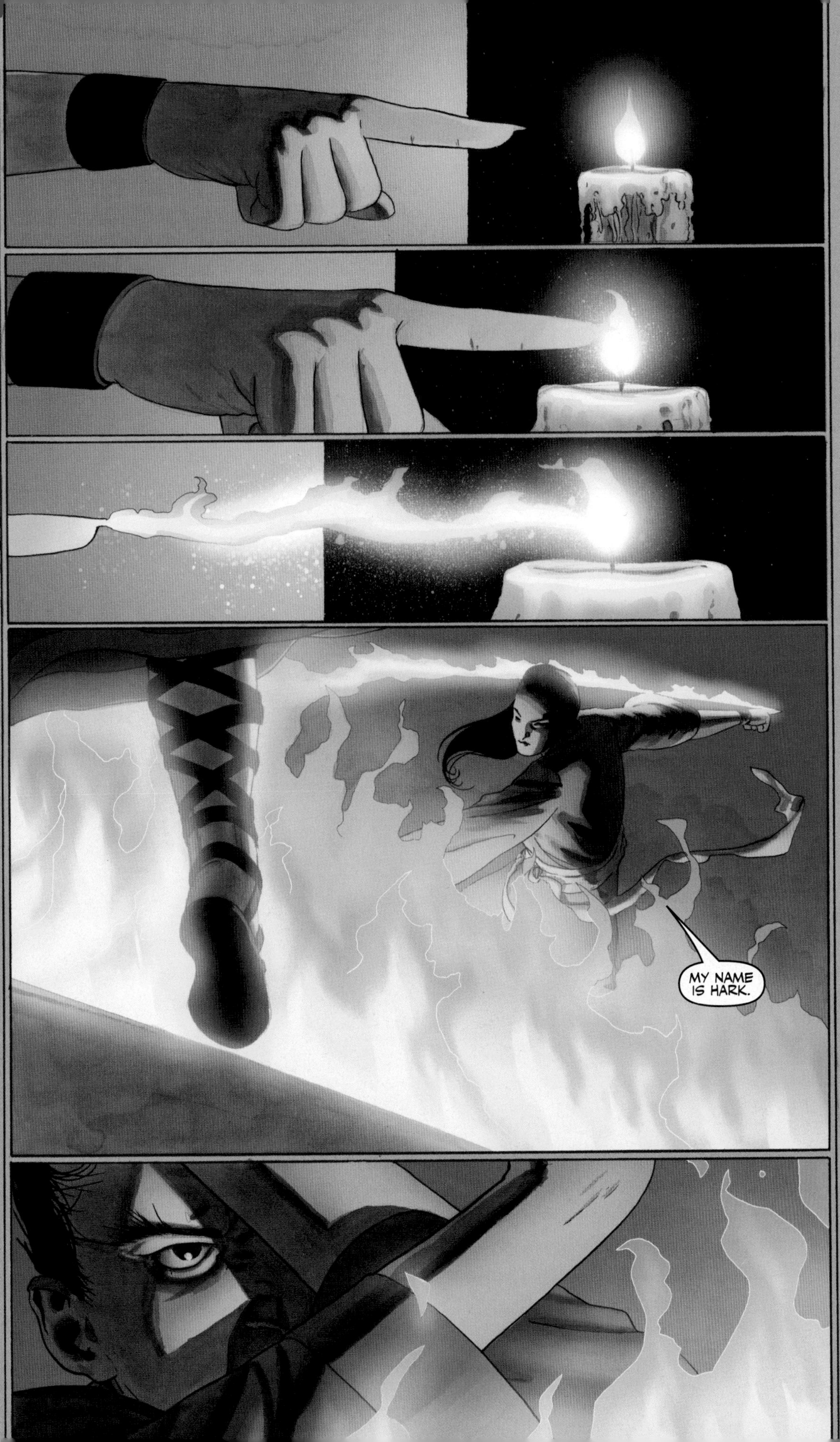
MY NAME IS HARK.

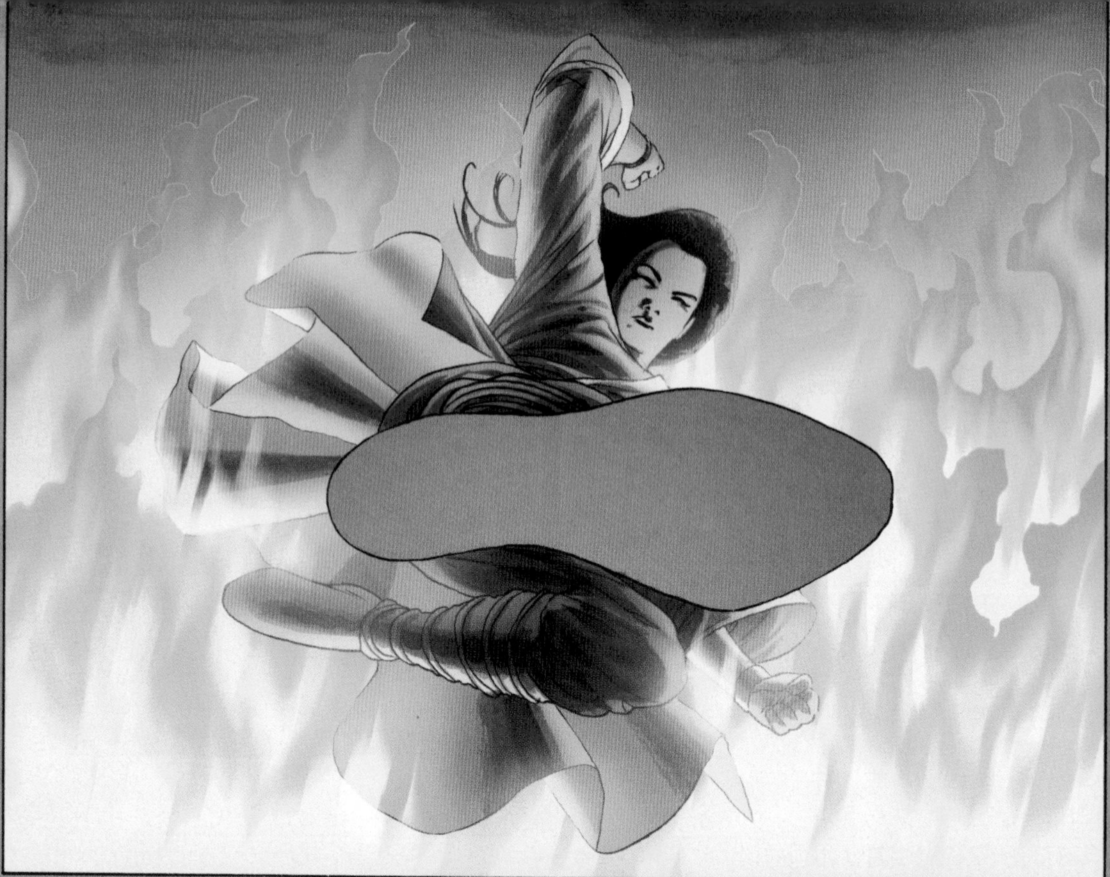

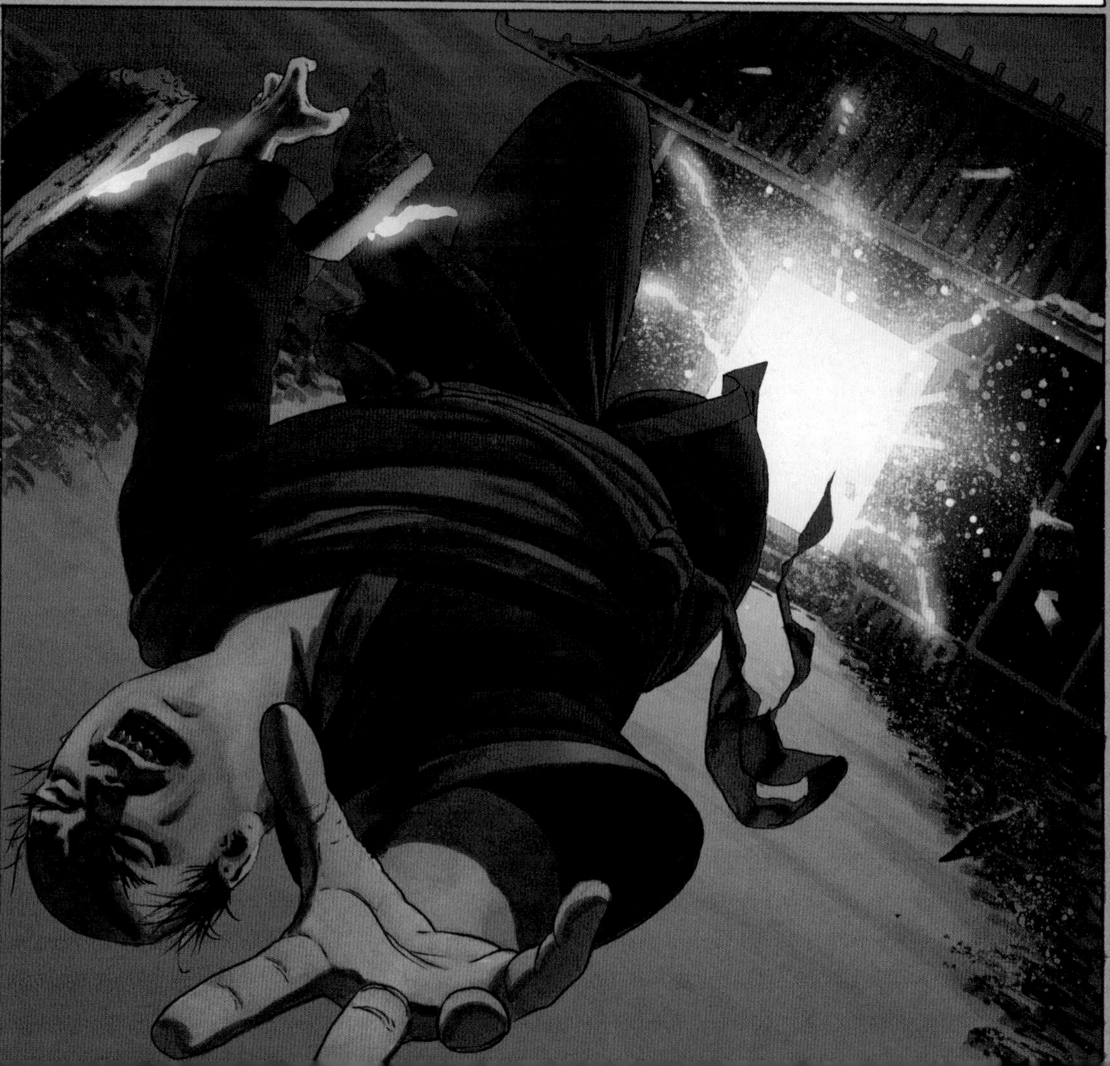

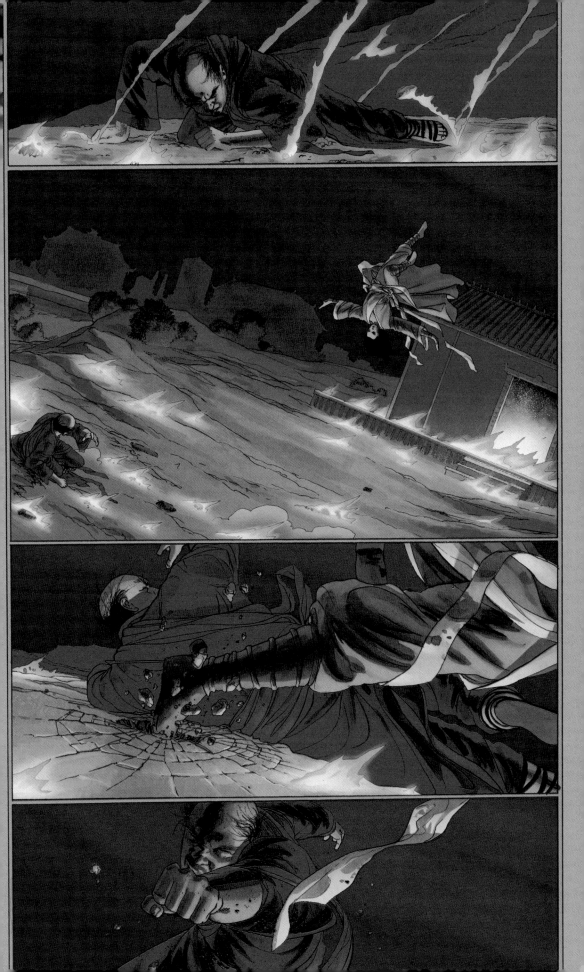

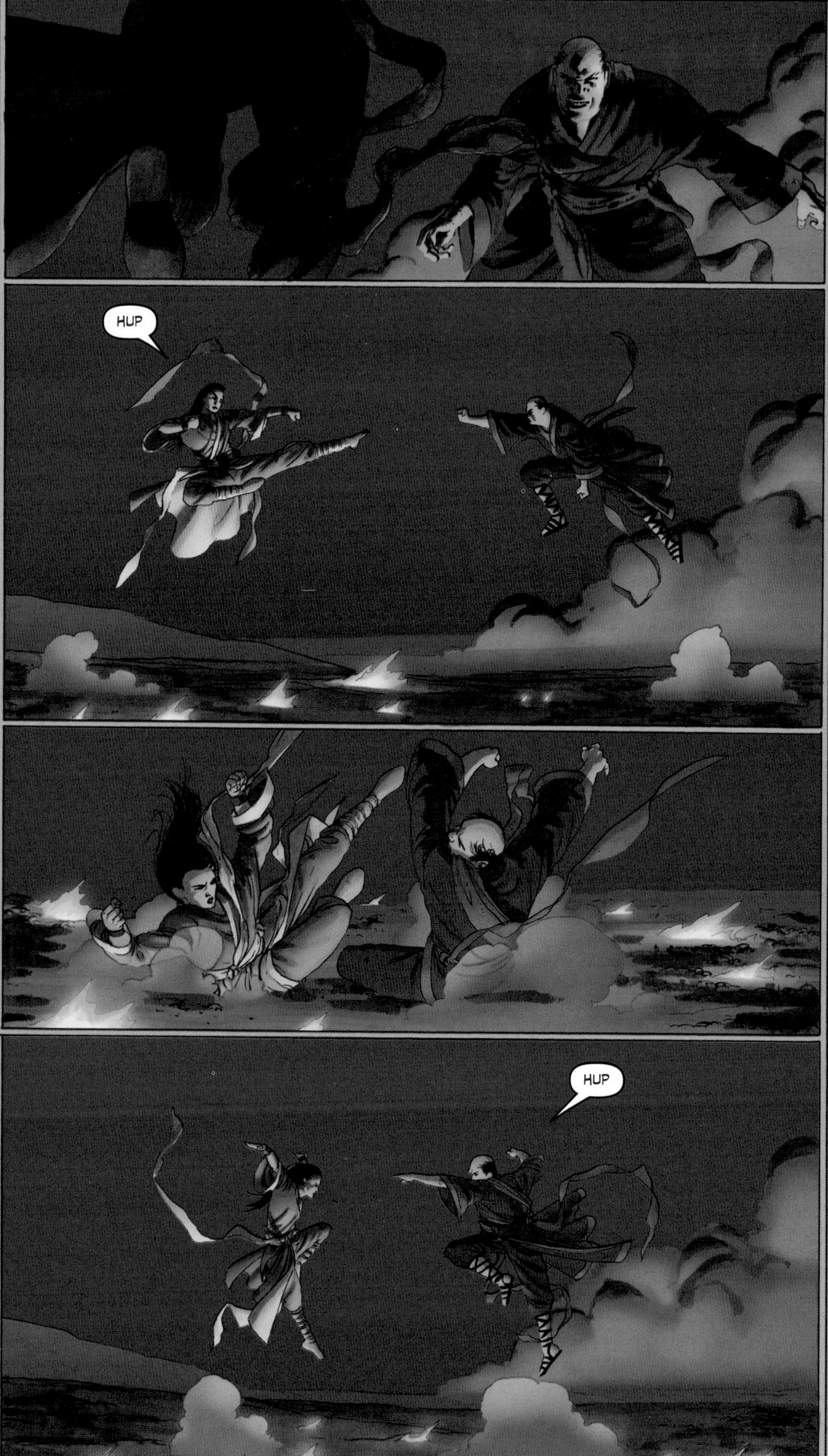
HUP
HUP

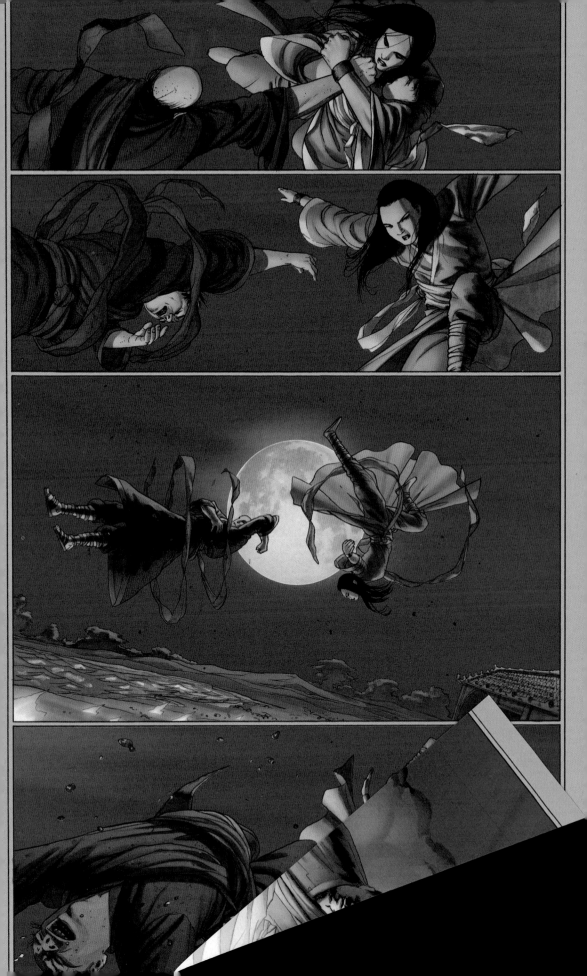

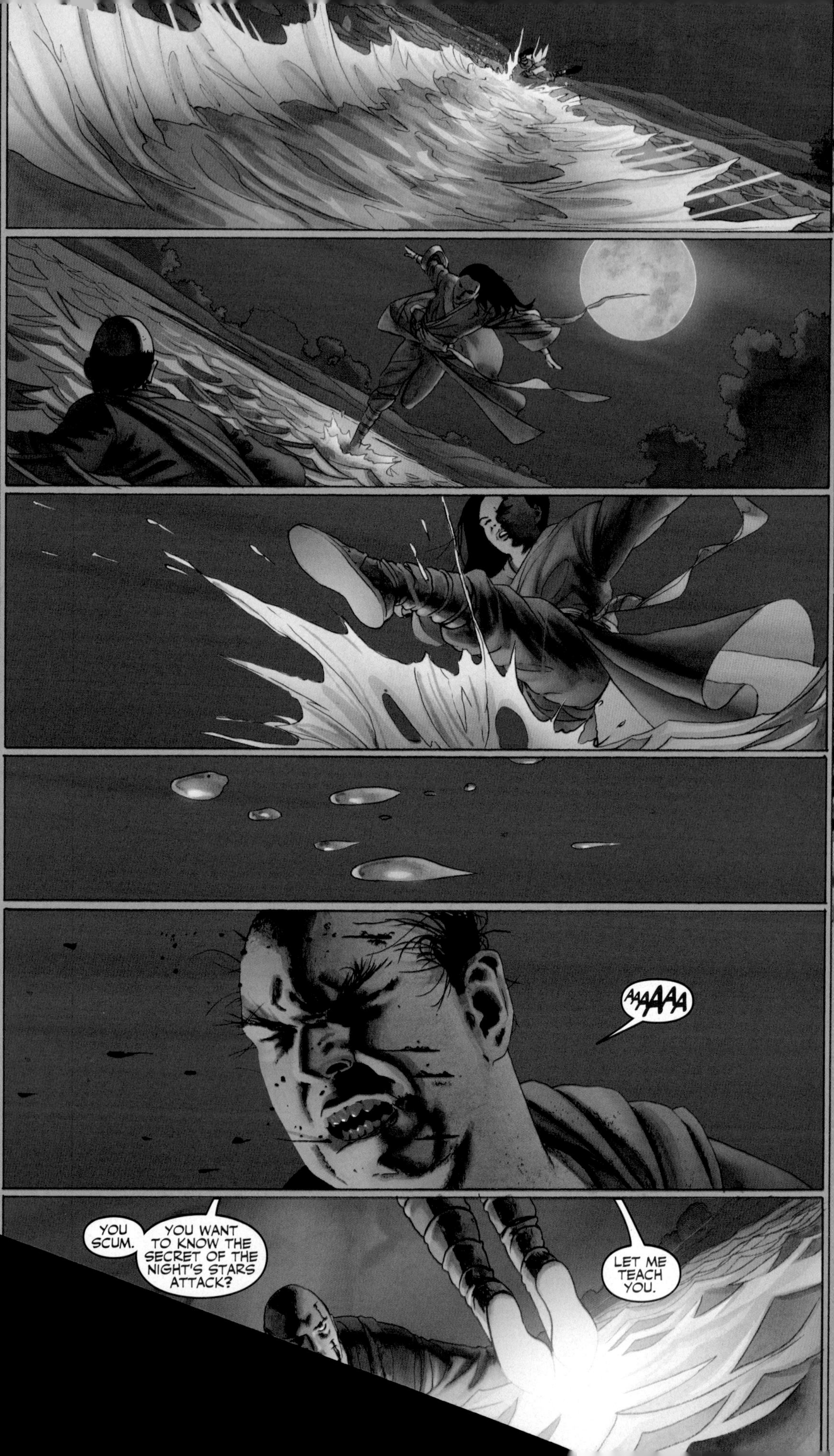
AAAAAA
YOU SCUM.
YOU WANT TO KNOW THE SECRET OF THE NIGHT'S STARS ATTACK?
LET ME TEACH YOU.

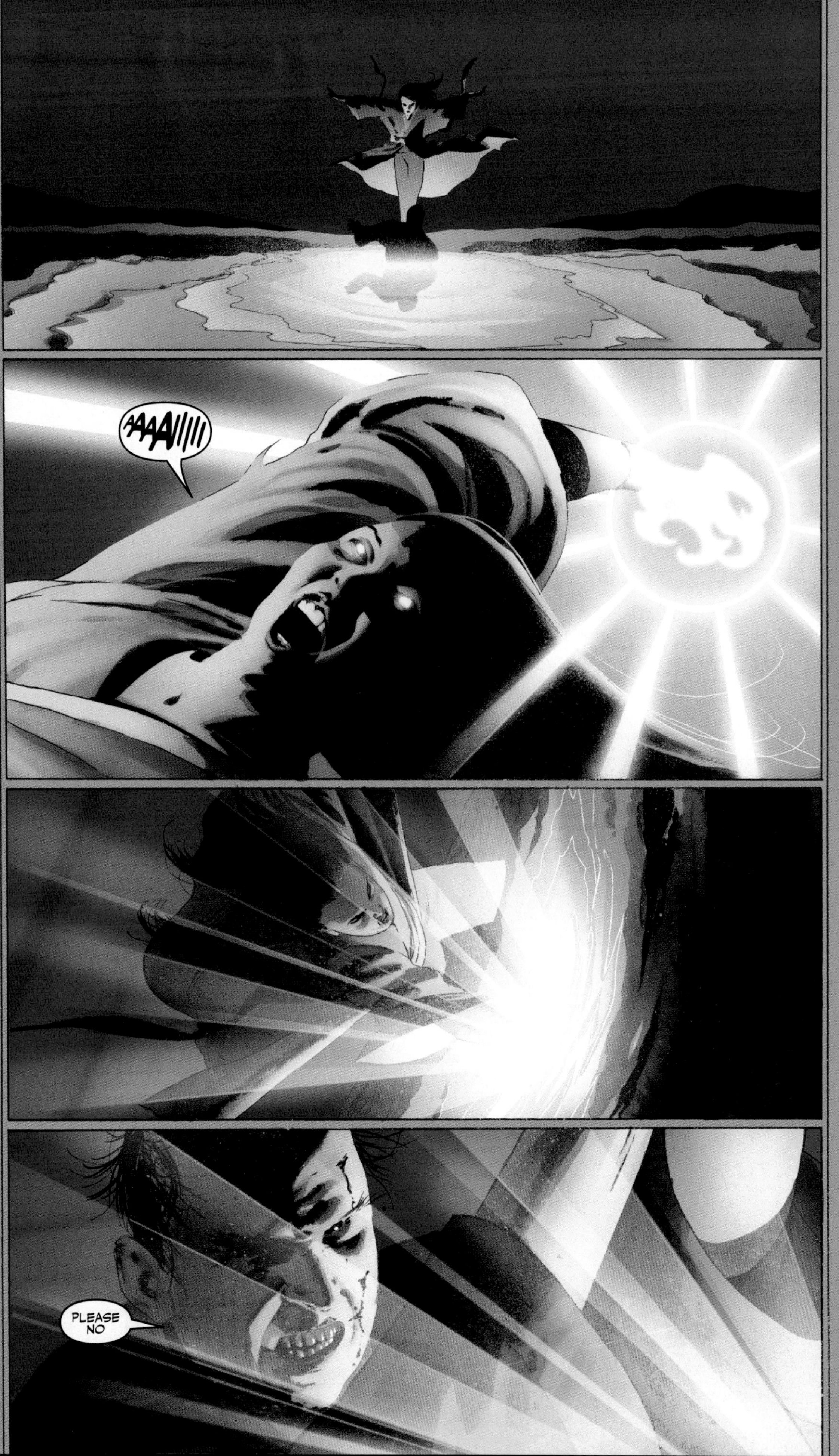
AAAAI!!!!!
PLEASE NO

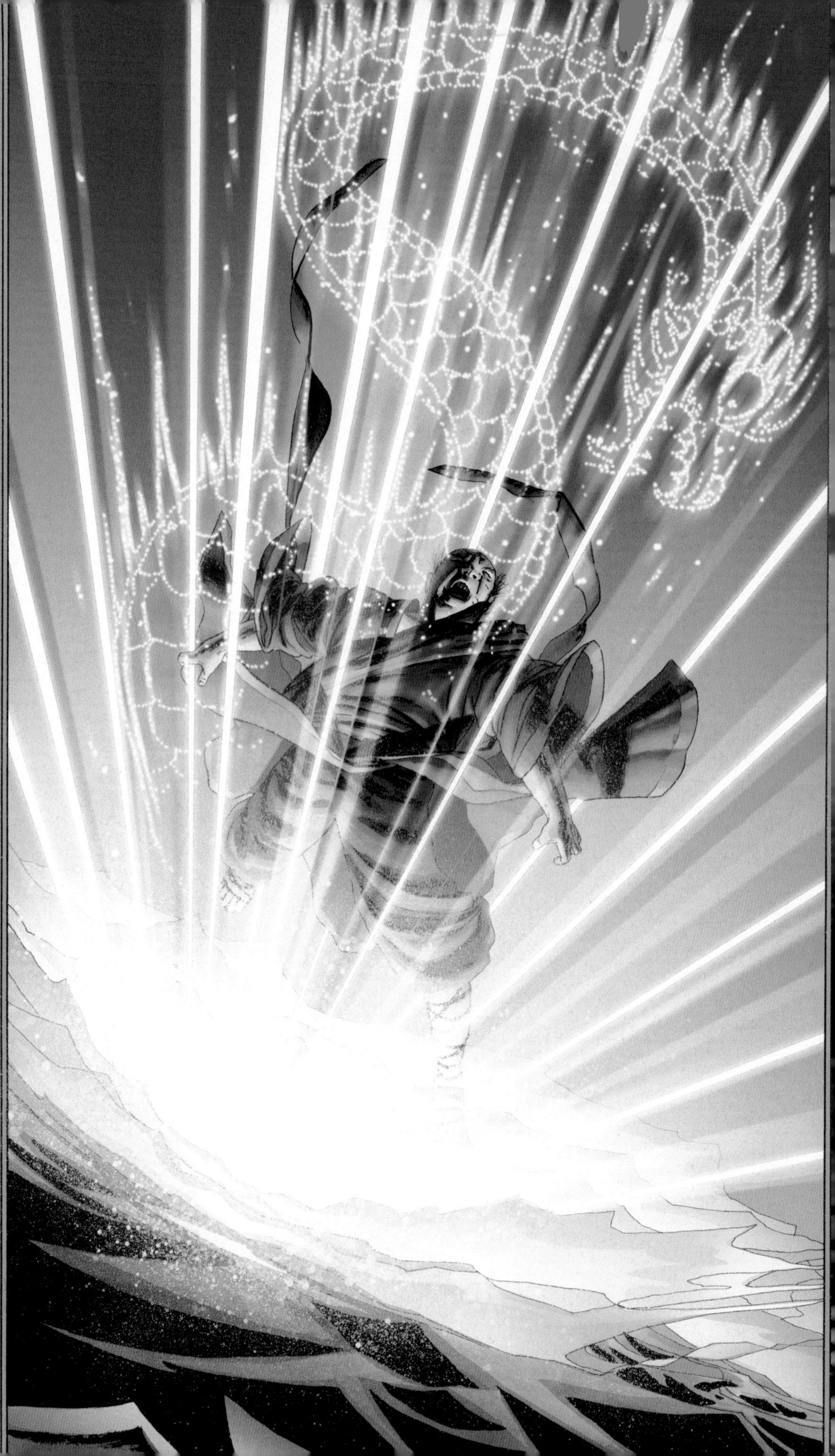

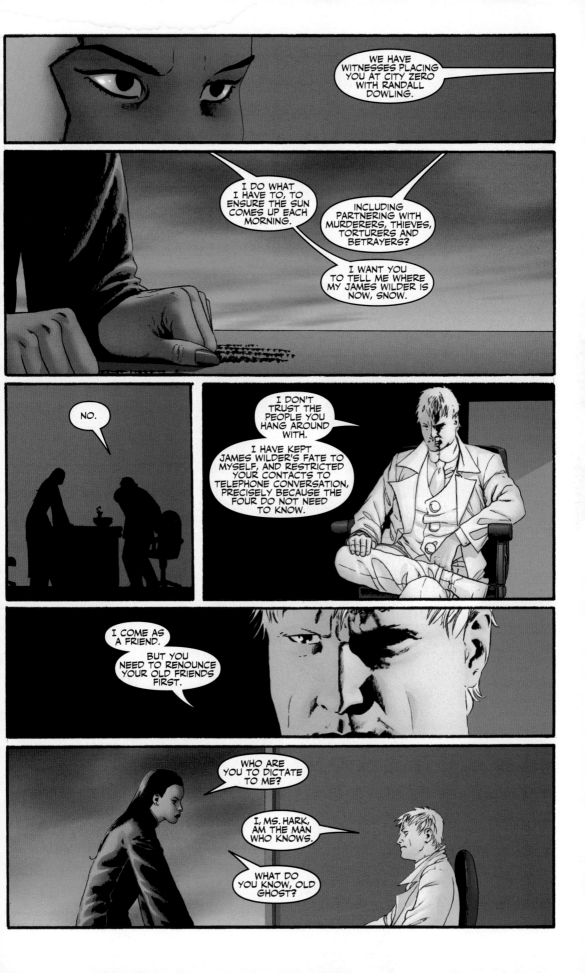

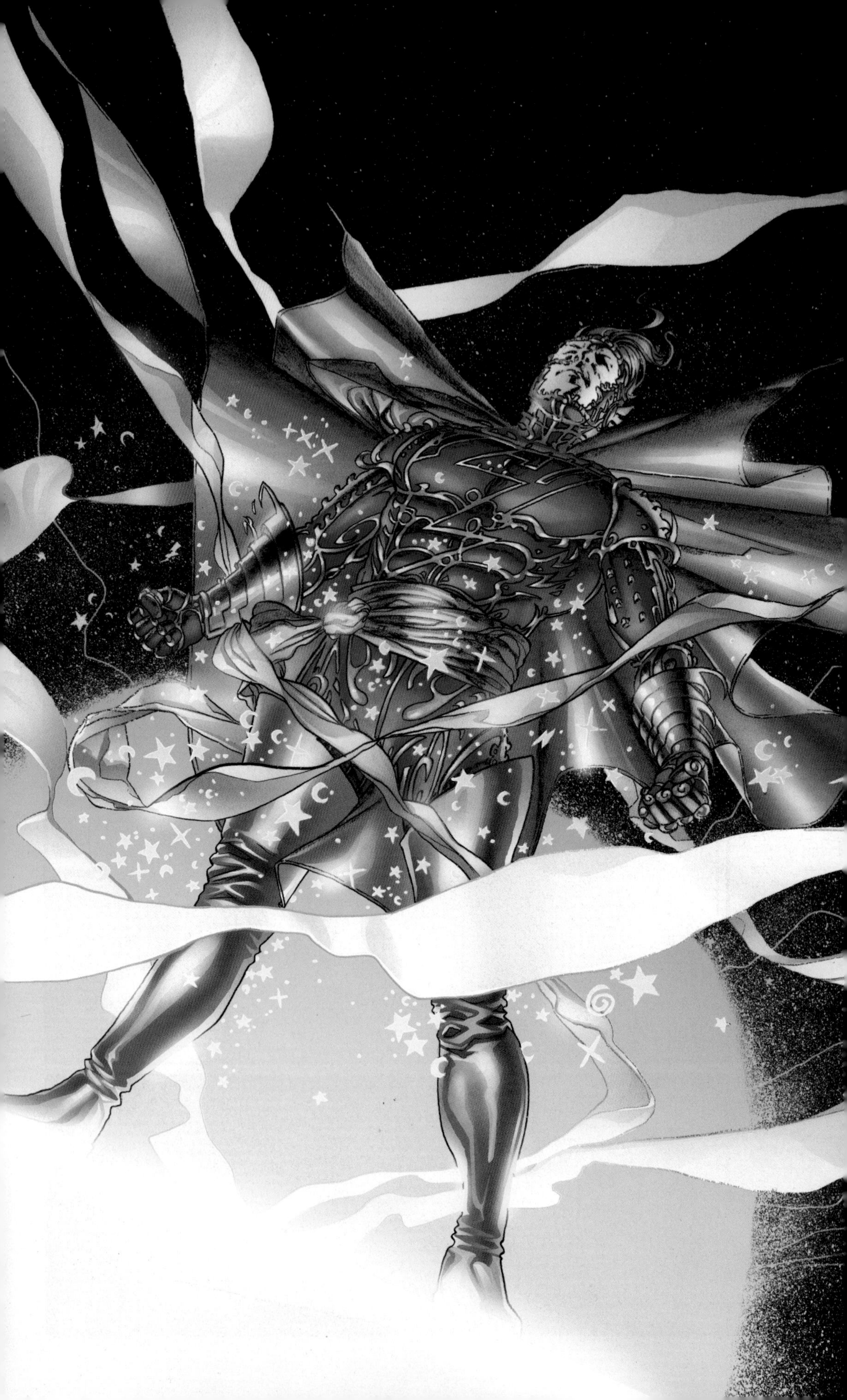

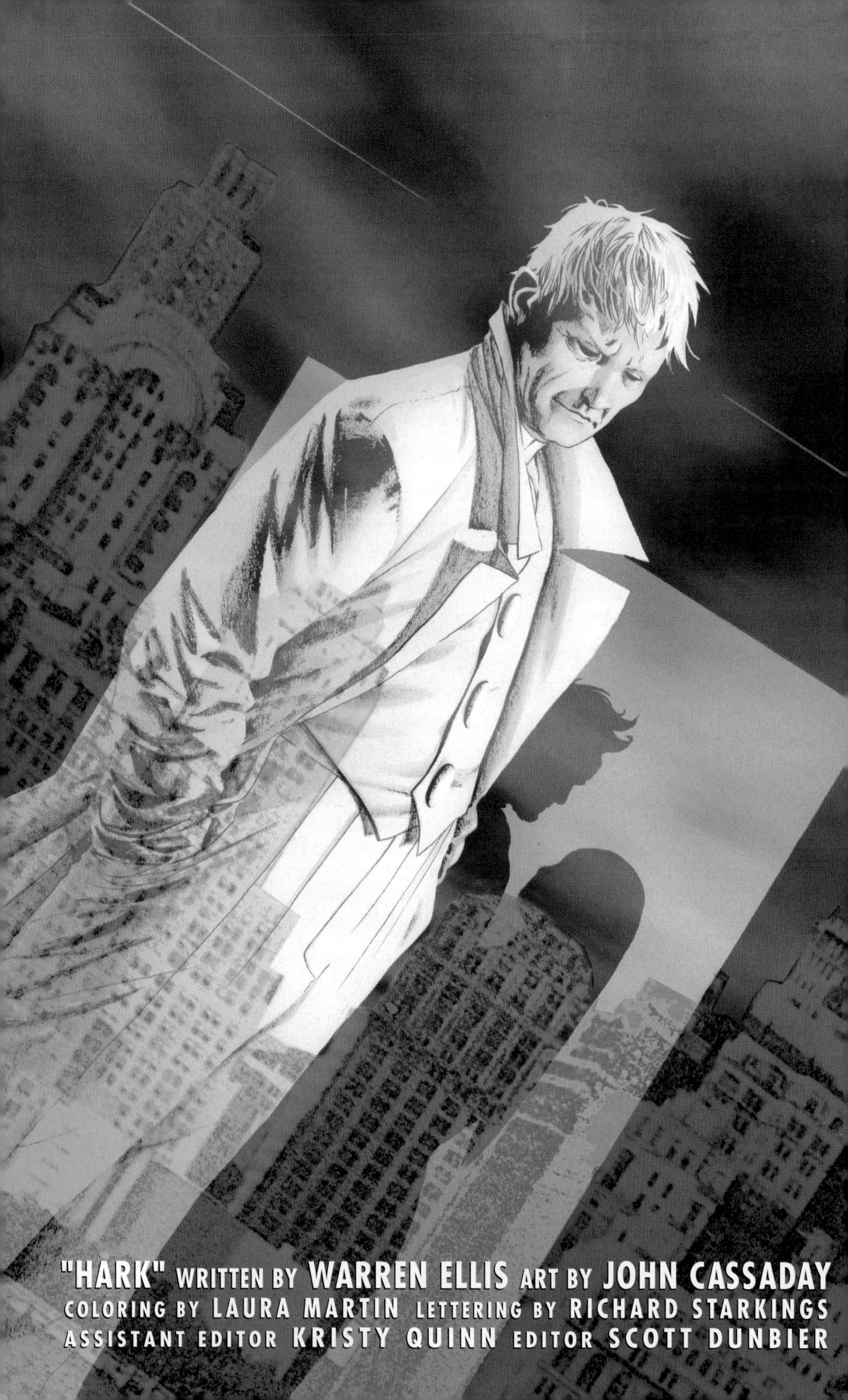

"HARK" WRITTEN BY WARREN ELLIS ART BY JOHN CASSADAY
COLORING BY LAURA MARTIN LETTERING BY RICHARD STARKINGS
ASSISTANT EDITOR KRISTY QUINN EDITOR SCOTT DUNBIER

A WildStorm Magazine
Chapter Seventeen
PLANETARY
ELLIS • CASSADAY • MARTIN
In the lost city of
Opak-Re

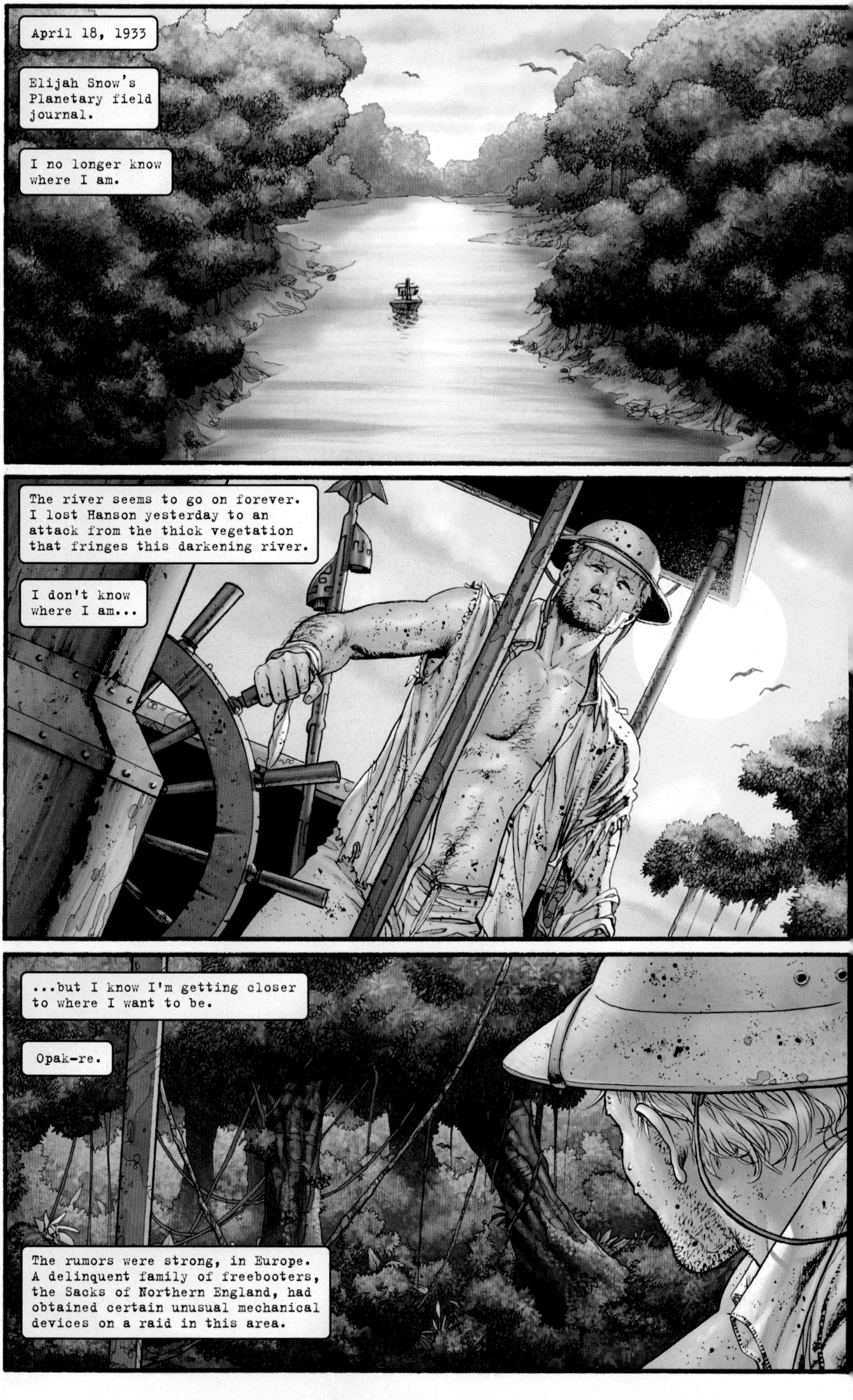
April 18, 1933
Elijah Snow's Planetary field journal.
I no longer know where I am.
The river seems to go on forever. I lost Hanson yesterday to an attack from the thick vegetation that fringes this darkening river.
I don't know where I am...
...but I know I'm getting closer to where I want to be.
Opak-re.
The rumors were strong, in Europe. A delinquent family of freebooters, the Sacks of Northern England, had obtained certain unusual mechanical devices on a raid in this area.

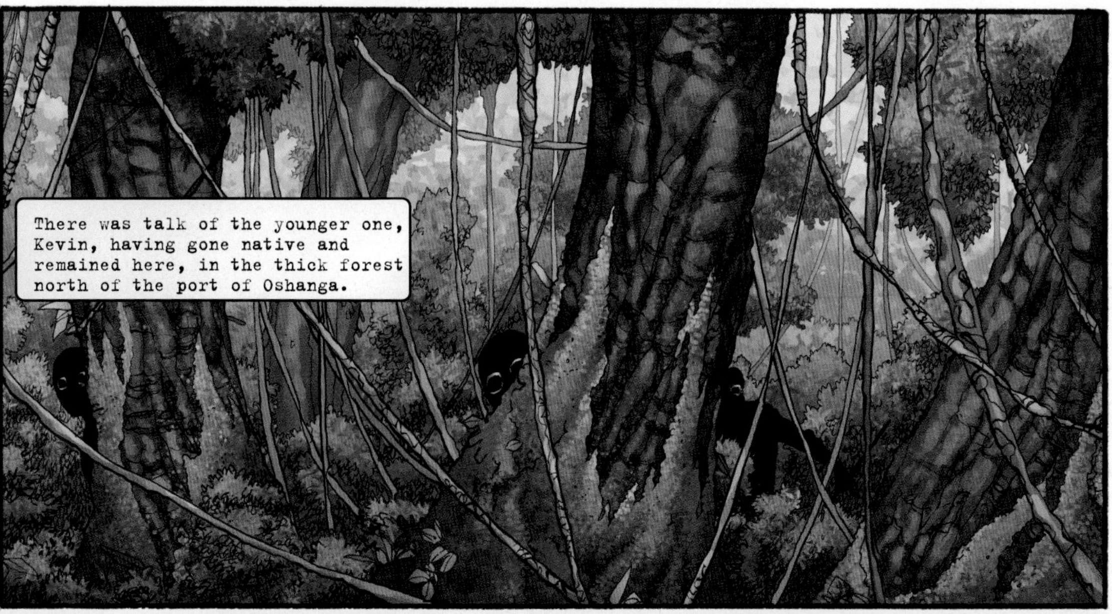
There was talk of the younger one, Kevin, having gone native and remained here, in the thick forest north of the port of Oshanga.

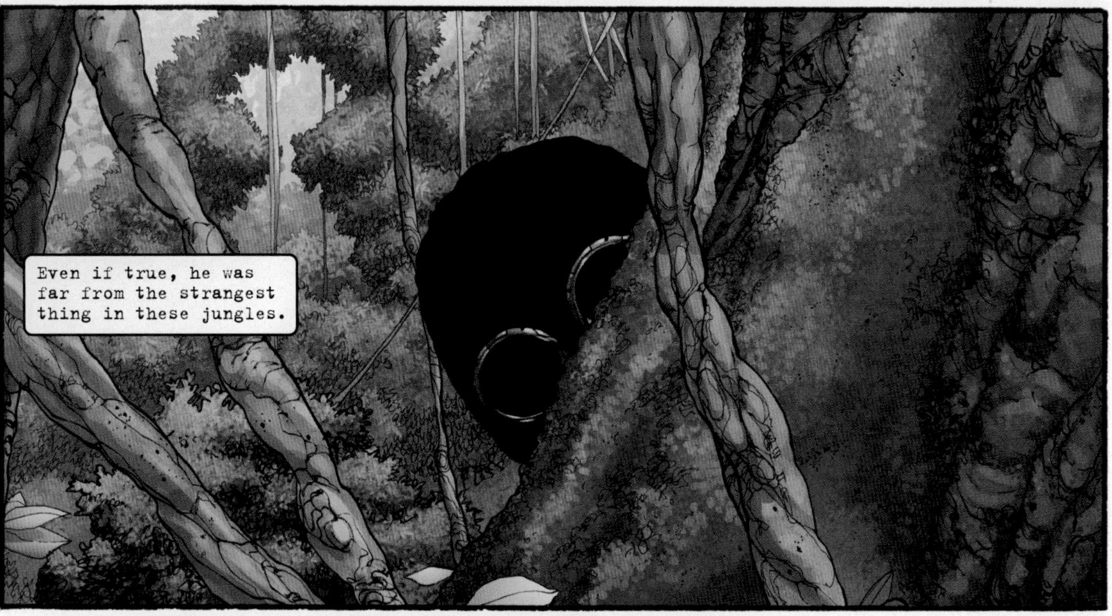
Even if true, he was far from the strangest thing in these jungles.

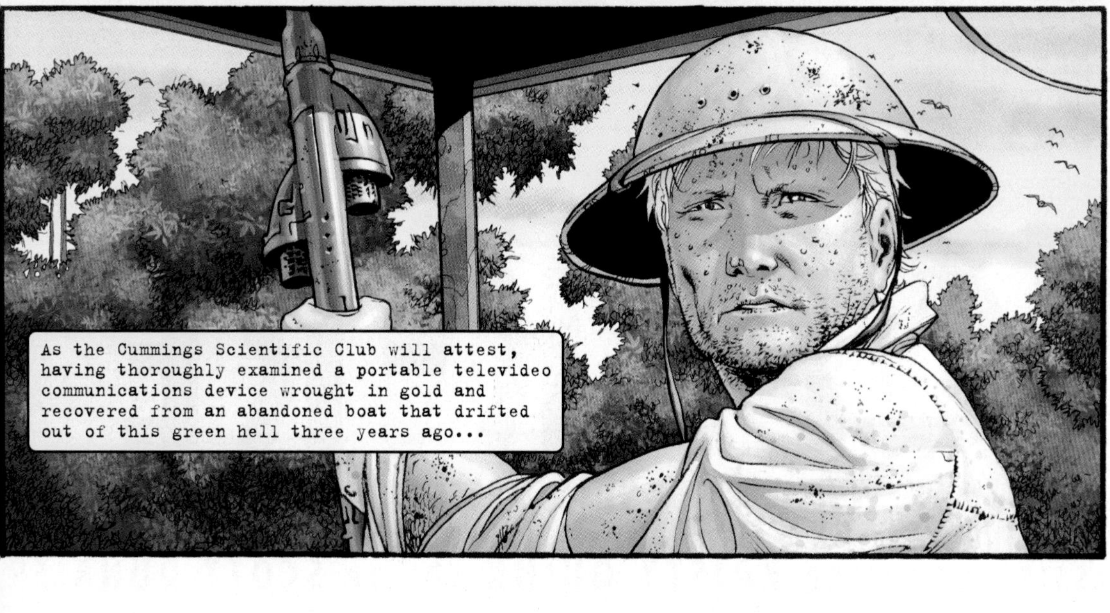
As the Cummings Scientific Club will attest, having thoroughly examined a portable televideo communications device wrought in gold and recovered from an abandoned boat that drifted out of this green hell three years ago...

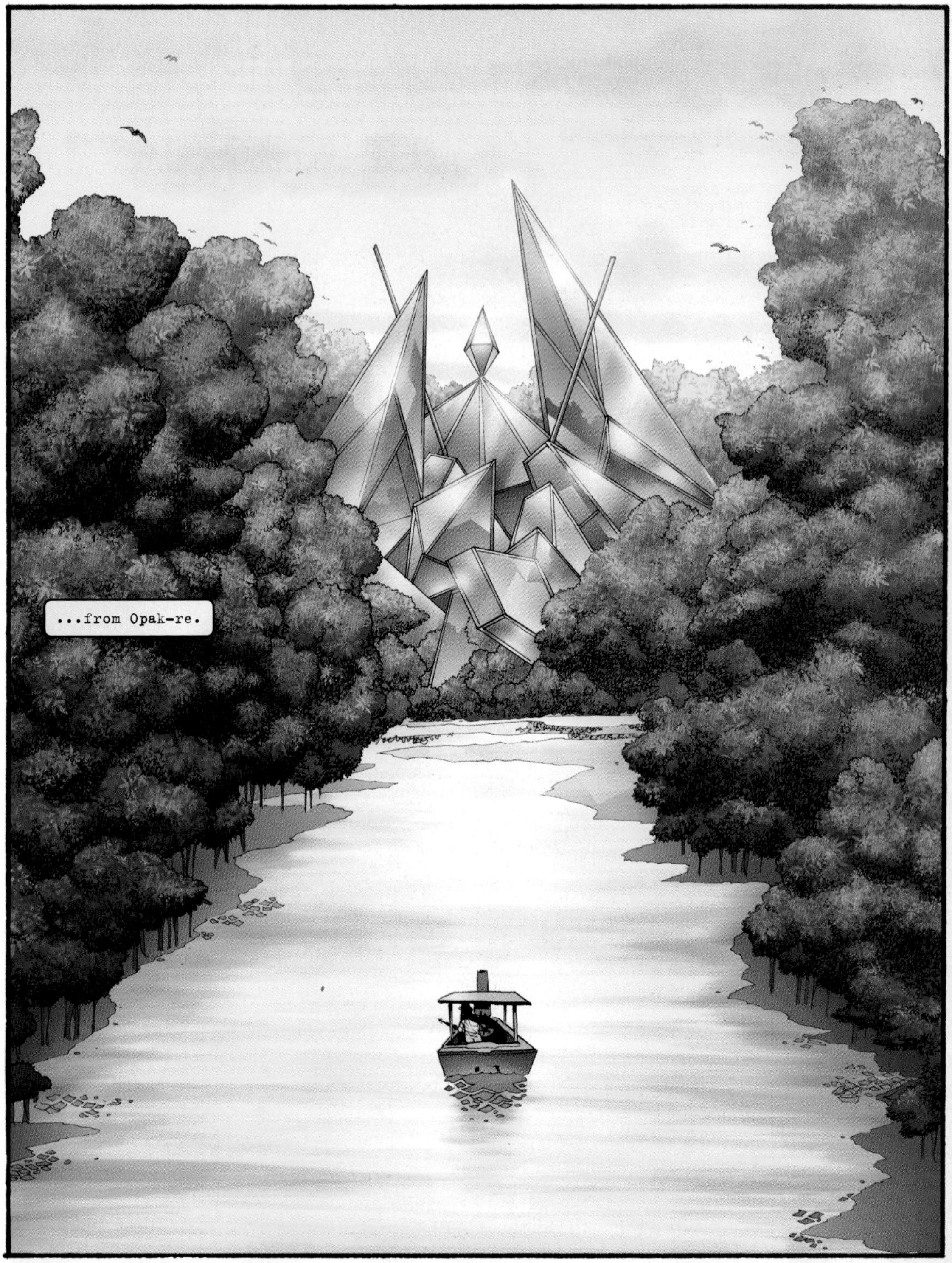
...from Opak-re.

"OPAK-RE"

WRITTEN BY WARREN ELLIS ART BY JOHN CASSADAY
COLORING BY LAURA MARTIN LETTERING BY RICHARD STARKINGS
ASSISTANT EDITOR KRISTY QUINN EDITOR SCOTT DUNBIER

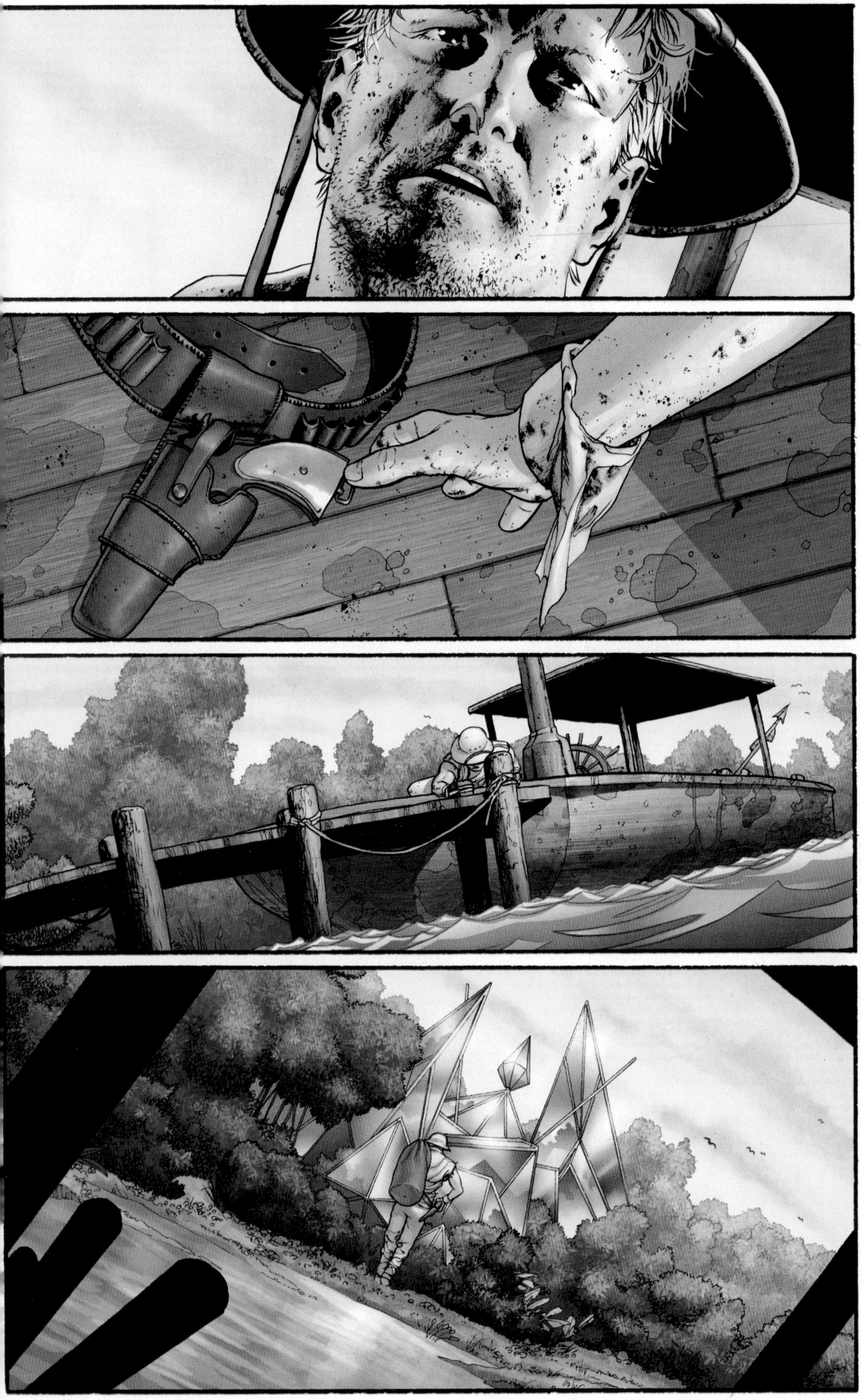

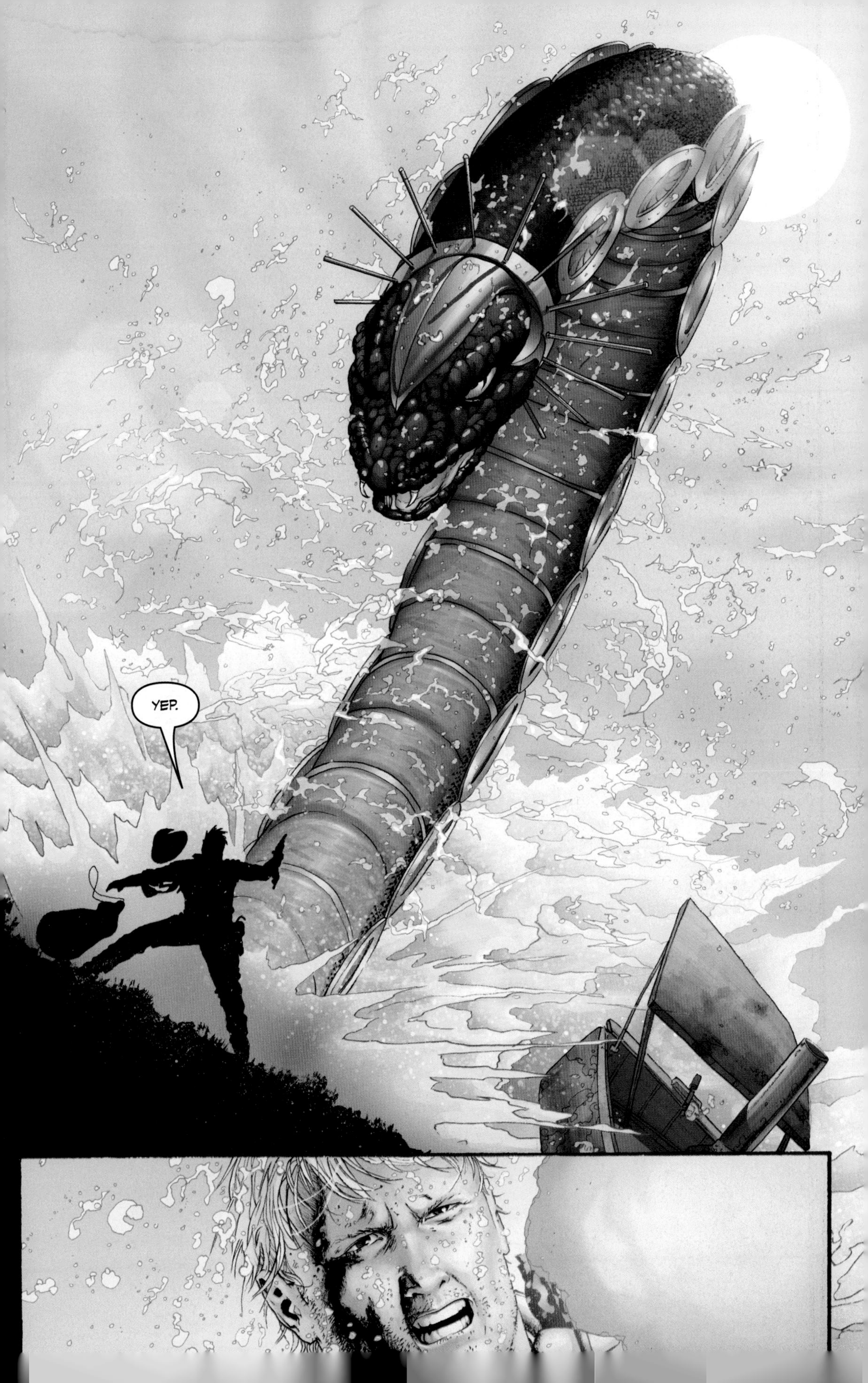
YEP.

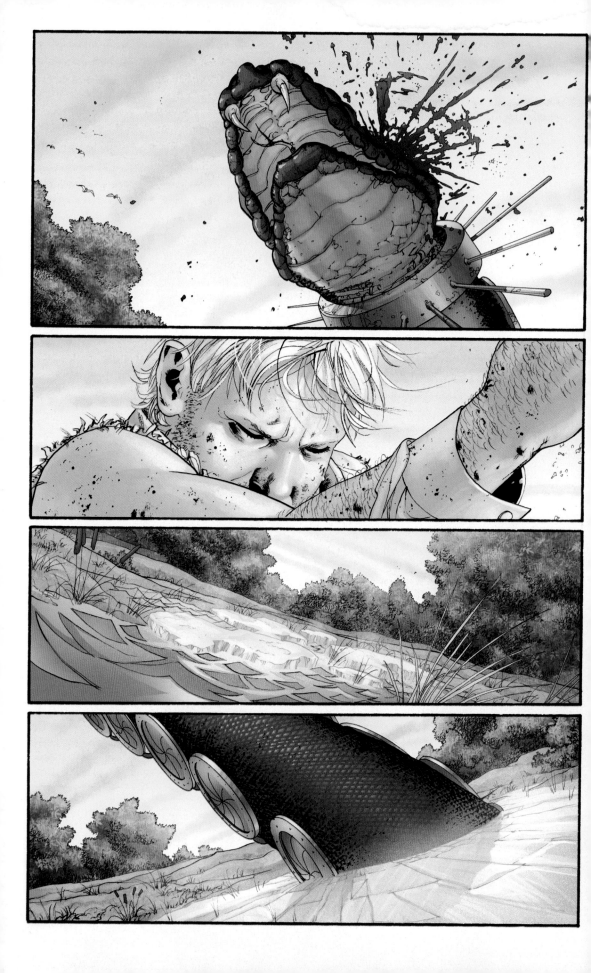

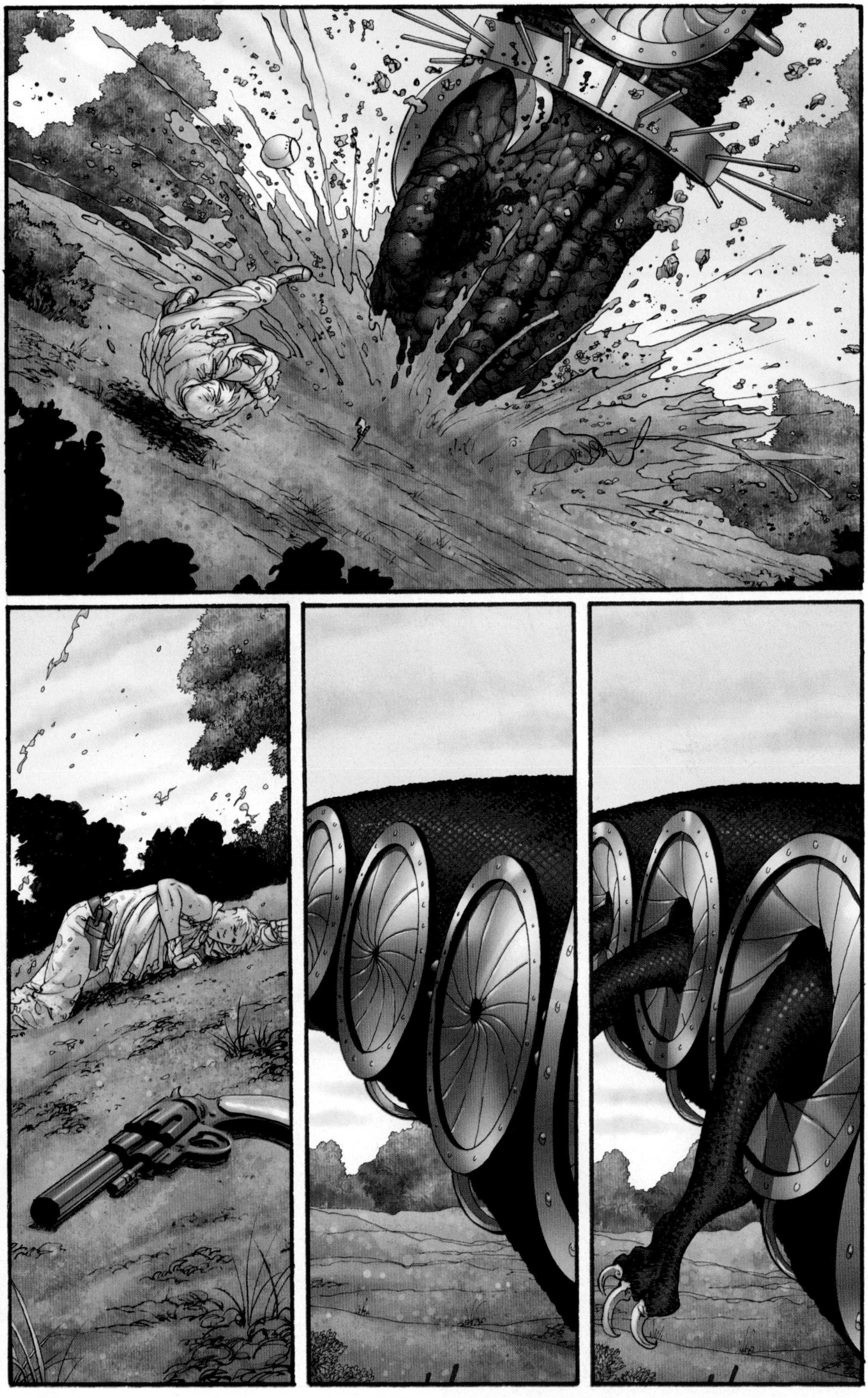

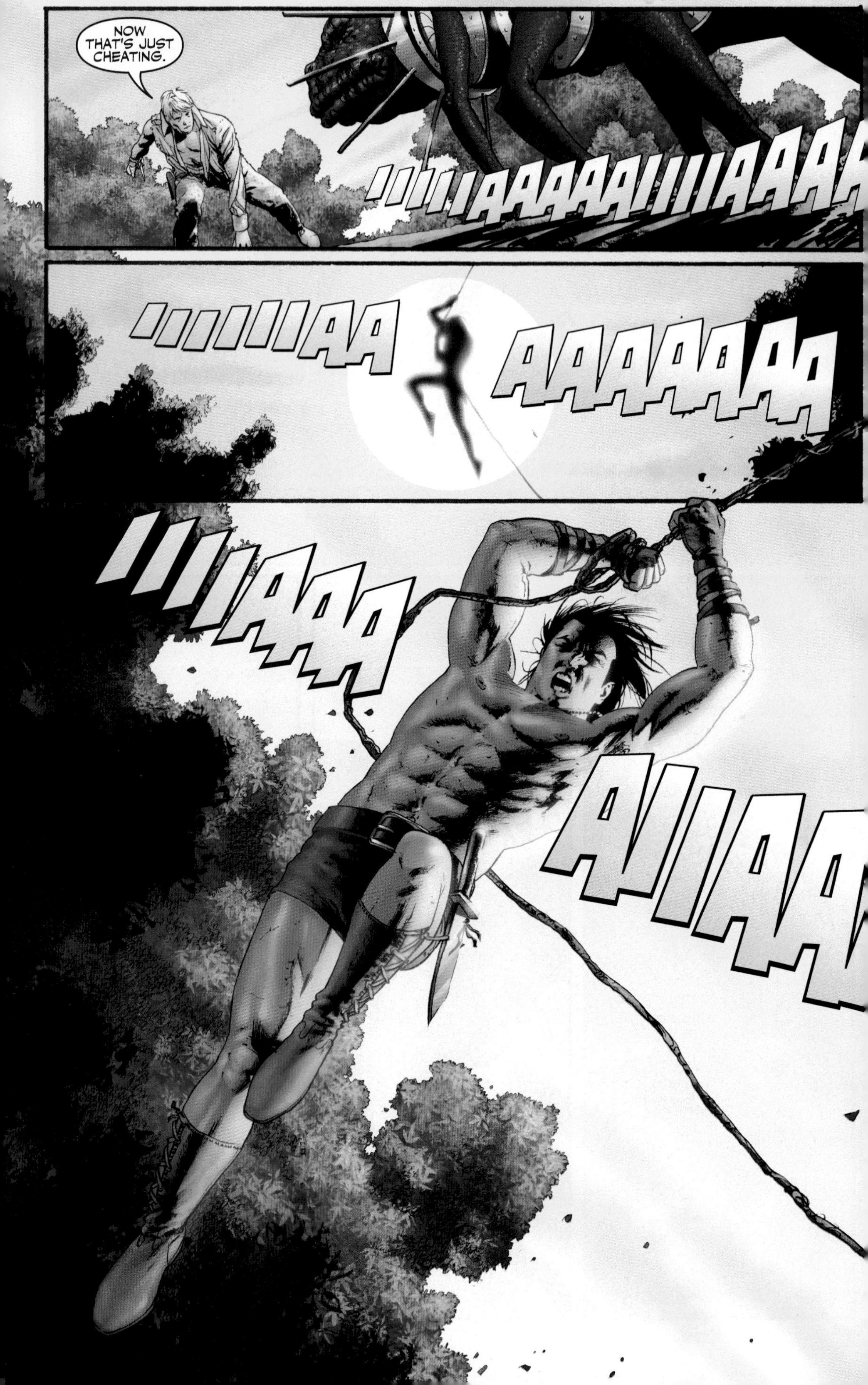
NOW THAT'S JUST CHEATING.
IIIIIAAAAAIIIIAAAA
IIIIIIIAA AAAAAAA
IIIIAAA
AIIAAA

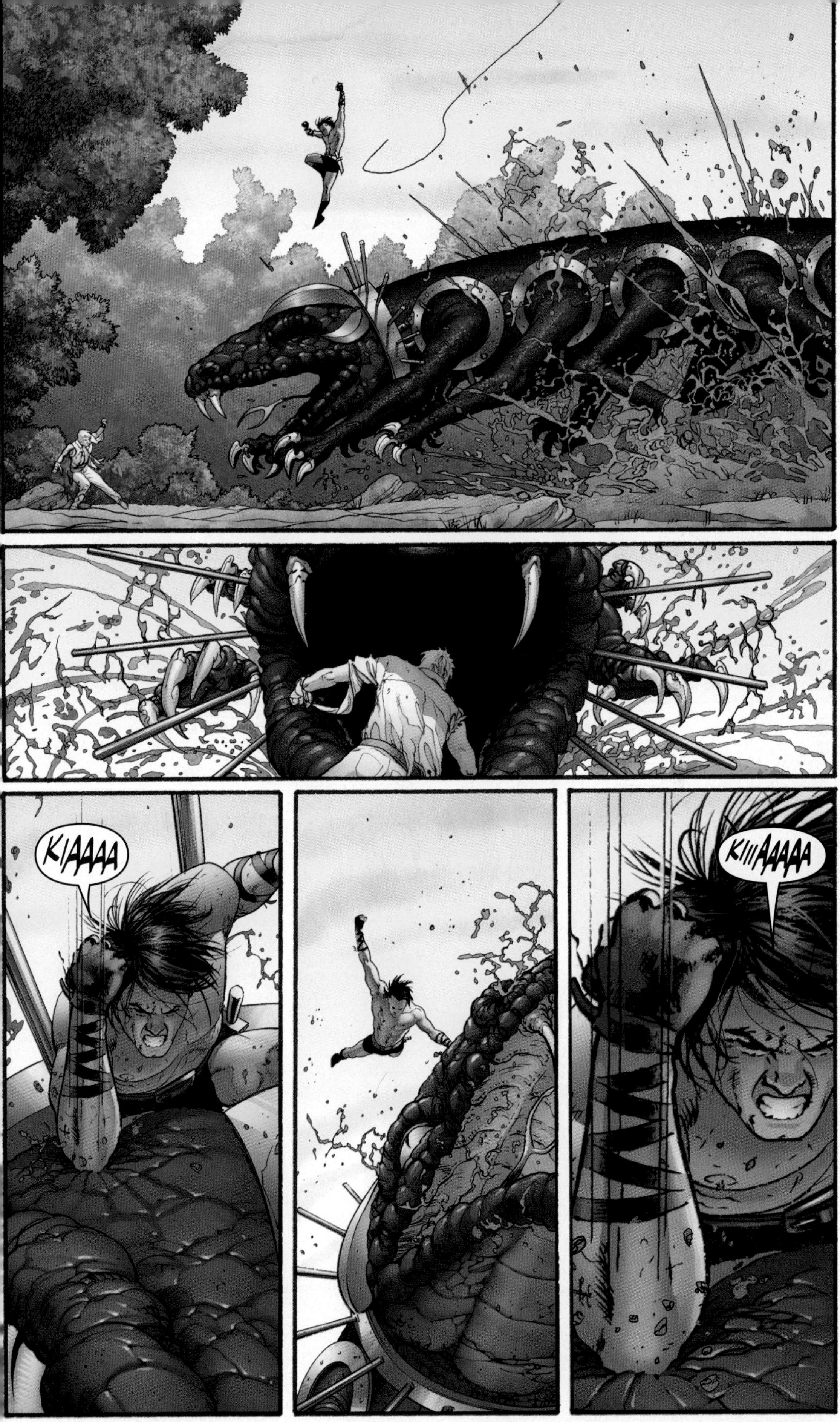
KIAAAA
KIIIAAAAA

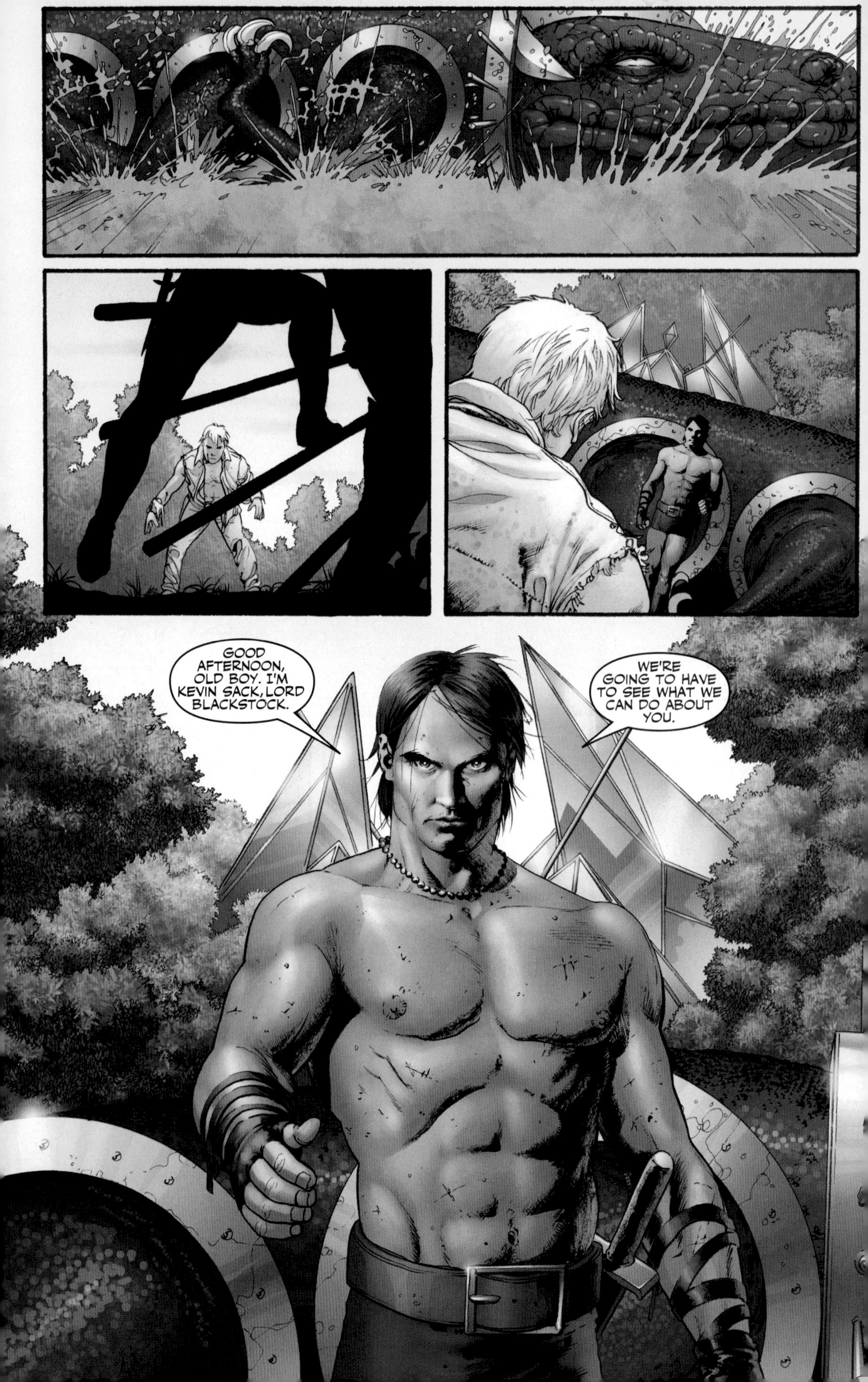
GOOD AFTERNOON, OLD BOY. I'M KEVIN SACK, LORD BLACKSTOCK.
WE'RE GOING TO HAVE TO SEE WHAT WE CAN DO ABOUT YOU.

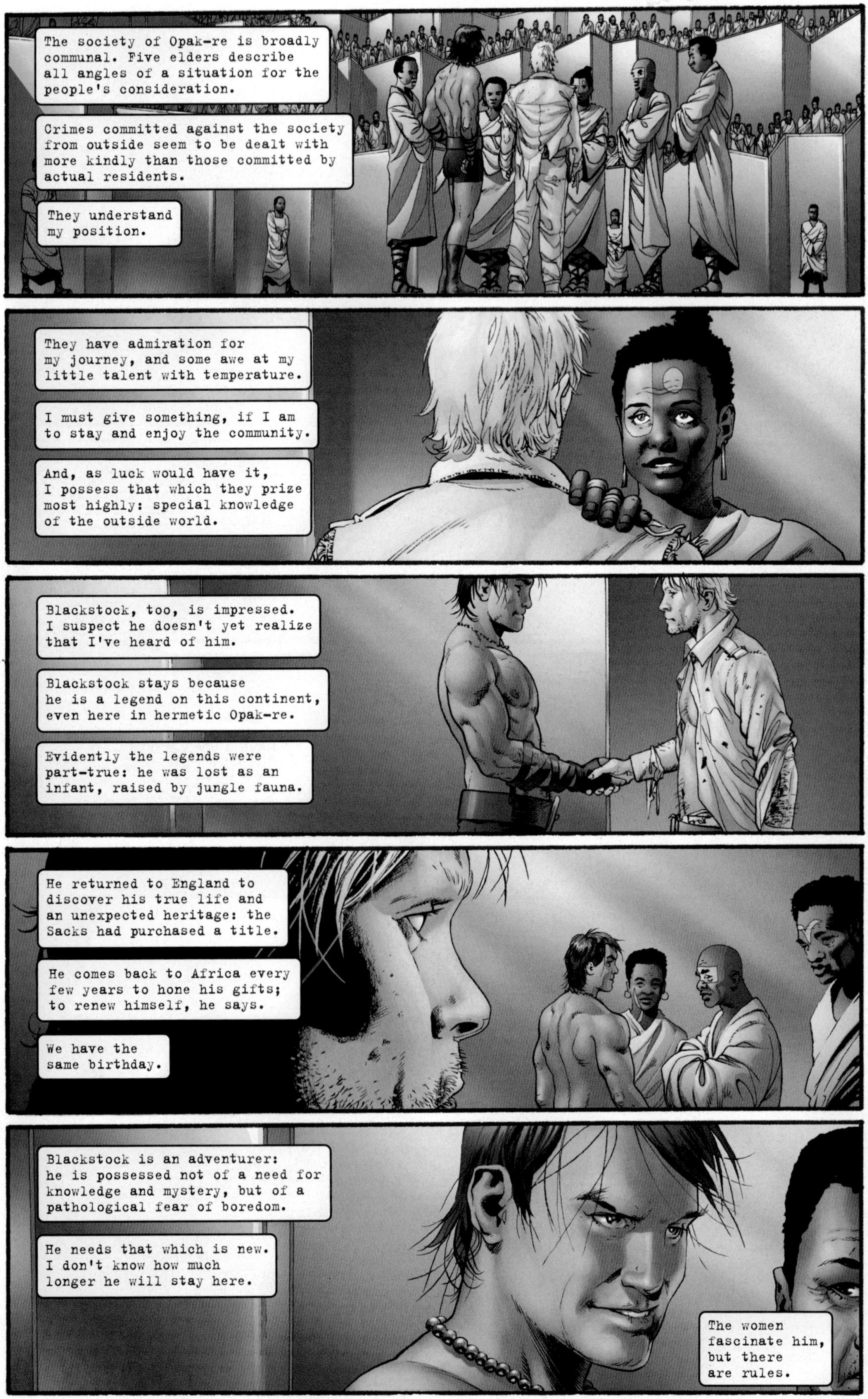
The society of Opak-re is broadly communal. Five elders describe all angles of a situation for the people's consideration.
Crimes committed against the society from outside seem to be dealt with more kindly than those committed by actual residents.
They understand my position.
They have admiration for my journey, and some awe at my little talent with temperature.
I must give something, if I am to stay and enjoy the community.
And, as luck would have it, I possess that which they prize most highly: special knowledge of the outside world.
Blackstock, too, is impressed. I suspect he doesn't yet realize that I've heard of him.
Blackstock stays because he is a legend on this continent, even here in hermetic Opak-re.
Evidently the legends were part-true: he was lost as an infant, raised by jungle fauna.
He returned to England to discover his true life and an unexpected heritage: the Sacks had purchased a title.
He comes back to Africa every few years to hone his gifts; to renew himself, he says.
We have the same birthday.
Blackstock is an adventurer: he is possessed not of a need for knowledge and mystery, but of a pathological fear of boredom.
He needs that which is new. I don't know how much longer he will stay here.
The women fascinate him, but there are rules.

I'm good with languages. Soon, I find the rules out for myself.

YOU MAY NOT REPRODUCE HERE, ELIJAH SNOW.

I HADN'T PLANNED TO. I HATE KIDS.

UNPLEASANT, BUT ACCEPTABLE. CHILDREN ARE OUR KINGS AND QUEENS.

BUT WE WISH OPAK-RE TO REMAIN OPAK-RE. WE HAVE NO NEED OF WHITE IN OUR WATER, DO YOU SEE?

YES.

NO CROSS-BREEDING.

THIS ISN'T GOING TO BE A CONCERN, ELDER.

AS YOU SAY. BUT BE AWARE. THERE IS INTEREST IN YOU.

I have never been the kind of man who knows when a woman is interested in him.

Therefore, Anaykah pinning me against a tree and nearly knocking out my back teeth with her tongue came as something of a surprise.

She was one of Opak-re's intellectuals, attended every one of my little storytelling sessions.

Far cleverer than I could ever be.

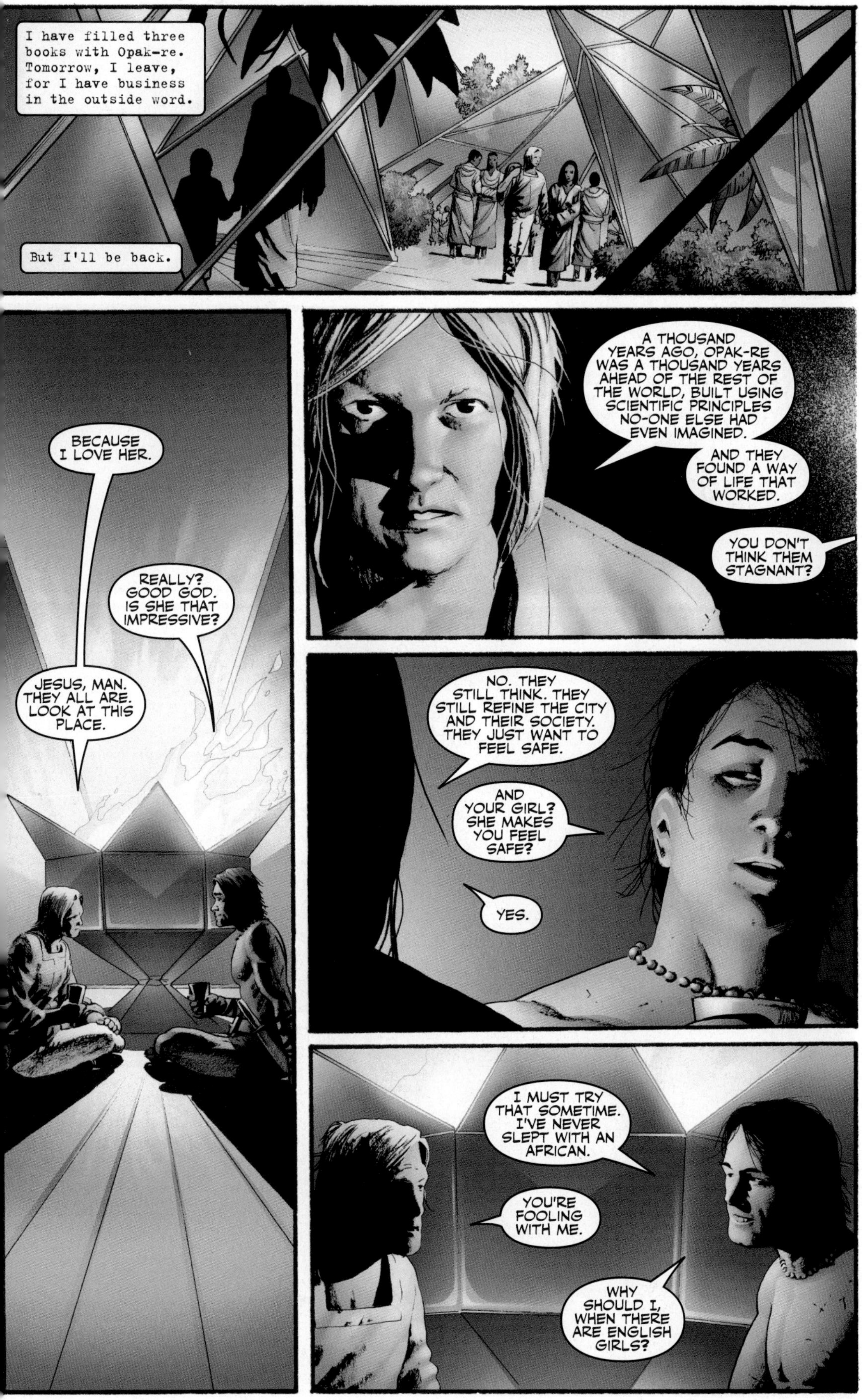
I have filled three books with Opak-re. Tomorrow, I leave, for I have business in the outside word.
But I'll be back.
BECAUSE I LOVE HER.
REALLY? GOOD GOD. IS SHE THAT IMPRESSIVE?
JESUS, MAN. THEY ALL ARE. LOOK AT THIS PLACE.
A THOUSAND YEARS AGO, OPAK-RE WAS A THOUSAND YEARS AHEAD OF THE REST OF THE WORLD, BUILT USING SCIENTIFIC PRINCIPLES NO-ONE ELSE HAD EVEN IMAGINED.
AND THEY FOUND A WAY OF LIFE THAT WORKED.
YOU DON'T THINK THEM STAGNANT?
NO. THEY STILL THINK. THEY STILL REFINE THE CITY AND THEIR SOCIETY. THEY JUST WANT TO FEEL SAFE.
AND YOUR GIRL? SHE MAKES YOU FEEL SAFE?
YES.
I MUST TRY THAT SOMETIME. I'VE NEVER SLEPT WITH AN AFRICAN.
YOU'RE FOOLING WITH ME.
WHY SHOULD I, WHEN THERE ARE ENGLISH GIRLS?

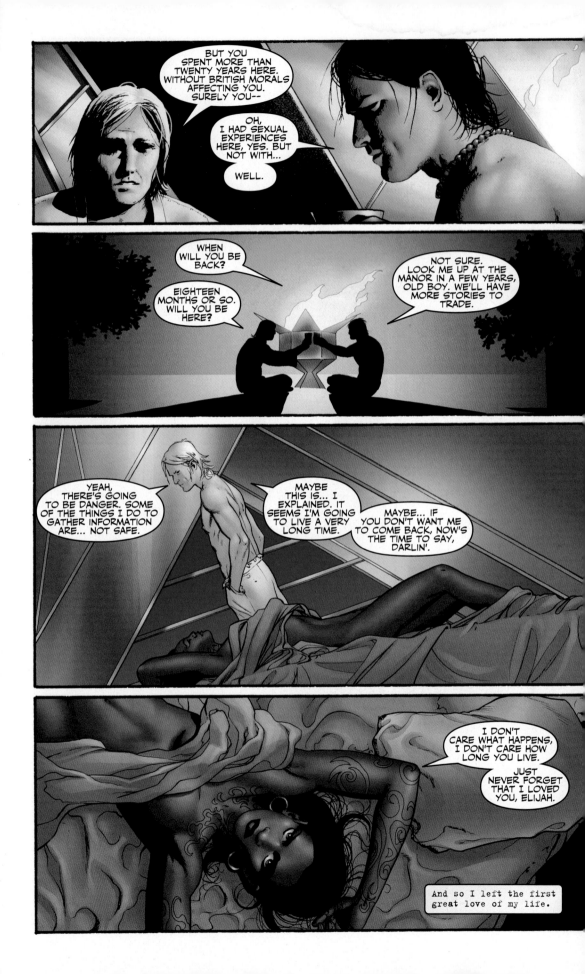

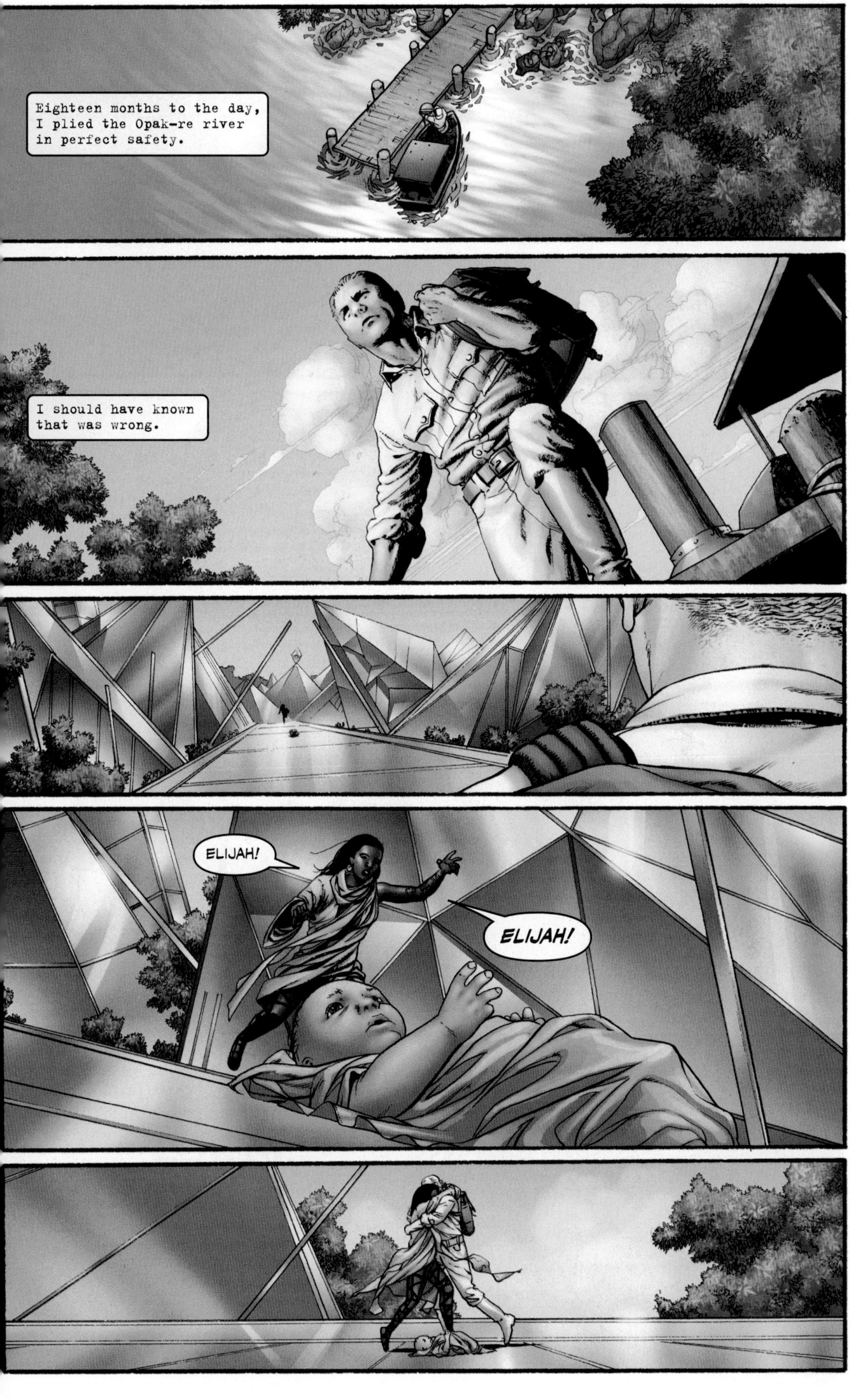
Eighteen months to the day,
I plied the Opak-re river
in perfect safety.
I should have known
that was wrong.
ELIJAH!
ELIJAH!

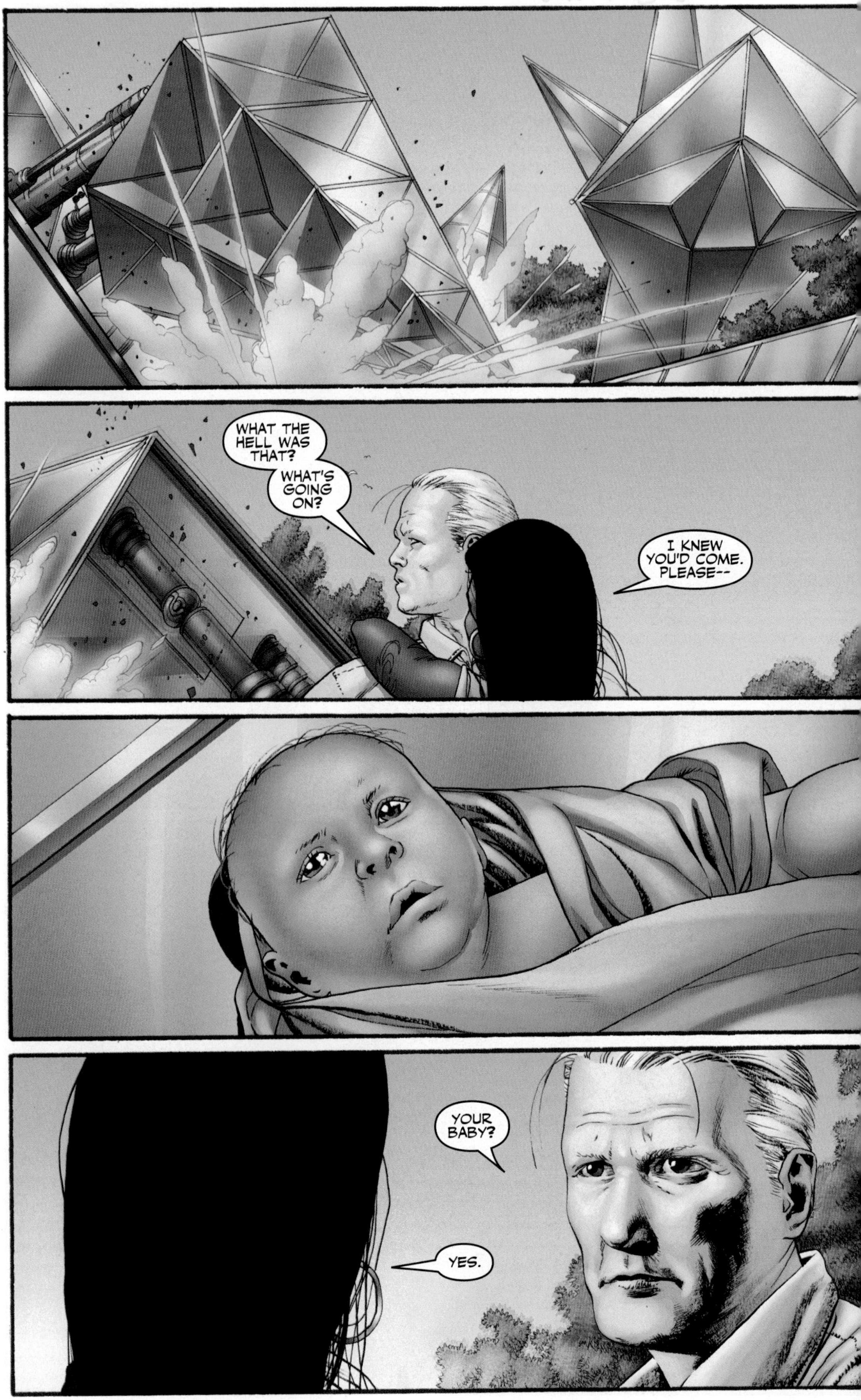
WHAT THE HELL WAS THAT?
WHAT'S GOING ON?
I KNEW YOU'D COME. PLEASE--
YOUR BABY?
YES.

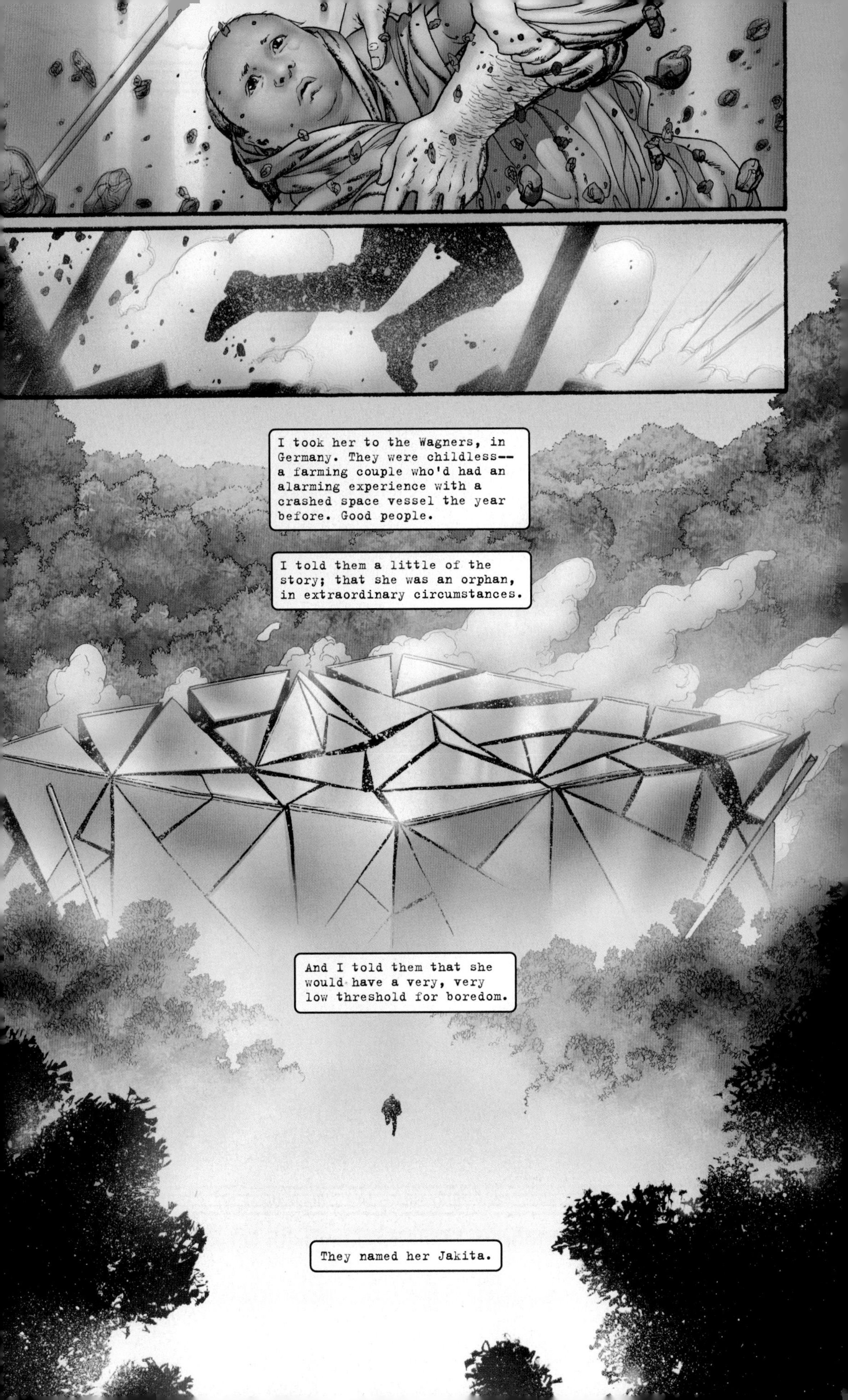
I took her to the Wagners, in Germany. They were childless-- a farming couple who'd had an alarming experience with a crashed space vessel the year before. Good people.
I told them a little of the story; that she was an orphan, in extraordinary circumstances.
And I told them that she would have a very, very low threshold for boredom.
They named her Jakita.

CHAPTER

PLANETARY 18

CHAPTER 18

THE GUN CLUB

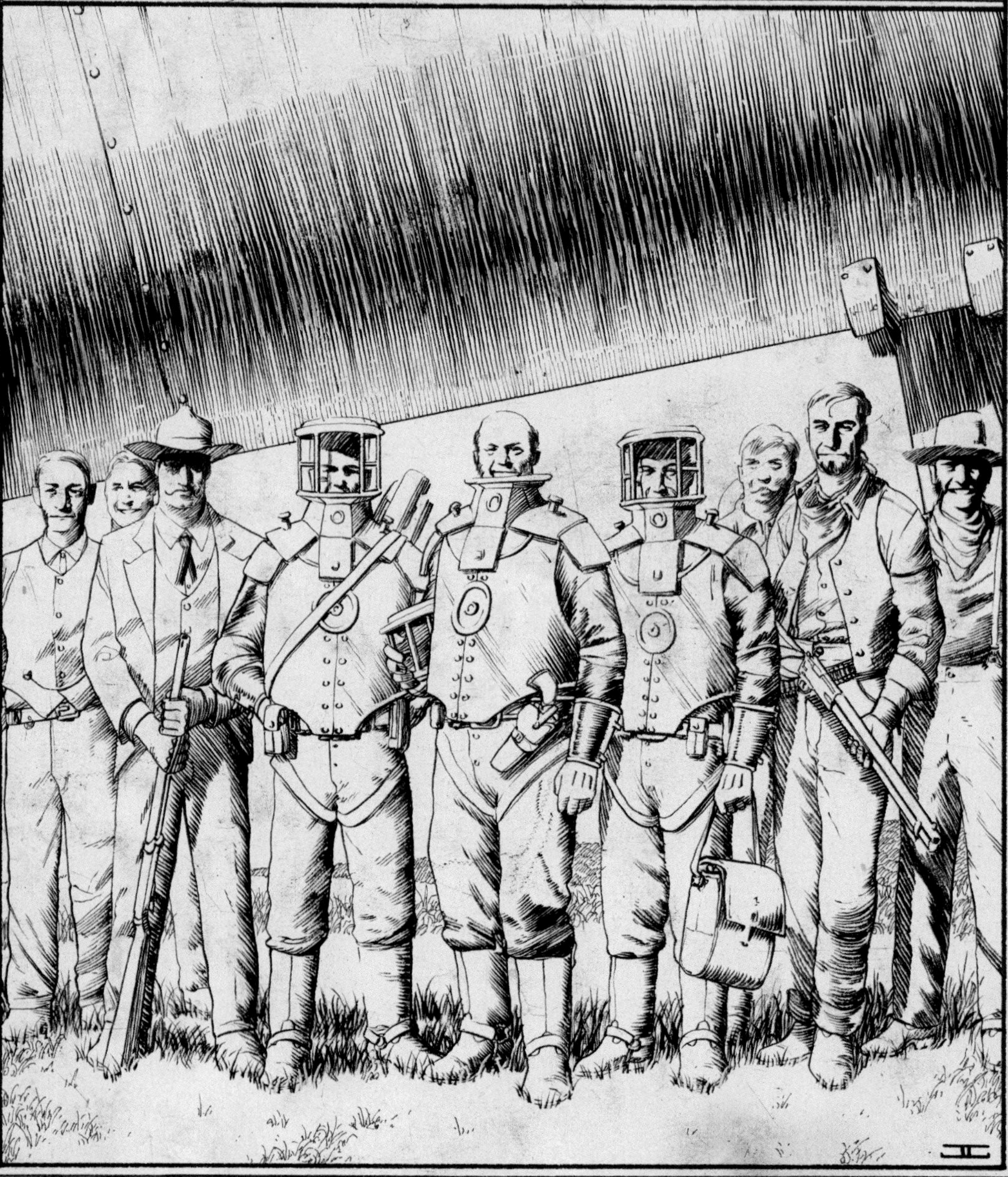

By W.G. Ellis and Johnny Mac Cassaday with Miss Laura J Martin

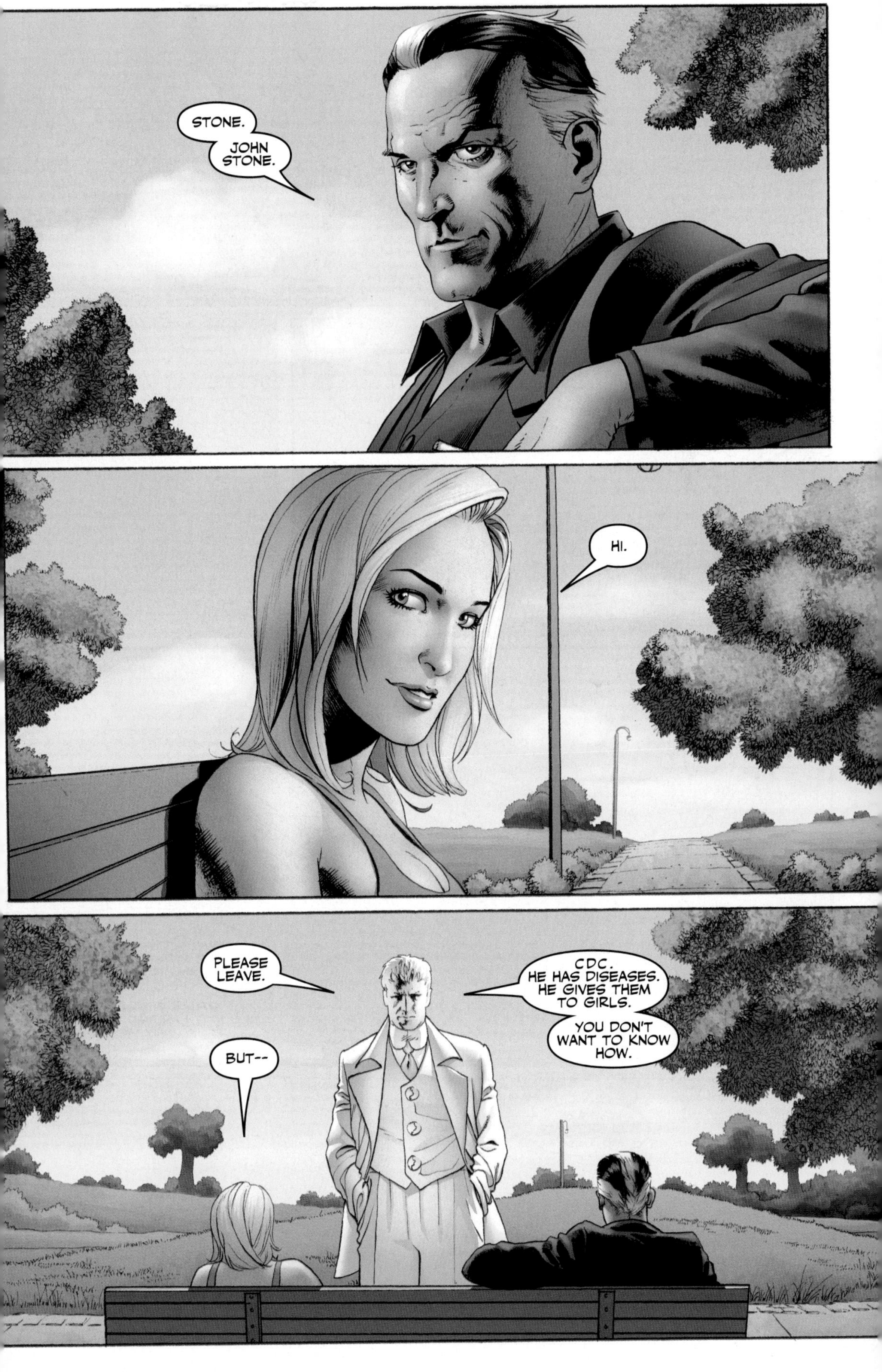
STONE.
JOHN STONE.
HI.
PLEASE LEAVE.
CDC. HE HAS DISEASES. HE GIVES THEM TO GIRLS.
YOU DON'T WANT TO KNOW HOW.
BUT--

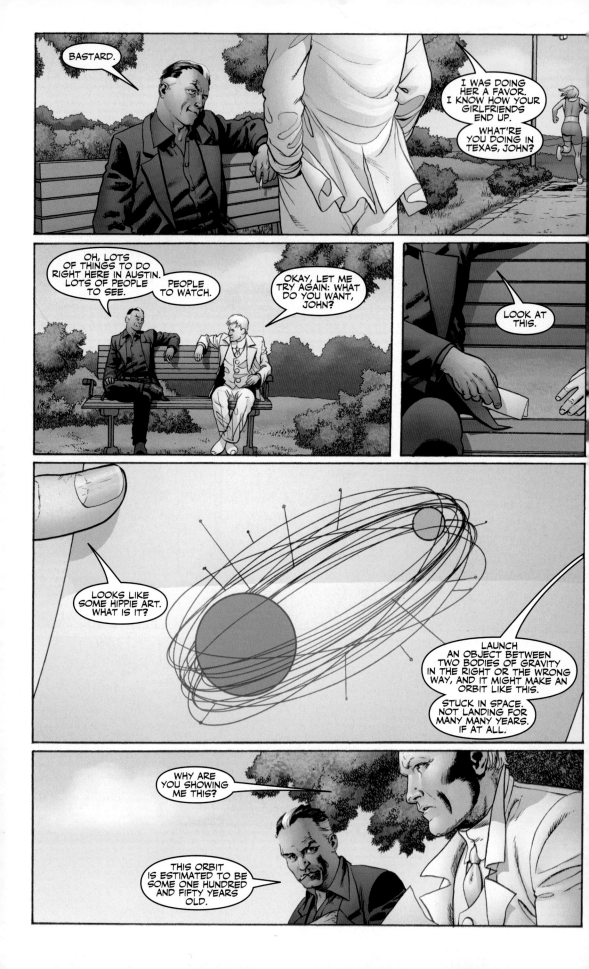

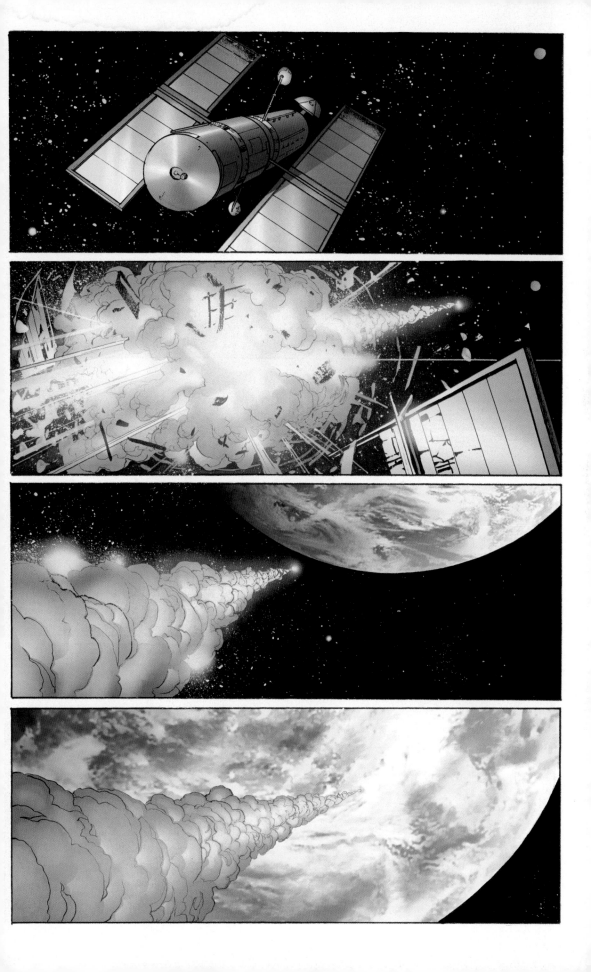

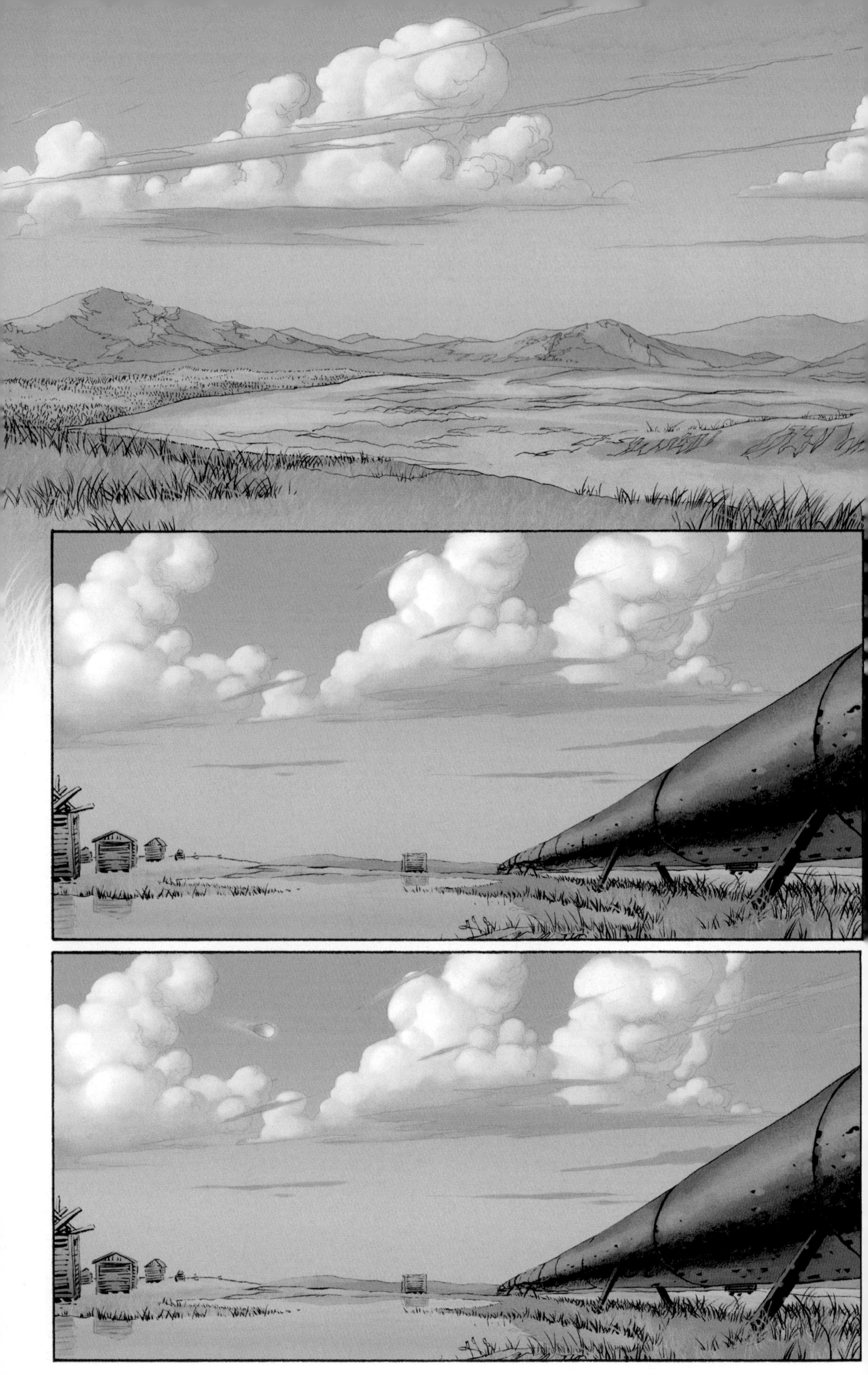

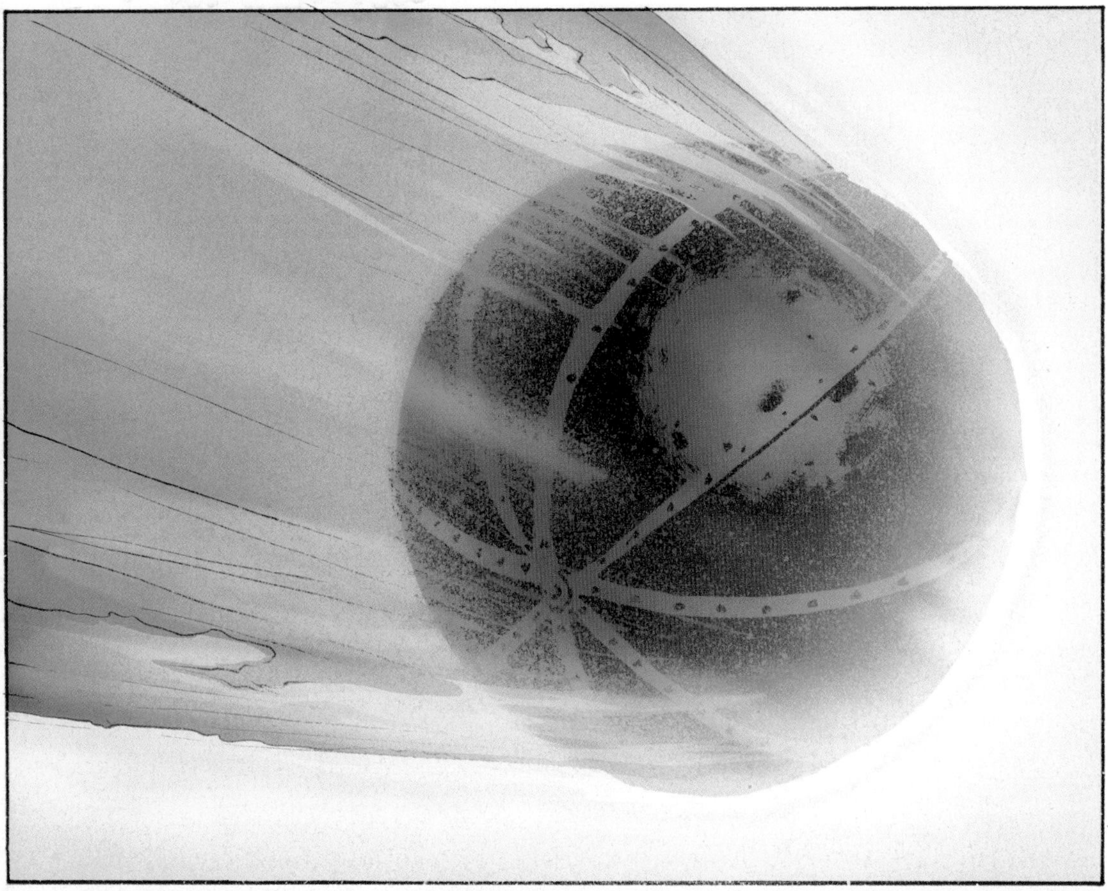

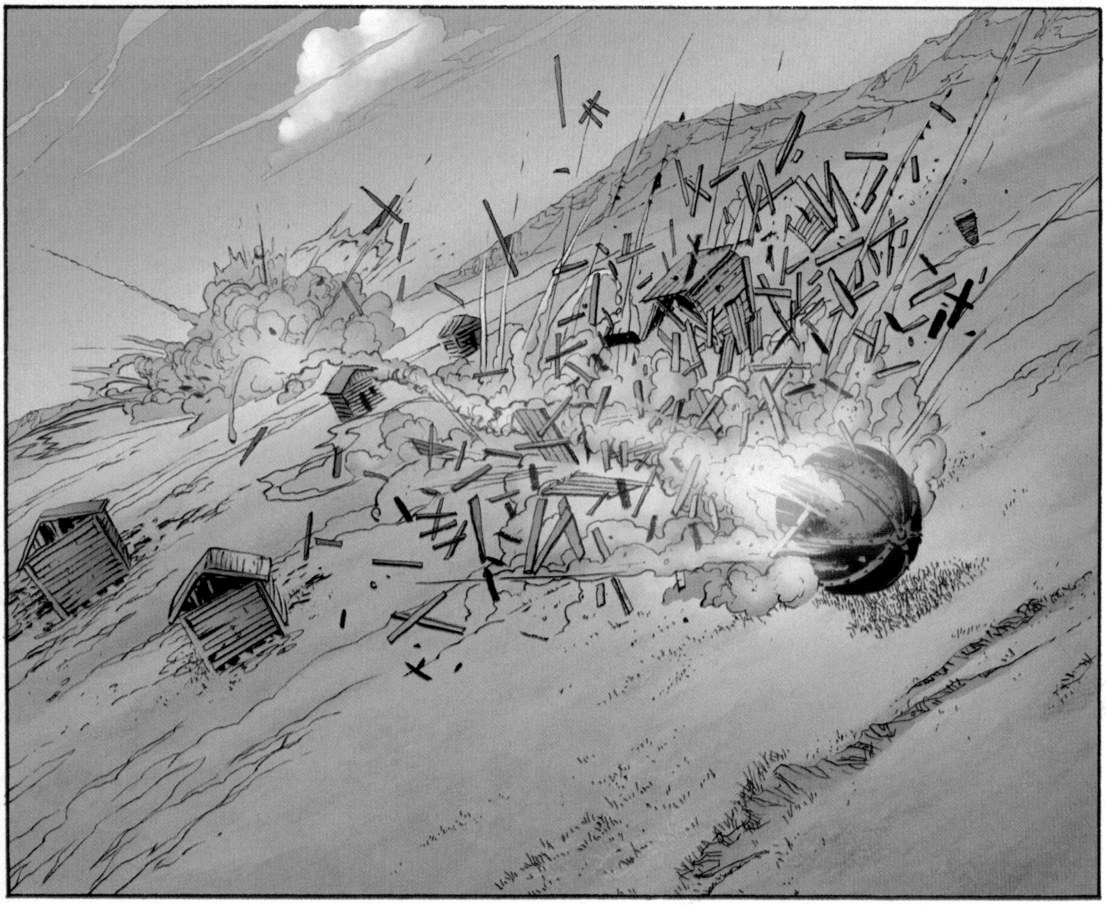

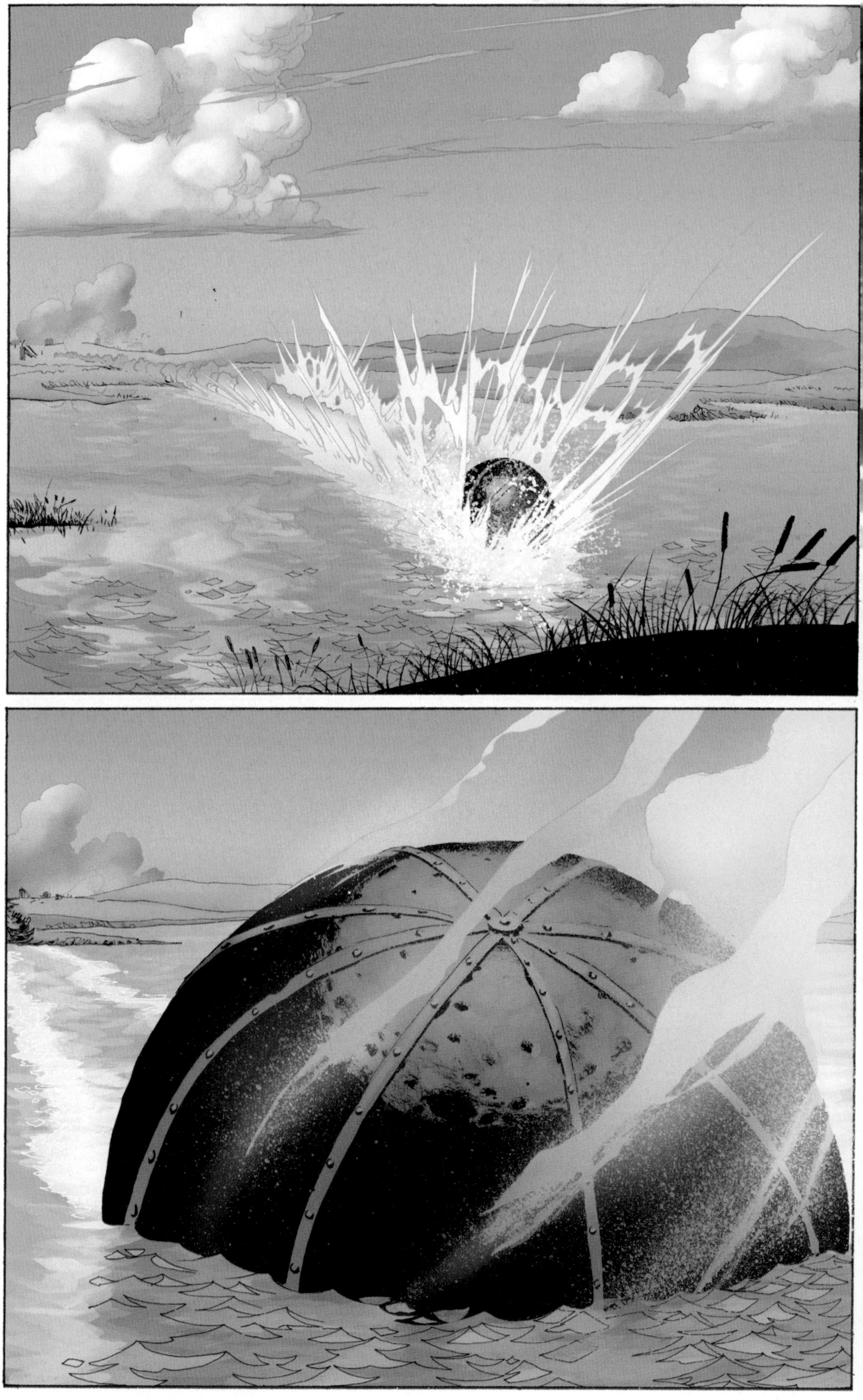

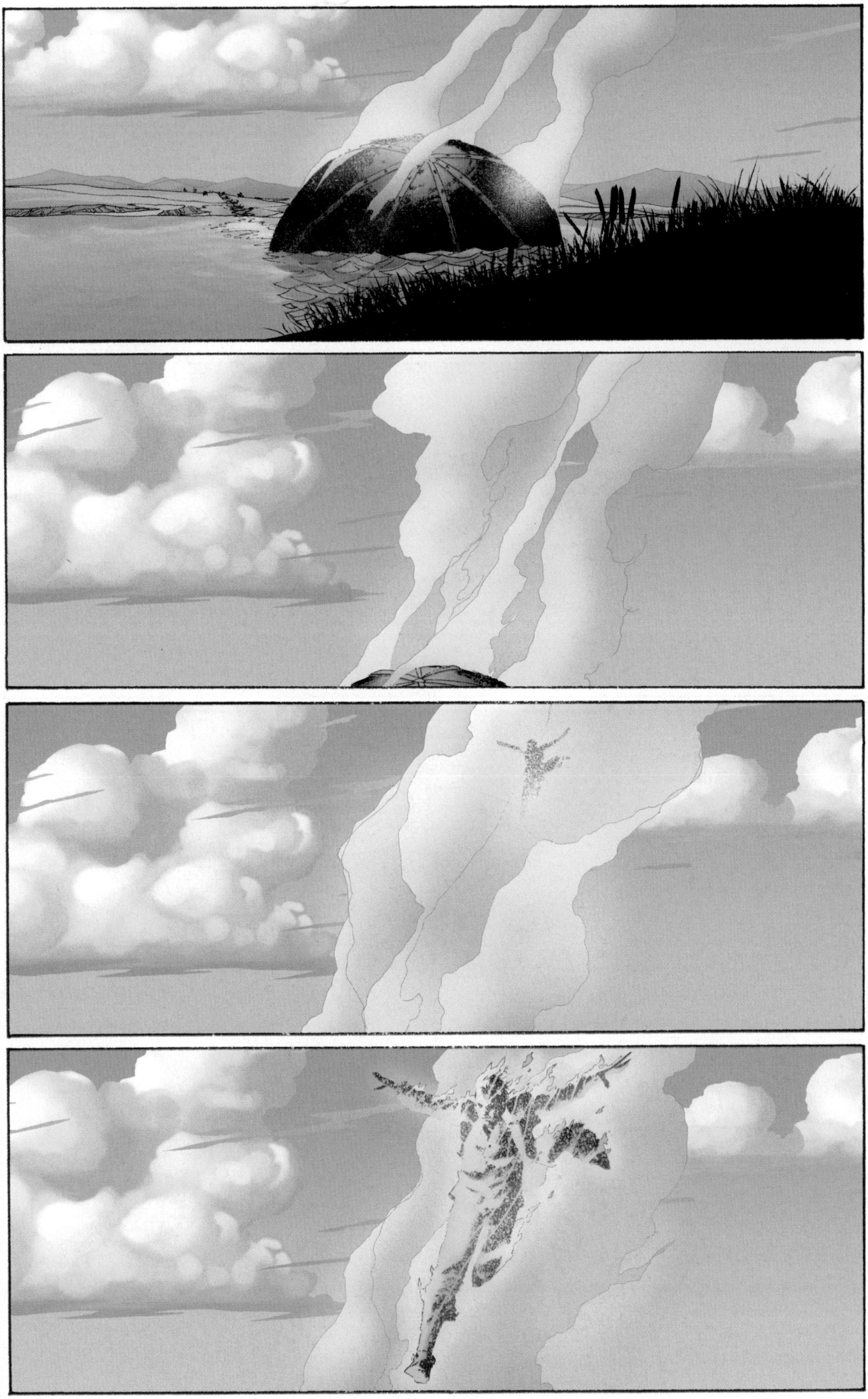

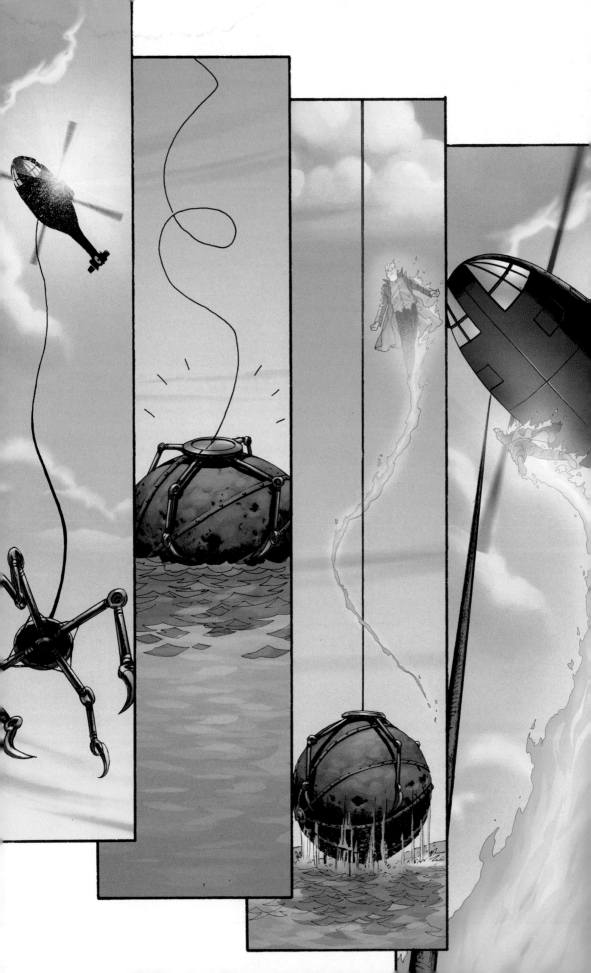

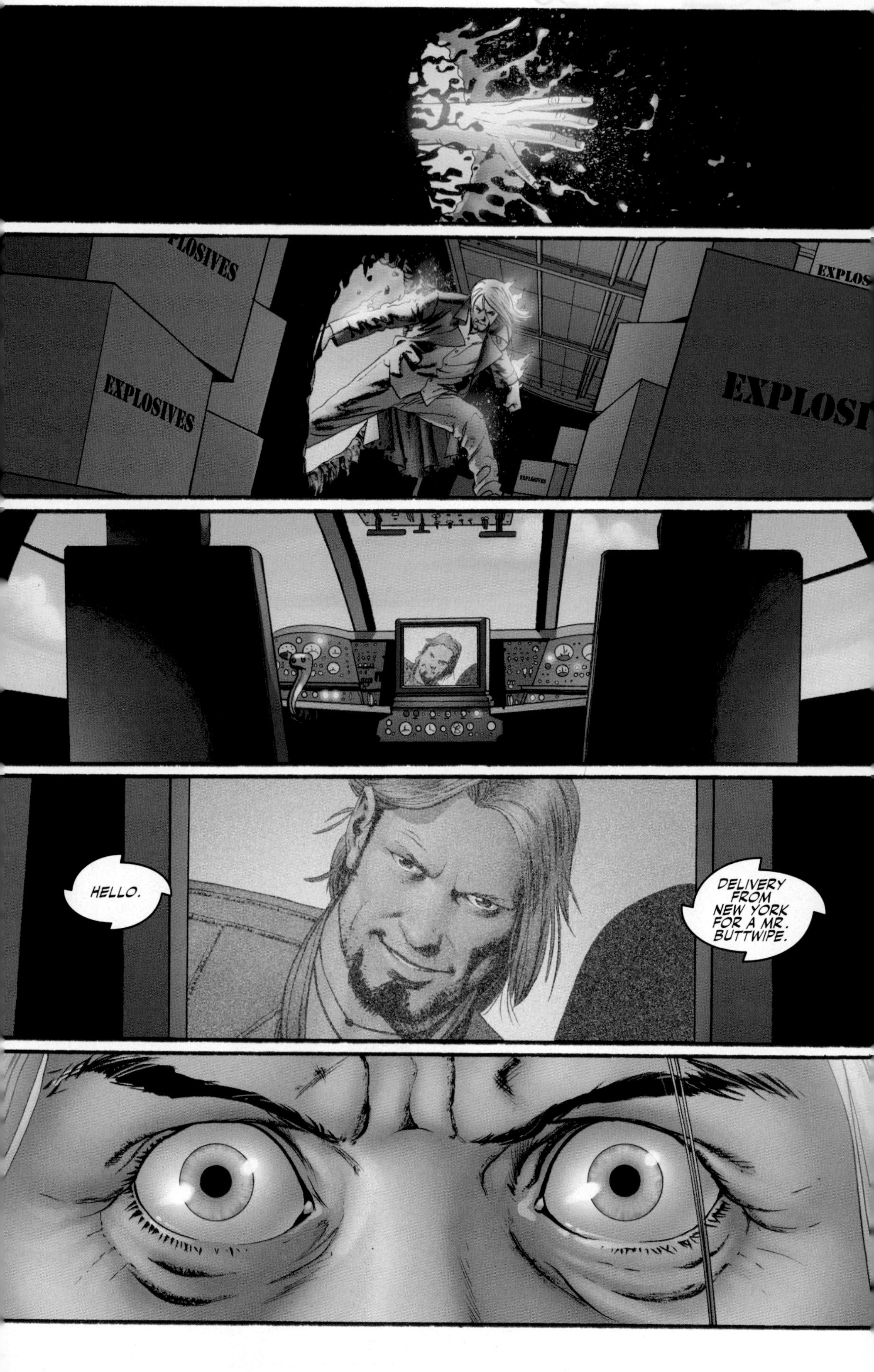
EXPLOSIVES
EXPLOSIVES
EXPLOSIVES
EXPLOSI
HELLO.
DELIVERY FROM NEW YORK FOR A MR. BUTTWIPE.

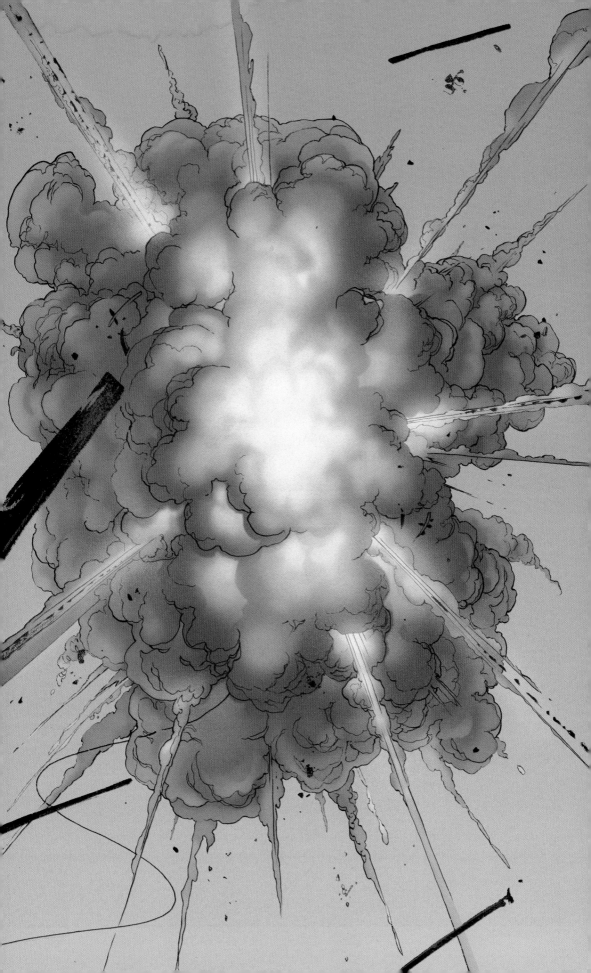

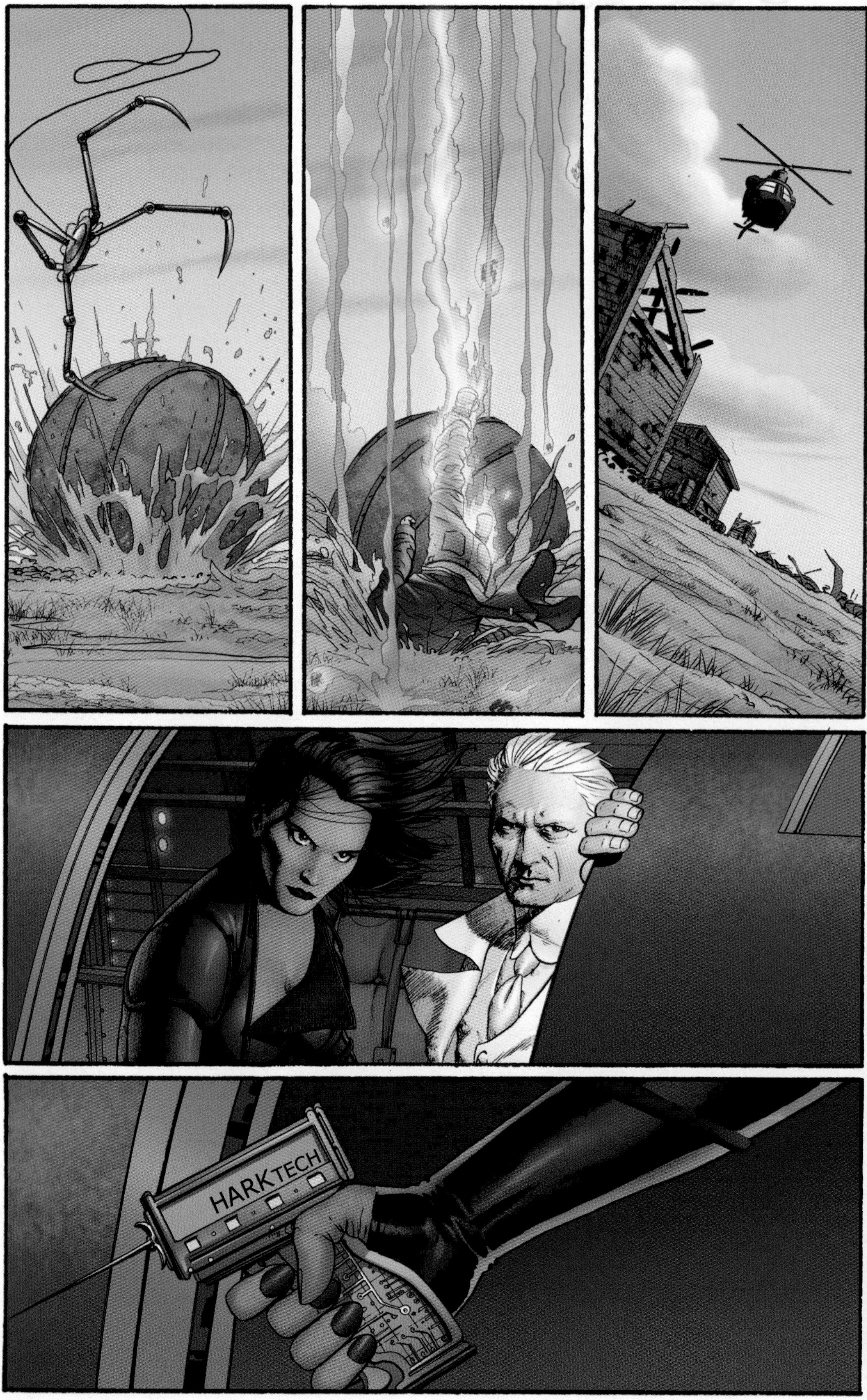
HARKTECH

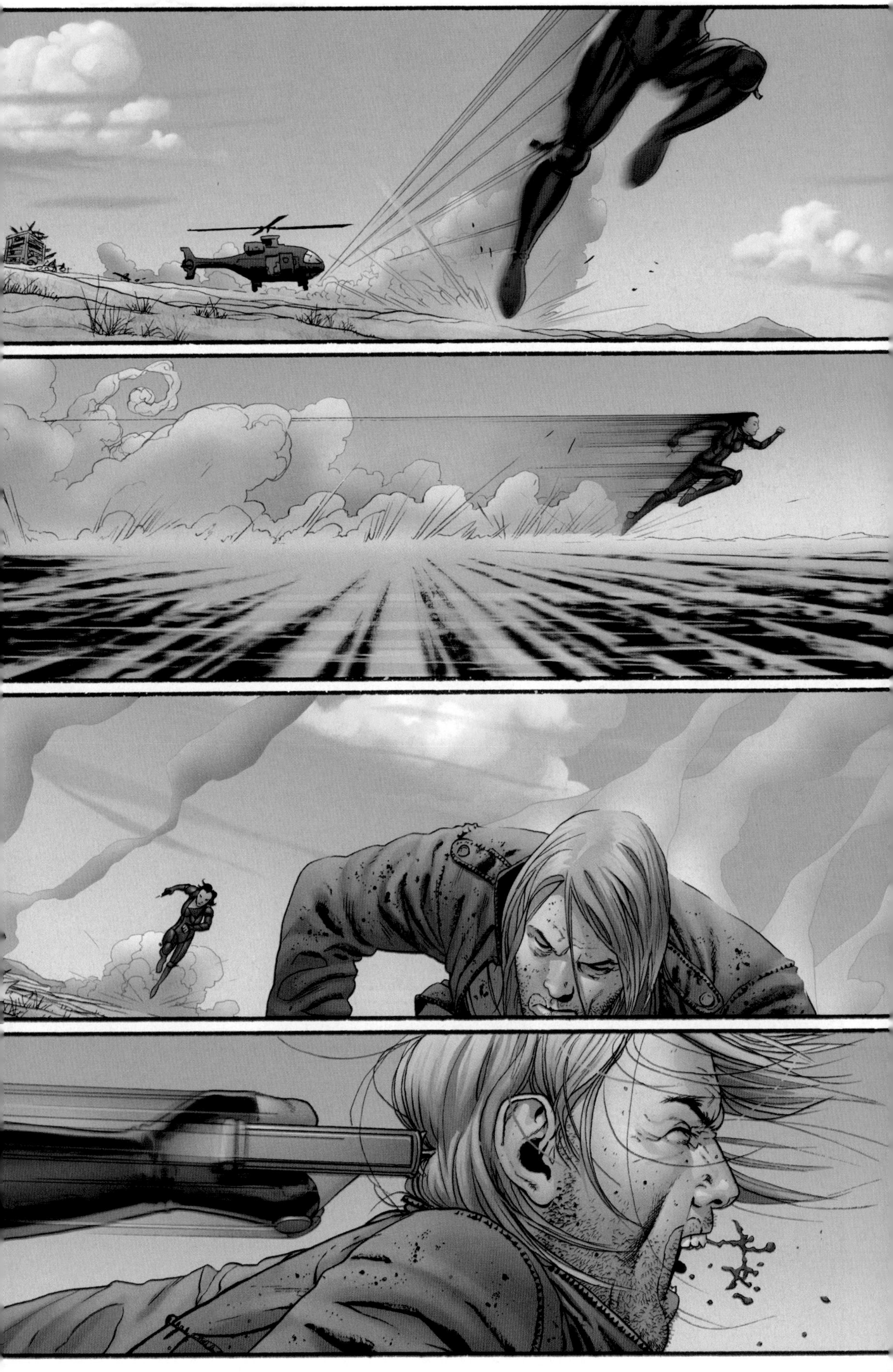

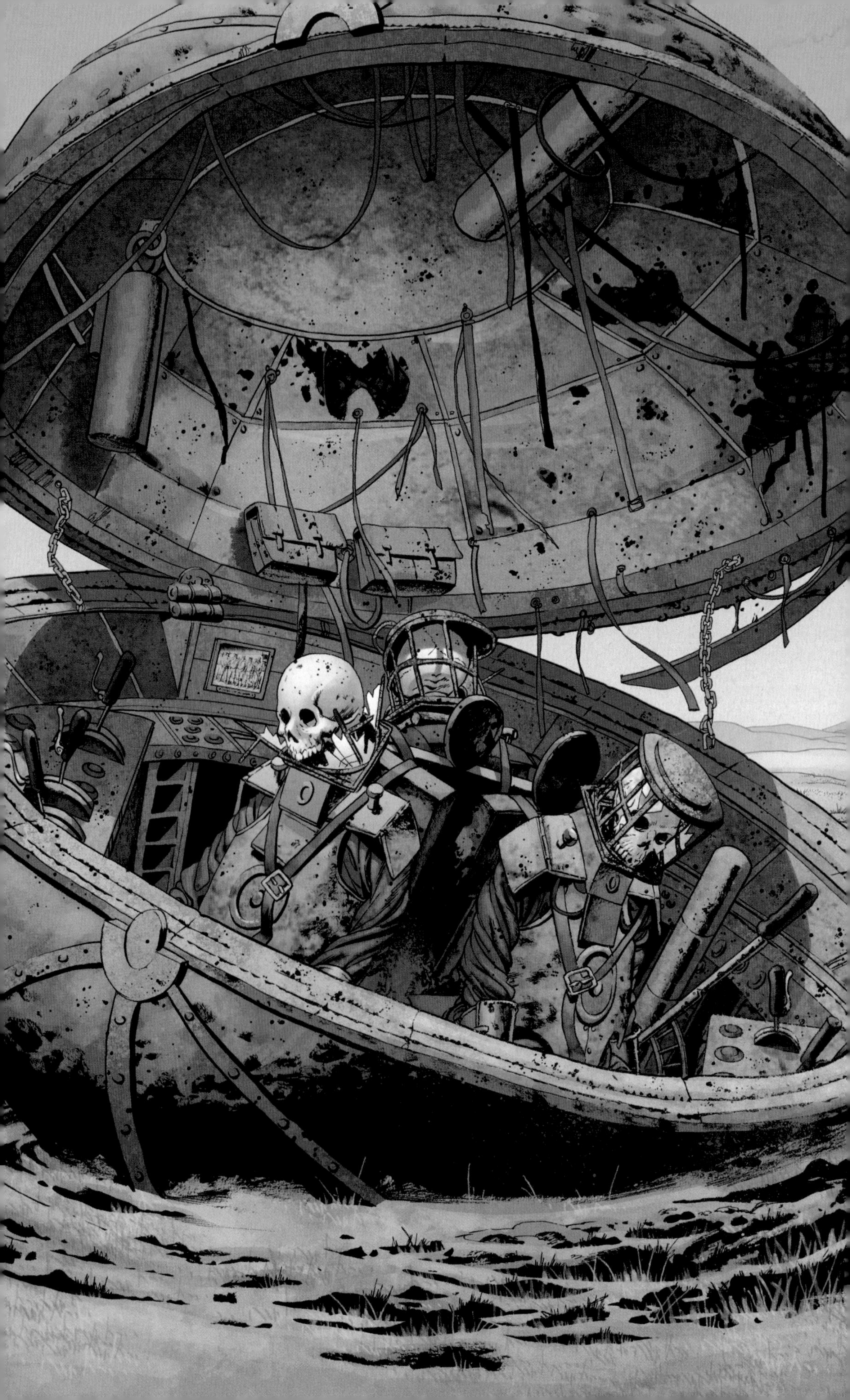

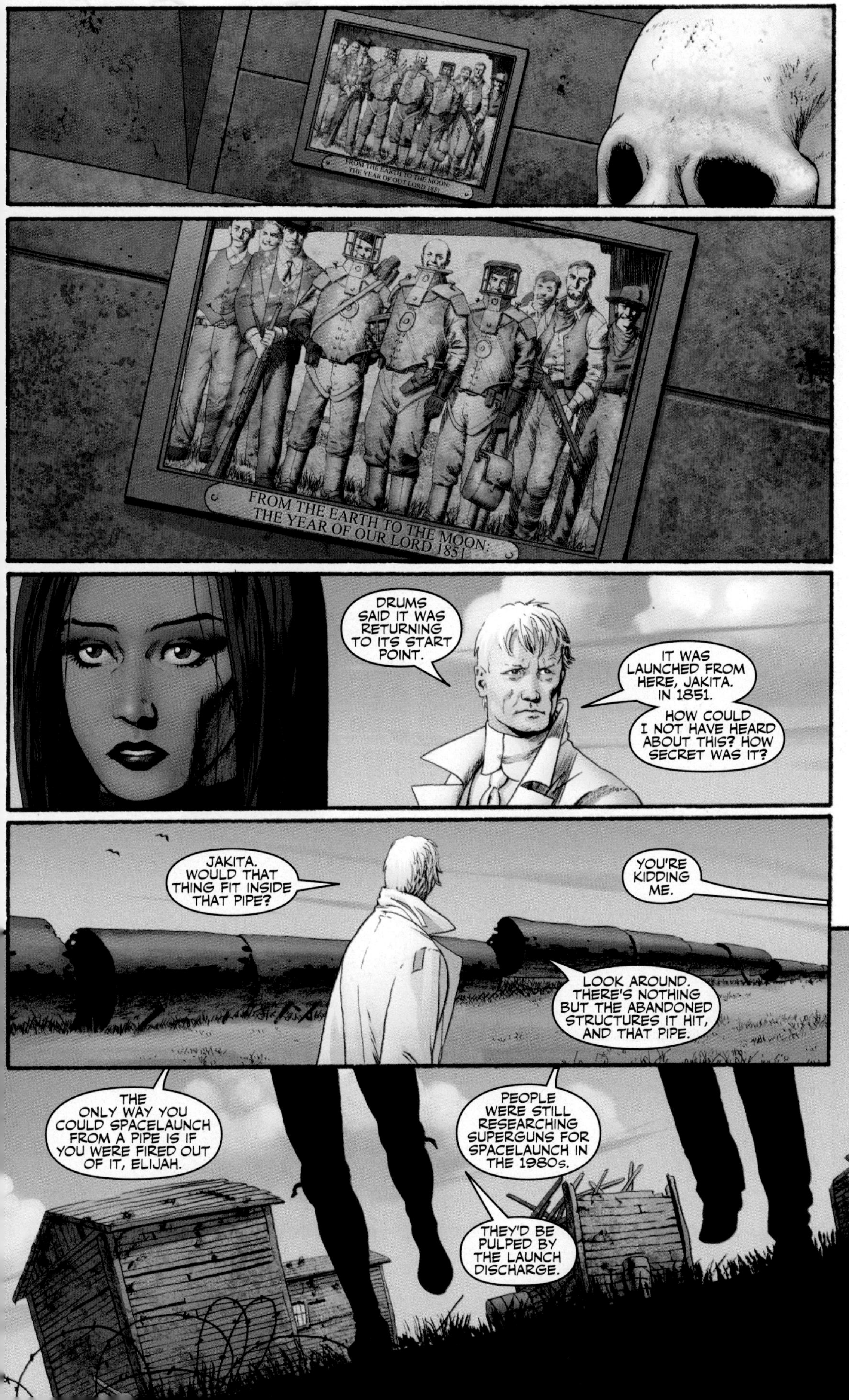
FROM THE EARTH TO THE MOON: THE YEAR OF OUT LORD 1851
FROM THE EARTH TO THE MOON: THE YEAR OF OUR LORD 1851
DRUMS SAID IT WAS RETURNING TO ITS START POINT.
IT WAS LAUNCHED FROM HERE, JAKITA. IN 1851.
HOW COULD I NOT HAVE HEARD ABOUT THIS? HOW SECRET WAS IT?
JAKITA. WOULD THAT THING FIT INSIDE THAT PIPE?
YOU'RE KIDDING ME.
LOOK AROUND. THERE'S NOTHING BUT THE ABANDONED STRUCTURES IT HIT, AND THAT PIPE.
THE ONLY WAY YOU COULD SPACELAUNCH FROM A PIPE IS IF YOU WERE FIRED OUT OF IT, ELIJAH.
PEOPLE WERE STILL RESEARCHING SUPERGUNS FOR SPACELAUNCH IN THE 1980s.
THEY'D BE PULPED BY THE LAUNCH DISCHARGE.

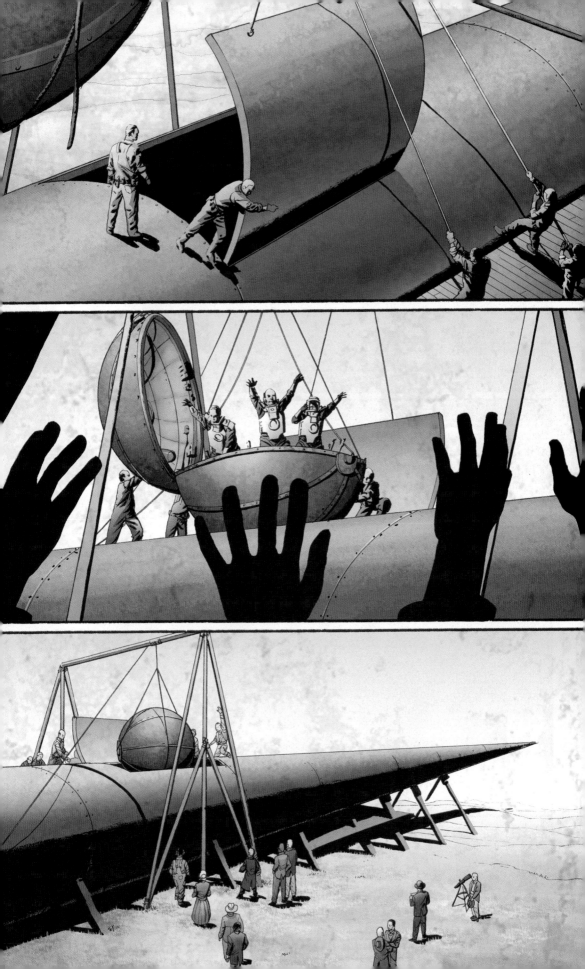

IMAGINE IT.

THEY LAUNCH A MOONSHOT WITH ALL THE AVAILABLE TECHNOLOGY AT THEIR DISPOSAL. IRON AND EXPLOSIVES.

BUT THEY'VE NO WAY TO CONTACT THE CAPSULE. ALL THEY CAN DO IS WAIT FOR IT TO COME BACK.

DAYS. WEEKS. SOME OF THEM DRIFT AWAY. MONTHS. MORE LEAVE.

YEARS PASS. AND THEY ALL REMAIN SILENT. THE LAUNCH SITE STANDS EMPTY.

AND I BET YOU THAT EVERY NIGHT, EVERY SINGLE ONE OF THEM LOOKED UP AT THE MOON AND WONDERED.

STRANGE WORLD. AND IT'S ALWAYS GOING TO BE THAT WAY.

THE GUN CLUB

WRITTEN BY **WARREN ELLIS** ART BY **JOHN CASSADAY**
COLORING BY **LAURA MARTIN** LETTERING BY **RICHARD STARKINGS**
ASSISTANT EDITOR **KRISTY QUINN** EDITOR **SCOTT DUNBIER**

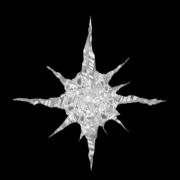

Warren Ellis was born and raised in darkest England. He has been cited by numerous critics as one of the finest creators currently working in the graphic narrative field. Among his many creations are **THE AUTHORITY, TRANSMETROPOLITAN,** and **GLOBAL FREQUENCY,** the last of which has been optioned for an episodic television program. The innovative and much renowned **PLANETARY,** done in collaboration with John Cassaday, is a work in progress.

John Cassaday was born in Texas, but New York City is his home. Highlights of his career include Captain America and Astonishing X-Men. John's first major work was for WildStorm, the much lauded western/horror series **DESPERADOES.** Shortly thereafter he began his collaboration with Warren Ellis on the groundbreaking and highly acclaimed **PLANETARY.**

Laura DePuy Martin has been employed by two comics' publishers and has freelanced for numerous others, winning awards for her work on **PLANETARY, THE AUTHORITY, JLA,** Universe-X, and Ruse. She is currently working on **PLANETARY,** Astonishing X-Men, I Am Legion, and The War, among other things. She lives in Tampa with her husband Randy and her two animal kids, Mina and Aku.

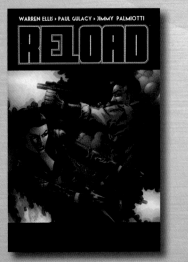